HUNTER OF
STORIES

HUNTER OF
STORIES

Eduardo Galeano

Translated by Mark Fried

NATION BOOKS
NEW YORK

Nation Books
116 East 16th Street, 8th Floor New York, NY 10003
http://www.publicaffairsbooks.com/nation-books
@NationBooks

Printed in the United States of America
Spanish-language edition published by Siglo XXI de España Editores, S. A., 2016.
First English-language Edition: November 2017
Published by Nation Books, an imprint of Perseus Books, LLC, a subsidiary of Hachette
Book Group, Inc.

Nation Books is a co-publishing venture of the Nation Institute and the Perseus Books.
The publisher is not responsible for websites (or their content) that are not owned by
the publisher.

Collages by Eduardo Galeano, inspired by anonymous artists of popular art and by
the work of April Deniz, Ulisse Aldrovandi, William Blake, Albrecht Dürer, Theodor
de Bry, Edward Topsell, Enea Vico, Pieter Brueghel the Younger, Hieronymus Bosch,
J. J. Grandville, Louis Le Breton, and Jan van Eyck.

PRINT BOOK INTERIOR DESIGN BY LINDA MARK.

The Library of Congress has cataloged the hardcover edition as follows:
Names: Galeano, Eduardo, 1940–2015, author. | Fried, Mark, translator.
Title: Hunter of stories / Eduardo Galeano ; translated by Mark Fried.
Description: New York : Nation Books, 2017.
Identifiers: LCCN 2017014189 (print) | LCCN 2017027554 (ebook) |
    ISBN 9781568589916 (ebook) | ISBN 9781568589909 (hardback)
Subjects: | BISAC: HISTORY / Latin America / South America. | LITERARY
    COLLECTIONS / Caribbean & Latin American.
Classification: LCC PQ8520.17.A4 (ebook) | LCC PQ8520.17.A4 A2 2017 (print) |
DDC 863/.64—dc23
LC record available at https://lccn.loc.gov/2017014189

ISBNs: 978-1-56858-990-9 (hardcover); 978-1-56858-991-6 (e-book)

LSC-C

10 9 8 7 6 5 4 3 2 1

This book is dedicated to the compañeros who helped me along the way: Alfredo López Austin, Mark Fried, Lino Bessonart, Carlos Díaz, Pedro Daniel Weinberg, and other friends. Always and above all, this book is dedicated to Helena Villagra.

Contents

Contents

Contents

Contents

x

Contents

Contents

Contents

xiii

Contents

Translator's Note

HUNTER OF STORIES WAS WRITTEN DURING THE LAST THREE years of Eduardo Galeano's life, most of it a few hours every day sitting quietly alone, pad and pen in hand, as he traveled across Latin America, Europe, and the United States for public appearances. A consummate performer, Eduardo drew energy from his readers even as the drudgery of travel exhausted him.

I last saw him in 2013 on his final visit to New York City, when he was already being treated for an aggressive return of the cancer that had cost him half a lung a decade before. Though he did not look well, his spirit was undiminished. He excitedly recounted what he had recently seen or heard, tales that confirmed his habitual optimism about the human condition and his eternal pessimism about the course of civilization.

Translator's Note

When an early draft of the book arrived on my desk at the beginning of 2014, sprinkled as it was with reflections on death, I realized how quickly his health was failing. By then, Eduardo had given up his itinerant lifestyle and was closeted at his home in Montevideo. He continued to rework and expand *Hunter of Stories* for much of that year, and I imagine his compulsive attention to detail and his delight in writing helped keep his mind off his illness.

Eduardo must have felt some urgency to tell the stories he had collected or imagined and to share the insights from a life fully lived. Yet the book retains his familiar tone of calm and delighted reflection, even when contemplating the prospect of leaving behind the world he critiqued so trenchantly and loved so dearly.

Mark Fried

Note from the Editor
of the Spanish Edition

EDUARDO GALEANO DIED ON APRIL 13, 2015. WE HAD signed off on the final details of *Hunter of Stories* the previous summer, including the cover image, the monster of Buenos Aires, which, as was his wont, he chose. He had spent 2012 and 2013 working on the book. Given that his state of health was not good, we decided to delay publication in order to protect him from the many tasks involved in any book launch.

During his last months he continued rewriting and polishing his texts, again and again, something that had always given him pleasure. He also began a new book, which he wanted to call *Scribblings*, a few stories of which he completed. After his death, when it was possible to move ahead with publishing

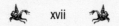

Note from the Editor of the Spanish Edition

Hunter of Stories, we reread the stories in that unfinished work and felt that a number of them had so much in common with those of *Hunter of Stories* that they should be incorporated into this volume. Some twenty of these "scribblings" are included here.

Eduardo was always a sober man, perhaps paying homage to the Welsh genes he so often denied, and he would rarely complain about his illness or his pains, even during his final days. A handful of the new texts seems to outline what he thought or imagined regarding death. They are so strong and beautiful that we took the liberty of adding a new section to the original manuscript and giving it the title of the poem he had chosen for the book's ending, which in fact ends the book: "I Crave, I Covet, I Yearn."

Besides these additions, we followed all of his indications, which, as usual, were obsessively and kindly detailed.

It is not easy to write the final word on this project, which benefited from the valuable commentaries and observations of Daniel Weinberg and the professionalism of Gabriela Vigo and the rest of the Siglo XXI team during the long editing process, all of whom must have been particularly motivated by the affection they felt and still feel for Eduardo.

I thank Helena Villagra for her priceless assistance in giving *Hunter of Stories* its final shape. Editing this book was a pleasant task, a reencounter with a beloved writer, and at the same time it was unavoidably difficult.

Carlos E. Díaz

Windmills of Time

Footprints

Wind smooths over the tracks of gulls.
Rain washes away human steps.
Sun bleaches the scars of time.
Storytellers seek the footprints of lost memory, love and pain that cannot be seen but are never erased.

Elegy to Travel

In the pages of *A Thousand and One Nights*, this advice appears:

"Get going, friend! Drop everything and get going! Of what use is an arrow if it never flies from the bow? How good would the melodious lute sound if it were still a piece of wood?"

Free

By day, the sun guides them. By night, the stars.

Paying no fare, they travel without passports and without forms for customs or immigration.

Birds are the only free beings in this world inhabited by prisoners. They fly from pole to pole, powered by food alone, on the route they choose and at the hour they wish, without ever asking permission of officials who believe they own the heavens.

Shipwrecked

The world is on the move.

On board are more shipwrecked souls than successful seafarers.

Thousands of desperate people die en route, before they can complete the crossing to the promised land, where even the poor are rich and everyone lives in Hollywood.

The illusions of any who manage to arrive do not last long.

Wind

It spreads seeds, guides clouds, tests sailors.

Sometimes it cleanses the air; sometimes it dirties it.

Sometimes it brings close what was far off and sometimes it scatters what was close by.

Invisible and untouchable, it caresses or strikes, whispers or roars.

Some think it says, "I blow wherever I wish."

But no one really understands.

Does it announce what is to come?

Weather forecasters in China are known as "mirrors of the wind."

Rice's Journey

In Asia rice is cultivated with meticulous care. At harvest the stalks are gently cut and gathered into bunches, so that evil winds do not carry off its soul.

The people of Sichuan remember the fiercest flood that has ever been or will be: it occurred in ancient times and it drowned the rice, body and soul.

Only a dog survived.

After the flood finally turned and the angry waters began to abate, he managed to reach shore, swimming hard.

The dog had a grain of rice stuck to his tail.

In that grain lay the soul.

Lost Breath

Before the before, when time was not yet time and the world was not yet the world, we were all gods.

Brahma, the Hindu god, could not bear the competition, so he stole our divine breath and concealed it in a secret hiding place.

Ever since, we have lived in search of our lost breath. We seek it in the depths of the sea and on the highest peaks.

From his great distance, Brahma smiles.

Stars

On the banks of the Platte River the Pawnee Indians speak of the origin.

Not even once had the paths of the evening star and the morning star crossed.

They wanted to meet.

The moon agreed to guide them to a rendezvous, but halfway there she threw them into the abyss, then spent several nights chuckling at her joke.

The stars were not discouraged. Desire gave them the strength to scale the precipice back up to the high heavens.

There, far above, they embraced so passionately that no one could tell which was which.

And from that incomparable coupling we wanderers of the world arose.

Encounters

Tezcatlipoca, Mexican god of the night, sent his son to sing alongside the crocodile musicians of heaven.

The sun was against it, but the black god, the outlawed beauty, paid no heed and brought together the voices of heaven and earth.

Thus were united silence and sound, chants and music, night and day, darkness and color. And thus they all learned to live together.

The New World

Ulysses, driven by the wind, might have been the first Greek to see the ocean.

I can only imagine his astonishment when his ship passed through the Strait of Gibraltar and before his eyes lay that immense expanse, guarded by the ever-open maws of monsters.

It would not have crossed the mariner's mind that beyond those salty waters and roaring winds lay a mystery even more immense and still without a name.

Satanic Diversity

In Peru, in the middle of the seventeenth century, the priest Bernabé Cobo finished writing his *History of the New World*.

Cobo set out in that voluminous work the reason why indigenous America had so many gods and such diverse versions of the origins of its peoples.

The reason was straightforward: the Indians were ignorant.

A century before, the scribe Juan de Betanzos, principal advisor of conquistador Francisco Pizarro, had revealed another, more powerful reason: Satan dictated what the Indians believed; that was why they did not share one religion and why they confused Good with Evil and had so many conflicting ideas.

"The Devil sends them thousands of illusions and ruses," he decreed.

Barbaric Customs

The British conquerors were cross-eyed with astonishment.

They came from a civilized nation, where women were the property of their husbands and owed them obedience, as the Bible insists, but in America the world was upside down.

They suspected the Iroquois women were libertines. Women had their own opinions and their own possessions. They had the right to divorce and could vote in community decisions. Husbands did not even have the right to punish the women that belonged to them.

The white invaders could no longer sleep in peace, for the customs of the pagan savages might prove contagious.

Mute

Indigenous divinities were the first victims of the conquest of America.

"Extirpation of idolatry" is what the victors called the war that condemned the gods to silence.

Blind

How did Europe view us in the sixteenth century?

Through the eyes of Theodor de Bry.

An artist from Liège who never set foot in America was the first European to draw the inhabitants of the New World.

His engravings were a graphic version of the chronicles of the conquistadors.

The images depicted a favorite dish of American savages: the flesh of Europeans, roasted over coals.

Seated in a circle around red-hot grills, they devoured arms, legs, ribs, and bellies and then licked their fingers.

Pardon the bother, but were those people hungering for human flesh really Indians?

In de Bry's engravings, all of them are bald.

In America, not a single Indian was bald.

The Monster of Buenos Aires

This is how the French priest Louis Feuillée saw it, or imagined it, and that is what he called it.

The monster was but one of the fearsome images that illustrated the account of his journey through South American lands, "kingdoms of Satan," from 1707 to 1711.

Deaf

A few natives came out to meet the Spanish conquistadors who first set foot on the sands of Yucatán.

According to Fray Toribio de Benavente, the Spaniards asked, in the language of Castile, "Where are we? What is this place called?"

The natives answered, "Tectetán."

The Spaniards understood them to say, "Yucatán."

And ever since, that is what the peninsula has been called.

But what the natives had said in their language was, "I don't understand you."

The Mighty Zero

Nearly two thousand years ago, the symbol for zero was engraved on stone stelae at Uaxactún and other Maya ceremonial centers.

The Mayans had gone farther than the Babylonians and the Chinese in developing the key that unlocked a new era in the history of science.

Thanks to the zero, these children of time, astronomical and mathematical sages, created precise solar calendars, becoming prophets able to predict eclipses and other marvels of nature.

Danger

Chocolate, ancient drink of the Indians of Mexico, provoked mistrust and even panic among the foreigners from Europe.

Physician Juan de Cárdenas proved that chocolate caused flatulence and melancholy, and the foam impeded digestion and provoked "terrible sorrows in the heart."

It was also suspected of abetting sin. Bishop Bernardo de Salazar excommunicated the ladies who drank chocolate during mass.

They did not give up the vice.

The Passion According to Cochabamba

When the child kissed his mother's nipple, a gush of milk and honey burst forth, but the breast ran dry when the father tried to suck.

And when mosquitos bit the father on his bald pate, the child caressed it, and from his scalp sprouted a rather handsome white hat of woven straw.

And when there was no work at the carpentry shop and they had nothing to eat, the child turned his body's excretions into empanadas of cheese and spiced chicken.

And when the family crossed the desert, suffering great thirst with not a drop to drink, the child kicked a pebble and from the earth flowed a spring of clear waters.

And when they reached fertile ground, he allowed the land to devour him, and down he sank and disappeared.

And on the third day, from the depths of the earth he reappeared, and he knew everything, absolutely everything that had occurred in his absence.

Thus it was in olden times, according to what I was told by truth-speaking women and men in the valley of Cochabamba.

The Explanation

Dominican friar Antonio de la Huerte wrote in 1547, regarding the strangeness of America: "One could say that on the day of Creation, the Lord's hand trembled a little."

Mother Nature Teaches

In the Amazon, mother nature gives classes in diversity.

The indigenous peoples identify ten soil types, eighty plant varieties, forty-three ant species, and three-hundred-ten species of birds, all within one square kilometer.

We Were Walking Forests

Every day the world loses a forest, murdered while only a few centuries old and still growing.

Barren deserts and uniform plantations spread far and wide, burying the world of green. Only a few peoples have been wise enough to keep up the language of plants that allows them to communicate with the fortress of the oak and the melancholies of the willow.

The Ceiba

In Cuba and other parts of the Americas the ceiba is a sacred tree, a tree of mystery. Lightning dares not touch it. Neither do hurricanes.

Inhabited by gods, it germinates at the center of the world and sends up the immense trunk that sustains the sky.

To cure the sky of its arrogance, every day the ceiba asks: "What feet would you stand on, if it were not for me?"

The Aruera

Warning to travelers: in the South American countryside, watch out for a tree called the aruera, from the indigenous *ahué*, meaning "evil tree."

A very touchy fellow is the aruera, who neither forgets nor forgives an affront.

One should not, one must not, cut a branch or sleep under its leafy crown without asking permission. Above all, it is forbidden to walk by it without offering a greeting.

If it is nighttime, you say, "Good morning."

If it is daytime, you say, "Good night."

Whoever fails in these obligations will be condemned to prolonged swellings and savage fevers, which sometimes kill.

Nobody Can Beat Grandpa

Good news for old folks still alive in this world: those who believe young trees have more and better wood are mistaken.

Giving testimony in California and other parts are sequoias, the largest trees in the world. These majestic grandfathers can live for three thousand years and still produce two billion leaves. They are the ones that best withstand lightning storms and six months of snow, and no disease can bring them down.

The Skin of Books

He gives us great pleasure, though he received little or none.

Ts'ai Lun, eunuch and member of the Chinese imperial court, invented paper. It was in the year 105, after much experimentation with mulberry bark and other plants.

Thanks to Ts'ai Lun, today we can read and write as we caress the skin of books and believe the words they speak belong to us.

Symbols

In 1961, while several international experts recommended outlawing the cultivation and consumption of coca leaves, there came to light in northeastern Peru the remnants of such leaves chewed thousands of years ago.

Chewing coca has long been a healthful custom in the high Andes. Coca calms nausea and dizziness and is the best remedy for exhaustion and certain diseases.

Besides, and this is not the least of it, the coca leaf is a symbol of Andean identity that only ill will confuses with the sorry chemical manipulation called cocaine.

Another chemical concoction, heroin, can be made from poppies. But to date, as far as we know, poppies remain a symbol of peace, remembrance, and patriotism in England.

Labor

In Tijuana, in the year 2000-something, the priest David Ungerleider heard confession from a hit man on the payroll of Mexico's cocaine-trafficking drug lords.

This professional, whose name was Jorge, was twenty years old and got paid $2,000 per killing.

He explained it thus: "I prefer living five years like a king to living fifty like an ox."

Five years later, he was also marked for death.

He knew too much.

Here's how the international division of labor in the cocaine trade works: so some can put it up their noses, others put up their bodies.

Urraká's Allies

In Panama's Veraguas Mountains, Urraká led the indigenous resistance.

He received a lot of help from rain, thunder, and wind.

Whenever the Spanish conquistadors advanced, rain ruined their powder and muskets; thunder roared and caused night to descend in the middle of day. The invaders lost their way and furious winds knocked them to the ground.

The Slingshot Boy

Juan Wallparrimachi Mayta, the warrior-poet, used neither a sword nor an arquebus.

Bolivia was not yet independent and not yet called by that name when he led the slingshot brigade under the command of Juana Azurduy. They launched a whirlwind of spinning lassos and death-dealing stones against the Spanish invaders.

The slingshot boys sang as they attacked. A chorus of voices intoned Juan's Quechua poems to the women he loved or hoped to love.

Loving you,
dreaming of you,
I shall die.

On the battlefield a bullet brought him down. He was twenty-one.

Túpac Amaru's Forebears

Near the middle of the eighteenth century, Ignacio Torote led a short-lived rebellion against the intruders who had come to the Peruvian jungle to steal souls and land.

At about the same time, Juan Santos Atahualpa's indigenous army was inflicting one crushing defeat after another on the Spanish troops, impeding their advance.

And it was not long after Juan Santos lay dying far from his impenetrable jungle home that young José Gabriel Condorcanqui took the name Túpac Amaru and rallied the largest indigenous uprising in the history of the Americas.

From rebellion to rebellion, defeat to defeat, history rolled on. When she says goodbye, she's really saying see you later.

Buenos Aires Was Born Twice

The first birth happened in 1536.

Still a newborn, the city died of hunger.

Then in 1580, where the Plaza de Mayo now stands, Buenos Aires was born again.

A densely populated part of today's city got its name because the Indians did not welcome the intruders. From the very beginning it was war. La Matanza was named for a massacre: the dead were Querandíe Indians, every one of them.

According to conquistador Juan de Garay, they were "angry natives."

The First Flute

A hunter got lost, once upon a time, in one of the labyrinths of the Amazon jungle.

After much wandering, he collapsed at the foot of a cigar-box cedar and fell asleep.

He was awakened by the sun and by music entirely new to him.

Then the lost hunter spied a woodpecker, red head, long neck, powerful beak, jabbing away at a branch.

The music came from the wind blowing through the holes the bird had drilled.

The hunter learned. Imitating wind and bird, he made the first American flute.

The Drum

From the coasts of Africa, in the hands and memory of slaves, it traveled to the plantations of America.

There it was outlawed, for the beating of the drum unbound the shackled and gave voice to those condemned to silence. The owners of men and property were well aware that such dangerous music, music that called down the gods, foretold rebellion.

That is why the sacred drum slept unseen.

Old Folks' Contest

A few millennia ago, give or take a year or two, the jaguar, the dog, and the coyote held a competition. Which of them was the oldest of the old? As a prize, the winner would get to eat the first food they found.

From a ramshackle cart bumping its way down a hill fell a bag filled with corn tortillas.

Who deserved the treasure?

Which of them was the oldest of the old? The jaguar said he had seen the world's first dawn. The dog said he was the only survivor of the great flood.

The coyote said nothing; his mouth was full.

A Storyteller Told Me

Once upon a time, somewhere in the jungle of Africa, lived a lion king, gluttonous and imperious.

The king forbade his subjects from eating grapes. "Only I may eat grapes," he decreed, and he signed a royal proclamation that his monopoly was the will of the gods.

The rabbit, deep in the thicket, then kicked up a tremendous ruckus, breaking branches, swinging from vines, screaming: "Even elephants will fly! The wind is going crazy! There's a hurricane coming!"

The rabbit urged the animals to protect the monarch by tying him to the stoutest tree.

Thus the lion king, tightly bound, was saved from the hurricane that never arrived, while the rabbit, scampering about the jungle, left not a single grape uneaten.

Samuel Ruiz Was Born Twice

In 1959, a new bishop arrived in Chiapas.

Samuel Ruiz, the newcomer, was horrified by the threat Communism posed to freedom.

In an interview, journalist Fernando Benítez suggested that the right to humiliate others did not deserve to be called freedom. The young bishop threw him out.

Don Samuel spent his first years teaching Christian resignation to Indians already condemned to slavish obedience. But as the years went by, reality spoke and taught, and Don Samuel was wise enough to listen.

After half a century as bishop, he became the religious arm of the Zapatista insurrection.

The natives called him the Bishop of the Poor, a successor to Fray Bartolomé de Las Casas.

Don Samuel said goodbye to Chiapas when he retired in 2000. But he took with him the embrace of the Maya. "Thank you," people told him, "now we walk with our heads held high."

José Falcioni Died Twice

In the year 1907, to break up an assembly of workers on strike, a double rank of riflemen from the Argentinian Navy fired their Mausers at the Community Hall in Puerto Ingeniero White.

Commander Enrique Astorga had given the order to shoot to kill.

José Falcioni, a worker who lived nearby but was not involved, had the bad fortune to be out and about, and a bullet pierced his lung.

A silent multitude accompanied him to Bahía Blanca cemetery.

They say the commander himself shoved his way through the crowd and put three more bullets into the body of the deceased.

Just in case.

Soil's Journey

The black soil of the Amazon is largely made up of "biochar," thanks to an ancient yet scorned practice of indigenous farmers in the jungle.

Biochar—charcoal made for fertilizer—never decomposes and draws additional sustenance from the thousand-and-one bits of earthenware that the farmers break apart and then bury, to return to the earth what from the earth has come.

Thanks to this act of religious gratitude, the soil regenerates continuously, from season to season, from hand to hand.

Indignant Earth

In May of the year 2013, for the first time in the history of Guatemala, an exterminator of Indians was found guilty of racist genocide. A civil court sentenced him to eighty years in prison.

General Efraín Ríos Montt was the next to last in a series of military dictators who specialized in massacring Maya Indians.

Shortly after the executioner received his sentence, the country's highest judicial authorities postponed it, only for an earthquake to hit the country. The earth rose up in fury against the impunity such killers habitually enjoy.

Homage

On Santa Lucía Hill, in downtown Santiago de Chile, stands a statue of the indigenous leader Caupolicán.

Caupolicán looks rather like a Hollywood Indian, which makes sense. The work was sculpted in the United States in 1869 for a competition to honor James Fenimore Cooper, author of *The Last of the Mohicans*.

The statue lost the contest, and the Mohican had to change countries and pretend he was Chilean.

Andresito

José Artigas, author of the first agrarian reform in the Americas, refused to accept that the poorest sons and daughters of these lands should be ambushed by independence. He scandalized colonial society by naming an indigenous man, Andresito Guacurarí, as governor and promoting him to the rank of commander.

Before Artigas was defeated by two slaveholding empires and three treasonous port cities, he learned of Andresito's death in battle.

Nothing ever caused him more pain. Andresito, his chosen son, was the bravest of his soldiers and the quietest. A silent Indian, whose actions spoke for him.

The Charrúas' Claw

In the year 1832, the few Charrúa warriors who survived the defeat of Artigas were invited to sign a peace treaty. The president of Uruguay, Fructuoso Rivera, promised them land.

Once the Indians had eaten well and drunk well, and were sound asleep, soldiers went to work. To save bullets, they killed the Indians with knives, and to save time, they dumped the bodies into a stream called Salsipuedes, which means "get out if you can."

Official history calls this deception a "battle." Today, whenever Uruguayans win a soccer trophy, we celebrate the triumph of "the Charrúas' claw."

Coffee's Journey

Captain John Newton sang hymns while piloting his ships across the sea, ships filled to bursting with slaves in chains.

"How sweet the name of Jesus sounds . . . "

Coffee had emerged in Ethiopia, millennia before, born from the black tears of the god Waka."

Perhaps the god was crying in advance for the misery coffee, like sugar, would bring to the millions of slaves stolen from Africa and worked to death in the name of other gods on the plantations of the Americas.

Cafés with History

At the café Bar El Cairo, located not in Egypt but in the Argentine city of Rosario, cartoonist and writer Roberto Fontanarrosa has a table. He died a few years ago, but you can always find him there, along with his dog Mendieta and his friend Inodoro Pereira.

The first group of Argentinean artists and writers was founded at the Café Tortoni in Buenos Aires.

The Brazilian Academy of Letters, presided over by novelist Machado de Assis, met at the Confeitaria Colombo in Rio de Janeiro.

At the Café Paraventi in the city of São Paulo, Olga Benário and Luiz Carlos Prestes dreamed up the Brazilian revolution.

During their time in exile, Trotsky and Lenin discussed the Russian revolution at the Café Central in Vienna.

Portuguese poet Fernando Pessoa wrote several of his master works in the Café A Brasileira in Lisbon.

While the twentieth century was being born, Pablo Picasso held the first exhibit of his works at the Café Els Quatre Gats in Barcelona.

In 1894, writer Ferenc Molnár threw the keys to Budapest's New York Café into the waters of the Danube so no one could lock the door.

In 1898, Émile Zola penned his famous open letter, "J'accuse," at the Café de la Paix in Paris.

In 1914, the socialist Jean Jaurès, who had declared war on war, was murdered in the Café du Croissant, also in Paris.

The epicenter of the 1919 insurrection against British occupation in Cairo was the Café Riche.

In 1921, the Sunset Cafe opened in Chicago, and there Louis Armstrong and Benny Goodman spread their musical wings.

Noon Splendor

There were fish never before seen, plants from no garden, books from impossible bookstores.

At the fair on Tristán Narvaja Street in Montevideo, there were mountains of fruit and city blocks of fragrant flowers of all hues. Bird musicians and human dancers vied for attention while preachers of heaven and orators of earth screamed words of doom from their soapbox mounts. The former proclaimed the hour of resurrection, the latter the day of insurrection.

Someone wandering among the stalls offered a hen for sale on a leash like a dog; another was selling a penguin blown off course to our beaches from the snows of the south.

There were long lines of exhausted shoes, mouths wide open and tongues hanging out. The shoes were sold in pairs and also singly, lone shoes for people with a lone foot. There were used eyeglasses, used keys, used dentures. The dentures sat in an earthen jar filled with water. Each customer reached in, selected one, popped it in and flapped his gums; if the denture did not fit, he returned it to the jar.

There were clothes for dressing up and clothes for dressing down, medals for athletes and for generals, clocks that kept whatever time you wished. And there were also the friends and lovers you stumbled upon without knowing you were looking for them.

Memory's fiesta, coming next Sunday at noon.

Memory's Helping Hand

In Saint Petersburg, when it was still Leningrad, I learned the history of that city's resurrection.

Between 1941 and 1944 Hitler's troops murdered it. Nine hundred days of continuous bombardment and blockade turned the city, once Queen of the Baltic, capital of czarist Russia, and cradle of the Communist revolution, into an immense ruin inhabited by ghosts.

Twenty years after that tragedy, I saw a city returned to its former self. Brick by brick, day after day, its citizens had built it anew. The plans for reconstruction came from photographs, sketches, old newspaper columns, and testimony from the residents of every neighborhood.

Memory gave birth to a city reborn.

Memory Is Not
an Endangered Species

The Mexican farmers organized in the Network for the Defense of Corn respond to queries: "Memory is our primary seed. Since people lost their love for corn, we don't even know where we're from."

A woman from the south of Veracruz, member of the same network: "Huge quantities of herbicide, insecticide, fertilizer and of course the earth gets sick. With all those chemicals the soil gets addicted."

Another: "Varieties are disappearing. Corn is not like it was before, when beans, chilies, tomatoes, and squash grew alongside it."

And an elderly farmer, nostalgic for the old flavors of rural life, concluded: "We no longer know how to read the rain, the stars, the delicacy of the air . . . "

Seeds of Identity

In the middle of the year 2011, more than fifty Peruvian organizations came together to defend the 3,250 varieties of the potato. Such diversity, the legacy of 8,000 years of peasant agriculture, faces a mortal threat from an invasion of genetically modified seed that would impose a few standardized varieties on behalf of powerful corporations.

What a paradox today's world is. In the name of freedom we are invited to choose between the same and the same, be it on the table or on television.

Divine Offering

Tunupa, the god of lightning who calls down the rain, is also a volcano that rules over the altiplano of the Andes.

At his feet lies an infinite white plain that looks like snow but is actually salt, and on his slopes blossom fields of quinoa.

"I brought quinoa to console the desperate," people say the volcano said.

He gave the tiny grains to the Aymara and Quechua people, who thus survived fierce sun and frost and were rescued from hunger.

Amnesia

Nicolae Ceausescu ran Romania's dictatorship for more than twenty years.

He faced no opposition because the population was too busy filling the prisons and cemeteries, but everyone enjoyed the right to endlessly applaud the Pharaonic monuments he built with volunteer labor in homage to himself.

Also exercising the right to applaud were notable politicians, like Richard Nixon and Ronald Reagan, both his bosom buddies, and the International Monetary Fund and the World Bank, which showered money and praise on a Communist dictatorship that obeyed their orders with no questions asked.

To celebrate his absolute rule, Ceausescu had a scepter carved from marble and gave himself the title "Conductor of the People."

As was the custom, no one disagreed.

But shortly thereafter, a hurricane of popular fury led to his execution in a ceremony of collective exorcism.

Then, magically, the favorite of the world's powerful became the bad guy of the picture.

It tends to happen.

Monster Wanted

Saint Columba was rowing across Loch Ness when an immense serpent with a gaping mouth attacked his boat. Saint Columba, who had no desire to be eaten, chased it off by making the sign of the cross.

Fourteen centuries later, the monster was seen again by someone living nearby, who happened to have a camera around his neck, and pictures of it and of curious footprints came out in the Glasgow and London papers.

The creature turned out to be a toy, the footprints made by baby hippopotamus feet, which are sold as ashtrays.

The revelation did nothing to discourage the tourists.

The market for fear feeds on the steady demand for monsters.

Ladies and Gentlemen!

"Only a few tickets left and they're going fast! Don't miss out!"

The first human zoos were founded in 1874 by German businessman Carl Hagenbeck. They spread nearly everywhere in Europe and were a huge success.

Not to be left behind, the Argentine Rural Society put on a spectacle of its own sixty-five years later. The ticket-buying public could enjoy a trip to prehistory and ogle a handful of nearly naked Macás Indians kidnapped from the Gran Chaco and displayed in a corral alongside the country's prize cattle.

Let's Go Out

At the end of the nineteenth century, many residents of Montevideo spent their Sundays on a favorite outing: an excursion to the jail and the insane asylum.

Contemplating prisoners and lunatics, the visitors felt certifiably free and sane.

Foreigner

In a community newspaper in Barcelona's Raval neighborhood, an anonymous hand wrote:

Your god is Jewish, your music is African, your car is Japanese, your pizza is Italian, your gas is Algerian, your coffee is Brazilian, your democracy is Greek, your numbers are Arabic, your letters are Latin.

I am your neighbor. And you call me a foreigner?

Aesop

Lilian Thuram, great-grandson of slaves on the island of Guadeloupe, asked his smallest child, "What does God look like?"

Without hesitation, the boy answered, "God is white."

Thuram was a great soccer player, a European and world champion, but that response changed his life.

He decided to leave the playing field and dedicate his best efforts to restoring black dignity across the world.

He decried racism in soccer and in education, which, except in the case of slave owners' descendants, drains children of their past.

And he delved into collective memory, which opened his eyes to endless discoveries. His work to reveal the hidden was laden with doubt and all but bereft of certainties, but he was not discouraged. Linking disparate studies, he demonstrated that Aesop may have been a black slave in Nubia, and he reminded us that there were black pharaohs in Egypt and hundreds of shrines in the Congo celebrating the Black Virgin, even if the Church said she was not black at all but only looked that way from the smoke of incense and the sins of the unfaithful.

A Fable from Aesop's Time

An old woman found an empty vessel shattered on the ground.

All that remained of the good Palermo wine was the aroma.

She sniffed the fragments of fine pottery again and again, with growing pleasure.

After imbibing many a lungful, she offered this flattery to the vanished wine: "If these are your footprints, how lovely must have been your steps."

If Larousse Says So . . .

In 1885, Joseph Anténor Firmin, a black Haitian, published in Paris a book of more than six hundred pages entitled *On the Equality of Human Races*.

The work had little distribution and evoked no response except silence. In those days, Larousse's *Grand dictionnaire universel* had the last word. It helpfully explained: "In the negro species, the brain is less developed than in the white species."

And Las Vegas Was Born

Back in the year 1950-something Las Vegas wasn't much. Its greatest attraction were the mushroom clouds sent up by the US Army, a spectacle the nearly exclusively white residents could enjoy from their porches. Also attracting audiences that were indeed exclusively white were the great black performers of the day, the stars of song.

Louis Armstrong, Ella Fitzgerald, and Nat King Cole were well paid, but had to slip in and out by the service entrance. The day Sammy Davis Jr. jumped into the swimming pool, the hotel manager ordered it drained and refilled.

Thus it was until 1955, when a millionaire opened what he called "the first interracial casino in the United States." Joe Louis, the legendary boxer, greeted the customers, by then white and black, and Las Vegas set off on the path to becoming Las Vegas.

The owners of the village soon to become the most sumptuous paradise of plastic were still racists, but they had made a discovery: racism is not good business. After all, a black man's dollars are as green as a white man's.

Would You Mind Repeating That?

Nowadays, the global dictatorship of the market gives orders that are rather contradictory: "Tighten your belts and drop your pants."

Commandments from on high are not much more consistent, truth be told. In the Bible (Exodus 20:13), God orders: "Thou shalt not kill."

And in the following chapter (Exodus 21:12–17), the same God orders us to kill and offers five different reasons for doing so.

The Golden Throne

As they tell it on Olympus, Zeus, the god of gods, and his wife Hera got into one of those domestic disputes that will age you a hundred years. Things were going from bad to worse when their son, Hephaestus, turned up uninvited and took his mother's side.

Cast out by his father, Hephaestus fell all the way to earth.

He found refuge in a cave and there he took up metalwork.

His masterpiece he dedicated to Mom.

It was a golden throne with but one defect: whoever sat in it would be enchained forever.

Illuminated Little Dictator

The man who burned the most books and read the fewest was the owner of the heftiest library in Chile.

Augusto Pinochet accumulated thousands upon thousands of volumes, thanks to the public monies he converted to funds for his personal use.

He bought books not to read them, but to have them.

An inexhaustible supply: it was like adding dollars to his accounts in Riggs Bank.

His library contained 887 works on Napoleon Bonaparte alone, all luxuriously bound. And sculptures of his favorite hero adorned the shelves.

Every book featured Pinochet's personal seal of ownership, his ex libris: a winged figure of Liberty bearing a torch.

To house the collection, he built the President Augusto Pinochet Ugarte Library at the Chilean Army's War College.

Invincible Little Dictator

Killing was a pleasure and it mattered little if the cadaver was a crow, a duck, or a Republican. But hunting quail was Francisco Franco's specialty.

One day in October 1959, the generalissimo killed 4,600 quail, thus breaking his own record.

Photographers immortalized that glorious day. At the feet of the victor, his spoils covered the earth.

The Terrorizer

Back in the years 1975 and 1976, before and after the coup d'état that imposed the most savage of Argentina's many military dictatorships, death threats flew fast and furious and anyone suspected of the crime of thinking simply disappeared.

Orlando Rojas, a Paraguayan exile, answered his telephone in Buenos Aires. Every day a voice repeated the same thing: "I'm calling to tell you you're going to die."

"So you aren't?" Orlando asked.

The terrorizer would hang up.

Purgatory

In July of the year 1936, at the height of his war against the Spanish Republic, Generalísimo Francisco Franco gave an interview to American journalist Jay Allen.

Franco said the victory of the cross and the sword was imminent: "We will go on at whatever cost."

"You will have to shoot half of Spain," the journalist suggested.

Franco replied: "I said whatever the cost."

The purgers worked hand in glove with confessor priests and soldiers. Spain had to be cleansed of rats, fleas, and Bolsheviks.

Closed Doors

In August of the year 2004, a shopping center caught fire in Asunción, Paraguay.

Three hundred ninety-six people died.

The doors were barred so that no one could escape without paying.

Invisible

In November of the year 2012, a factory fire burned 110 workers alive in Bangladesh. They labored in sweatshops and had neither rights nor security.

In April of the following year, another Bangladeshi sweatshop conflagration burned 1,127 workers alive.

They were invisible, like the slaves in other parts of this globalized world.

And practically invisible were their wages, a dollar a day.

In full view, however, are the outrageous prices charged for the clothing their hands produced for Walmart, JCPenney, Sears, Benetton, H&M . . .

The First Strike

It broke out in Egypt, in the Valley of the Kings, on November 14 in the year 1152 BC.

The protagonists of the first strike in history were the stonecutters, carpenters, masons, and draftsmen building the pyramids, who dropped tools until they received the wages they were due.

Long ago, Egypt's workers won the right to strike and also free medical attention for workplace accidents.

Until recently we knew nothing or nearly nothing about this.

Perhaps because others might follow their lead.

The Windbreak

The priest Thomas Müntzer led the peasant insurrection of 1525 in Germany.

This enemy of princes and of the lords of land and war rallied droves of men who refused to be the property of other men.

Martin Luther cursed his renegade disciple as a fool: "I would not believe in Müntzer, even if he swallowed the Holy Spirit, feathers and all."

Müntzer responded: "I would not believe in Luther, even if he swallowed a hundred thousand Bibles whole."

Müntzer's revolution occupied land, burned castles, confronted both the army and the high priests, but within the year it was over.

The victors killed thousands of rebellious serfs and cut off Müntzer's head, which they displayed in the central square of the imperial city of Mühlhausen as a lesson to all.

Echoes

In the middle of the seventeenth century, agrarian communities that defied the all-powerful nobility spread across the fields of England and survived.

Centuries have passed and the words spoken and written by one of the communities' stalwarts, Gerrard Winstanley, still resound:

Thy Father is the Spirit of Community and thy Mother is the Earth.

In the beginning of Time, the great Creator Reason, made the Earth to be a Common Treasury, but not one word was spoken that one branch of mankind should rule over another.

Every man and woman shall have the free liberty to marry whom they love, if they can obtain the love and liking of that party whom they would marry.

If the earth were set free from kingly bondage, many secrets of God and his works in nature would be made public, which men nowadays keep secret to get a living by. But when commonwealth's freedom is established, then will knowledge cover the earth, as the waters cover the seas.

Was Order Restored?

Workers on general strike in November of the year 1922 committed the crime of occupying the city of Guayaquil without firing a shot. The few days they governed were more peaceful than any before in that part of the world. Those born to obey took the place God had reserved for those born to rule, and that is simply not done. The president of Ecuador called for "order and tranquility, cost what it may."

The announcement soon came that order had been restored.

Now every November wooden crosses bob in the current of the Guayas River, set afloat to commemorate the workers murdered and thrown into the waters by presidential decree.

Nests United

Maybe mutual aid and community awareness are not human inventions.

Housing cooperatives, for example, might have been inspired by birds.

In southern Africa and elsewhere, birds by the hundreds have always built their nests together, sharing the labor of all for all. They begin by erecting a large straw roof, under which each couple weaves its nest, linked to the rest in a grand apartment block that reaches the highest branches of the trees.

The Other School

Ernesto Lange grew up in the region of San José in the Uruguayan countryside.

As a child, sparrows kept him company. At dusk thousands of them congregated in the trees to bid goodbye to the departing sun, and after night fell they continued singing.

The sparrows were rather ugly, but the music of the choir that gathered without fail to give thanks to the sun for its warmth and light was lovely.

Ernesto's story made me remember something I saw many years ago in a park in Gijón: there, lone peacocks, the most beautiful of birds, displayed their astonishing fans of colored feathers and howled disconsolately, each in solitude, while darkness grew and the day withered.

The Activist

Laudelina de Campos Mello, granddaughter of slaves, was born in 1904.

From the age of twelve she had to take charge of her five younger brothers.

Her black skin did not help her find employment in the city of São Paulo, but she managed to cook and clean in several private homes, from dawn to dusk, taking her brothers with her.

Granny Nina, as she became known, was twenty when she was elected president of the domestic workers' union.

From then on she dedicated her life to helping women who, like her, were born already condemned to perpetual servitude.

She died at the age of eighty-six.

At her funeral there were no speeches.

All of her fellow workers were there and they said goodbye with song.

The Seamstress

She sewed the best doublets in the city of La Paz, elegant bulwarks against the cold. In quality and taste, nothing could compare with her creations.

But Simona Manzaneda's mastery reached far beyond that. This seamstress of delicate hands and soft words plotted against the colonial power. Between the basted layers of her many skirts and amid their many folds, she hid maps, letters, instructions, and messages that helped win freedom for the land now known as Bolivia.

Simona sewed and conspired until someone gave her away.

They cut off her braids and shaved her head. Mounted on a burro, she was paraded naked in the city's main plaza, and after fifty lashes she was shot in the back.

Not a moan escaped her. She knew her death was no mistake.

The Dangerous Woman

In November of the year 1976 agents of Argentina's military dictatorship shot up Clara Anahí Mariani's home and murdered her parents.

She was never heard from again, although her name figures on a list of "subversive delinquents" compiled by the Intelligence Division of the Buenos Aires Provincial Police.

Her record says: "Extremist."

She was three months old when that record was filed.

Look Who's Looking

In the days of Al Capone, spying was frowned upon in the United States, since it violated citizens' freedom and privacy.

Years later, surveillance has become a patriotic duty.

Nearly everyone agrees spying is the proper way to foil the troublemakers who serve the cause of international terrorism by invoking human rights. As in the case of several dubious individuals who happen to be friends of the author of this book.

Admirable Heroes, Unwanted Guests

At the beginning of the nineteenth century, the leaders of Chile's struggle for independence openly admired the indigenous resistance that was the toughest bone the Spanish conquistadors had to chew.

The earliest patriots identified with the Mapuche warriors Caupolicán and Lautaro.

Barely a few years later, the largest newspapers were already applauding the war against the Indians, whom they called "unwanted guests in the Chilean fatherland."

Now the papers call them "terrorists" for defending lands still being stolen from them.

Leeches

For several centuries leeches were among Europe's main imports.

Doctors believed the worms cured the ill by sucking their blood.

Common sense finally determined that bloodletting weakens the sick and hastens death.

Even so, modern leeches, made over to look less repulsive, now operate as honorable companies in many fields, and will suck your blood for a fee as they conduct you to the cemetery.

Hallelujah

A midday hour in mid-1972 was witness to a memorable religious ceremony in the city of Quito.

It was a huge story in the papers, on television and radio, and the city's gossipers spoke of nothing else.

The liturgy reached its culminating moment when the sizable gathering, faces bathed in tears and accompanied by a blaring bugle, sang the national anthem as the honoree slowly ascended to the summit of the Shrine of the Heroes.

There on high, the altar built especially for this grand occasion glowed brightly in the sun.

At its center, wreathed in flowers, lay the honoree: the first barrel of Ecuadorean oil extracted by Texaco.

The crowd, on its knees, paid its devoted respects.

General Guillermo Rodríguez Lara, a dictator with a generous soul, who had made a gift of the country's oil to the company, declared: "We are going to plant oil! A new era has begun!"

Not long after, the truth came out. June 26, 1972, marked the beginning of arguably the worst massacre of nature in the history of the Amazon.

The Virgin Mary Privatized

What is not profitable does not deserve to exist, not on earth and not in heaven.

In the year 2002 the Virgin of Guadalupe, mother and symbol of Mexico, was sold not once, but twice.

In March the multinational company Viotran promised to pay $12 million for the rights to the Virgin's image for five years. The contract, signed by the abbot of the Basilica of Guadalupe with the backing of Cardinal Norberto Rivera, conferred blessings on all the religious articles the company would produce.

Then in July a Chinese businessman named Wu You Lin secured the Virgin's trademark for a much lower price and for a much longer period.

No one knows who she belongs to anymore.

The Welcome

For a few short days in the year 1982, the Uruguayan city of Fray Bentos was Hollywood.

A crowd, the likes of which had never been seen, cheered the city's first black limousine carrying an Arab sheikh, Abubaker Bakhashab, trailed by an eye-popping retinue of women dressed for a thousand and one nights.

During his stay in Uruguay, the savior of our flagging economy handed out promises left and right: fabulous investments, jobs galore, top wages, and juicy interest rates for anyone who would like to double his savings in the time it takes to say "amen."

No one could resist, until the night the sheik and his entire retinue evaporated without a trace.

Not even one of the many rings that weighed down his fingers remained as a souvenir, though he did paper the city with rubber checks.

That fleeting visit turned out to be prophetic: in short order powerful foreign companies turned up with the noble intention of repeating the story.

The Gates of Paradise

In the year 2009, the town of Moatize in Mozambique woke up to find itself the richest source of coal in the world.

Lifelong residents had to abandon their favorite haunts, devoured by companies come from afar to celebrate the discovery.

The mines drank up all the water and turned the town into a branch office of hell.

Farmers are still awaiting the fertile land they were promised.

What they got were fields of stone.

A Visit to Hell

Some years ago, during one of my deaths, I paid a visit to hell.

I had heard that in the underworld you can get your favorite wine and any delicacy you want, lovers for all tastes, dancing music, endless pleasure . . .

Once again, I was able to corroborate the fact that advertising lies. Hell promises a great life, but all I found were people waiting in line.

In that endless queue, snaking out of sight along narrow smoky passages, were women and men of all epochs, from cavemen to astronauts.

All were condemned to wait. To wait for eternity.

That's what I discovered: hell is waiting.

My Face, Your Face

According to those in the know, dolphins can recognize themselves in the mirror.

Any dolphin can identify the image he sees.

Our cousins, chimpanzees, orangutans, and gorillas, also peek in the mirror and have no doubt: this is me.

For us, things are more complicated, especially on those unfortunate depressing days only good for bad news or nail soup. When a day like that begins, all we can think is: Who is that guy looking at me? Who the hell's face am I shaving?

Masks

In West Africa, masks disclose the truth. Faces obscure, while masks reveal.

Depending on your vantage point—direct or in profile, close up or from afar, from above or below—by the magic of their art masks uncover the many in the one, the lives and deaths in every life. For each of us is multiple and masks have not learned how to lie.

This Shoe

Rafael Bieber picked it up: "This shoe, the one you're looking at, has a story."

He told me it had belonged to a patient who had trouble breathing.

Sometimes a machine or medication opened his lungs for a time, but then the air would abandon the suffocating man, no matter how much he implored it to come back.

One night in his distress, the fellow threw this shoe at the windowpane. At last, air came into his house and into his body, and he slid into a deep sleep after so many enemy nights.

When he awoke the floor was littered with shards of glass.

But they were not from his window, not from a window at all: they were what remained of the mirror, his mirror, shattered into a thousand pieces by this shoe.

The Doctor

Shennong, the Chinese god of farmers, felt deep compassion for the victims of polluted water and toxic plants. He taught farmers to distinguish drinkable from undrinkable, edible from inedible, and by saving lives he became the divine patron of Chinese medicine.

How would Shennong carry on his charitable work nowadays, when even ducks have asthma, doves suffer allergies, and herons have to spit out the poisoned water of the rivers?

Peace upon the Water

The world's fairest court, also the oldest in Europe, is not made up of jurists.

The Water Tribunal of Valencia, founded in the year 960, meets every Thursday at noon in the doorway of a cathedral that was once a mosque.

Its sensible rulings do not descend from above or come from afar: the judges, who resolve any conflicting claims on the water from the eight irrigation canals that supply Valencia's orchards, are local farmers who work their own land.

The canals, like the court, are a legacy of Muslim Spain.

Once upon a Time,
There Was a River

The Ganges was born from the seven steps of the god Vishnu, who left his footprints on the stones of the seven regions across India.

The river was the incarnation of Ganga, prettiest of the goddesses, who had her house amid the stars until she took it into her head to come live in this murderous world.

Only a few years ago, pilgrims visited the Ganges to drink the waters of immortality.

Today, that water kills.

Still sacred, but now one of the most polluted rivers on earth, the Ganges sickens whoever drinks from it or eats the food irrigated by its waters.

Once upon a Time,
There Was a Sea

It was a lake, and because it was one of the four largest in the world, they called it a sea, the Aral Sea.

Inundated by industrial waste and runoff from chemical fertilizers, abandoned by the rivers engineers diverted, not much of it is left.

Its waters have turned brackish, and brine has sterilized its shores.

A few boats, once for fishing and now ghosts, lie some distance inland.

Occasionally, voices announce the resurrection.

No one believes them.

We'll Have to Change Planets

God forbid that India should ever take to industrialization after the manner of the West. The economic
imperialism of a single tiny island kingdom (Britain) is
today keeping the world in chains. If an entire nation
of 300 million took to similar economic exploitation, it
would strip the world bare like locusts.

—Mahatma Gandhi, October 1926

A Nation Called Garbage

In 1997 a sailor named Charles Moore discovered a new archipelago made entirely of garbage, nearly three times the size of Spain.

The islands of this immense dump in the North Pacific feed on plastic debris: bottles, bottle caps, wrappers, fragments, and whatever other junk the cities of civilization chuck into the open sea.

In 2013 a campaign was launched to bestow nationhood on the new country, which might as well have its own flag.

Sorcerers' Apprentices

From the beginning of the millennium, in laboratories worthy of Dr. Frankenstein, experts have been working to save humanity.

They set themselves up in the Cayman Islands, not to evade taxes as suspicious minds might think, but rather to invent new ways of solving global warming and other scourges.

To cool the earth, they have tried shooting sulfur into the stratosphere, seeding the clouds. To end the plague of bug bites, they have propagated millions of sterile male mosquitoes, genetically modified, who dupe the females with promises of love but can never reproduce.

Autoism

With television proffering auto bodies more erotic than human ones, the deification of wheels has spread like a disease across the globe and our legs have withered from disuse.

At the beginning of this century, an international survey revealed an eloquent fact: asked what crime would hurt the most, most people answered to have their car stolen and not get it back.

A Riddle

A group of friends were invited to a feast on one con-dition: they would have to eat blindfolded.

After the meal, the cook commanded: "Each mouth shall say what it has eaten."

Most of them answered, "It tasted like chicken."

That was the only animal not on the menu, but no one argued. After all, not even chicken tastes like chicken anymore, since everything tastes like everything else and nothing at all. In these days of mandatory uniformity, chickens are mass produced, as are shrimp and fish.

As are we.

The Price of Devoutness

Twenty-five thousand elephants are murdered every year, crushed with ax-blows or shot from helicopters, their tusks turned into objects of religious veneration.

Ivory for making heavenly angels and earthly saints commands a very high price.

From slaughtered elephants come the most lavish sculptures of the Holy Virgin and Child, the sacred Child who symbolizes Goodness and Piety, while the most moving images of Jesus on the Cross are carved from the tusks of the massacred beasts.

Prophecies

Who was it that a century ago best described today's global power structure?

Not a philosopher, not a sociologist, not a political scientist either.

It was a child named Little Nemo, whose adventures were published in the *New York Herald* way back in 1905, as drawn by Winsor McCay.

Little Nemo dreamed about the future.

In one of his most unerring dreams, he traveled to Mars.

That unfortunate planet was in the hands of a businessman who had crushed his competitors and exercised an absolute monopoly.

The Martians seemed stupid, because they said little and breathed little.

Little Nemo knew why: the boss of Mars had seized ownership of words and the air.

They were the keys to life, the sources of power.

Magicians

In the year 2014 the International Monetary Fund issued an infallible prescription to save the world from economic crisis: *lower the minimum wage*.

Experts at the IMF had discovered that reducing the minimum wage would create more jobs for young people, who would earn less but then make up the difference by working more.

We all should be thankful for such generous minds. However, days keep going by, years too, and their ingenious recipe has yet to be brought to bear on a global scale.

Very Brief Synthesis of Contemporary History

For several centuries subjects have donned the garb of citizens, and monarchies have preferred to call themselves republics.

Local dictatorships, claiming to be democracies, open their doors to the steamroller of the global market. In this kingdom of the free, we are all united as one. But are we one, or are we no one? Buyers or bought? Sellers or sold? Spies or spied upon?

We live imprisoned behind invisible bars, betrayed by machines that feign obedience but spread lies with cybernetic impunity.

Machines rule in homes, factories, offices, farms, and mines, and also on city streets, where we pedestrians are but a nuisance. Machines also rule in wars, where they do as much of the killing as warriors in uniform, or more.

Diagnosis of Civilization

Somewhere in some jungle, someone commented: "Civilized people are so strange. They all have watches and none of them has any time."

Report on the Health of Our Times

Medical science calls the malady suffered by more than a few tourists "Jerusalem syndrome."

Certain visitors to the holy city, the ceremonial hub of three religions, experience a sudden divine revelation: they become characters in the Bible and from a perch on any chair or public bench they declaim sermons, dictated by God, which reveal the eternal punishments that await the disobedient in the flames of hell.

Far from Jerusalem, a similar malady often afflicts occupants of the White House and presidents elsewhere, who proceed to exterminate sinners on direct orders from heaven.

Wisdom/1

I remember her; I can see her still: Pepe Barrientos's mom, rocking in her rocking chair, surrounded by greenery at her bungalow in the neighborhood of Buceo.

Her eyes, sunk in dusky skin crisscrossed by a thousand wrinkles, lit up mischievously when Pepe and I loudly complained about so-called friends in the neighborhood or at work, who thought they deserved to go farther than anyone else, and feigned a hug just to elbow their way ahead.

The old woman, who spoke little and said much, gave her verdict: "Pity the poor souls who spend their lives comparing themselves to others."

Wisdom/2

Incite Pereyra works at the Argentino Hotel in Piriápolis. While Helena and I are having breakfast and reading the paper, he comes over, coffee pot in hand. He talks as if he were old and wise, but he's young and clever: "For the latest news, there's nothing like an old newspaper. People say silent movies couldn't speak. How stupid can you get. They didn't speak because silence was better."

What the River Told Me

Back around 1860-something, the forces of order strung Gauchito Gil up by the feet and slit his throat.

Ever since, in Corrientes and other provinces of Argentina's North, shrines honor his memory. People come to ask for his help getting through their hard lives and warding off death.

Gauchito Gil, sanctified by his devotees, was condemned for crimes invented by the lords of land and war. The only crime he really committed was desertion: he refused to join the ranks of Argentinean, Brazilian, and Uruguayan troops that invaded Paraguay and in five years left no home standing and no adult male alive.

"I am not going to kill my Paraguayan brothers," said Gauchito Gil, and that was the last thing he said.

The Hero

Orlando Fals Borda told me this sad story, which occurred in Colombia during the Thousand Days' War.

As the twentieth century was being born, General José María Ferreira was battling the enemy near the Magdalena River. In an astute maneuver, the general marched in the opposite direction of his troops and took refuge in the hollow of a ceiba tree, the only tree standing in the immense emptiness.

Curled up into a ball, he waited.

Bullets meant for him whizzed by and he began to mumble prayers, begging, "Ceiba, ceiba, do not abandon me," until suddenly he lost control of his body. Then he muttered, "If blood smells like shit, I'm wounded."

At least only the ceiba heard him.

She knows to keep a secret.

The Chronicler

On August 18, 1947, in the neighborhood of San Severiano in Cádiz, a stockpile of torpedoes exploded.

Juan Martínez, nicknamed the Parakeet, told the story of that calamity as only someone from Cádiz could: "Two sailors were standing watch at the gate. They ended up like cigarette paper stuck to the wall."

"A little kid did somersaults in the air and landed without a stitch on."

"It was nuts. If you didn't feel like shooting yourself, you wanted to hang yourself; everybody was so afraid they were shitting themselves."

"I was about to have a drink, but the neck of the bottle slumped over and was pointing at the ground."

"On the bridge the explosion blew the head off a donkey and the rest of him kept on walking."

"What saved us were the city walls. They sent the blast straight up to the heavens. I saw stars racing to get out of the way."

But ten days later, in the ring at Linares, the famed bullfighter Manolete was gored to death. And in Cádiz no one spoke another word about the catastrophic explosion.

A Lawsuit

In July of the year 2004 the town of San Roque in Cádiz split in two: half sided with the cow, which was private property, and half backed the donkey, which belonged to the town.

A citizen had brought suit alleging that the donkey had pursued the cow with dishonest intent. The cow, fleeing such advances, had stepped off a cliff and fallen to her death. The donkey's lawyer alleged the cow had provoked his client by going into the field utterly naked, its teats in full view.

The lawyer of the deceased cow demanded compensation, insisting his client had been the victim of sexual harassment.

Other lawyers stuck their judicial noses into the matter. In the process, the late cow and the donkey sank into oblivion.

A Most Prestigious Account

Julius Caesar was a war correspondent who covered his own campaigns.

For posterity he wrote a very meticulous account of his successes.

Commentaries on the Gallic War is his best-known work. In time, that paean to the military merits of the author, who never considered the sacrifices of his uncomplaining and tireless soldiers, became a classic.

Julius Caesar, emperor and god, chronicler of himself, used his considerable literary talent to pay homage to an invasion that killed a million Gauls and condemned the survivors to slavery.

The Silent One

In Spanish they call him the Barber, though he does not do shaves or haircuts.

He lives in the depths of a tropical sea and never leaves it.

His shop, guarded by anemones and colorful sponges, sits beside a coral reef.

Waiting in a long line are fish, filthy with bacteria, parasites, and fungus.

He cleans them in utter silence.

The bluespine unicornfish is the only barber in the world who doesn't talk. Not a word, ever.

The Storyteller

The Alligator of Sanare was born in a tiny settlement near Barquisimeto, home of the many ghosts that kept him company as a child.

He speaks of them in his stories:

the spirit that made bats sing,

the man-eating goblin who lived in a calabash,

the five devils that cured cases of fright,

the warlock who would twist your neck around so you could only walk backward,

the ghoul that knocked over mountains by lassoing them with a rope,

the wizard who hunted pigeons so high in the sky they took years to fall to earth,

and the one that used a winged jacket to fly from town to town, until the Yacambú River stole it because it was tired of flowing and wanted to fly.

The Singer

Ever since that day long ago, when he was born in a sandhill in Oruro, the armadillo wanted to sing.

At the first drops of rain, he set out on his short sluggish legs to the edge of the pond to listen to the frogs singing happily.

The armadillo did his best to join in. Frogs, crickets, and birds all mocked his growling voice.

And so it went, until the day the wizard Sebastián Mamani offered him the divine gift of song, if he, in return, would hand over the shell on his back.

That was how the shell, liberated from the body, became a musical instrument.

Through it, the armadillo, which also answers to the name *quirquincho*, began to sing. And sing he does.

The Musician

In Kanchi, holy city of the Tamils of India, lived and dreamed the most off-key flutist in the world.

He was paid very well to play very poorly.

In the service of the gods, his flute tormented the devils.

The inhabitants of Kanchi kept him chained to a tree so he would not run away. From Kerala, Mysore, and other places fabulous offers rained down.

Everyone wanted the master of the impenetrable art of being awful.

The Poet

She was called Phillis because that was the name of the ship she came on, and Wheatley because it was the name of the merchant who bought her.

She was born in Senegal in 1753.

In Boston, slave traders put her up for sale: "Seven years old! She'll make a great brood mare!"

Naked, she was poked and prodded by many hands.

At the age of thirteen, she was already writing poems in a language not her own.

No one believed she was the author.

At the age of twenty, Phillis was interrogated by a tribunal of eighteen illustrious gentlemen in frocks and powdered wigs. She had to recite texts by Virgil and Milton, plus several passages from the Bible, and she had to prove that her own poems were original.

Seated in a chair, she endured her long examination. Finally, the tribunal relented: she was a woman, she was black, and she was a poet.

The Defective Woman

In Montevideo at the beginning of the nineteenth century, Captain José Bonifacio Toledo paid three hundred pesos for an eighteen-year-old black woman named Marta.

She was well-behaved, "free of vices and defects," according to the man who sold her, but a few days later the buyer demanded his money back. Marta did indeed have one defect, the worst of all: she fled at the first opportunity, leaving no trace of her footsteps.

After many escapes, her new owner put her in chains, imprisoning her wrists and ankles in iron cuffs.

The defective woman did not complain. In silence, she accepted her punishment.

A few days later, she vanished.

In the cell were four iron rings and a long chain, all intact.

Nothing was ever heard of her again.

The Baptism

American physician Samuel Cartwright christened the mental disorder that drove slaves to take flight.

This form of insanity had no remedy, but thanks to the doctor's good will, at least it had a name: drapetomania.

The Kidnapped Woman

In the middle of the year 1911, the *Mona Lisa* disappeared from the Louvre.

When it resurfaced after a two-year search, it was evident that the experience had not diminished the most mysterious smile in the world; being stolen only enhanced its prestige.

The Lady with the Magnifying Glass

She was a novelist and an archaeologist.

Whether unraveling a baffling crime or excavating ruins thousands of years old, Agatha Christie faced the same challenges.

The titles of her books are telling: *Murder in Mesopotamia, They Came to Baghdad, Death on the Nile, Murder on the Orient Express* . . .

Perhaps she suspected the ancient civilizations of hiding the thievery that stoked their rise. Perhaps curiosity drove her to chase down hidden clues, to trace the footprints covered in lies. Detective Hercule Poirot, her invention, lent her his magnifying glass.

The Idol

When she retired from the movies, the whole world was widowed.

She was born with a different name, and she was rightly dubbed the Divine One, the Swedish Sphinx, the Viking Venus for her frosty beauty.

Half a century after her goodbye, Justo Jorge Padrón, a Spanish poet who spoke Swedish with a Canary Islands accent, was looking at the display in a record store window in Stockholm when he spotted the reflection of a tall and haughty woman wrapped in white fur standing behind him.

He turned and saw her raised chin, her large dark glasses. He told himself yes, told himself no, she was, she wasn't, she might be, and out of curiosity he asked, "Excuse me, madam, but . . . aren't you Greta Garbo?"

"I was," she said.

And with the unhurried bearing of a queen, she moved off.

The First Female Referee

Her name is Léa Campos and she is Brazilian. Once she was a beauty queen in Minas Gerais and still she is the only woman to have refereed professional soccer in the stadiums of either Europe or the Americas.

Even though she had her license, diploma and all, after four years of courses and exams, the whistles of protest from indignant machos in the terraces resounded louder than her own.

The referee was always a he, not a she. But the male monopoly ended in 1967, when Léa became commander-in-chief on the field, and twenty-two men were obliged to obey her orders and submit to her punishments.

Several higher-ups in Brazilian soccer were quick to denounce the sacrilege. A few threatened to resign, while others invoked dubious scientific evidence to demonstrate that a woman's inferior bone structure could never withstand such an arduous task.

Another Interloper

John was Jane? A woman occupied Saint Peter's throne for two years, one month and four days?

Some say that beginning in the year 855, the pope who led the Vatican was really a popess. Was she? Was she not? Historical fact or only legend? Why does this possibility still provoke the indignation of the Church? Why does it still scandalize the public?

Other religions have gods and goddesses, priestesses as well as priests. Might that be why some view those religions as mere superstition?

I would say, well, what do I know? But I wonder: don't the single men perched at the pinnacle of Churchly power get bored?

Bless You, Dalmiro

I have the good luck to live on a street named for an artist, the Uruguayan musician Dalmiro Costa. A miracle, given that nearly all Montevideo's streets bear the names of military officers, politicians, and appalling figures from world history.

The Right to Plunder

In the year 2003 a veteran Iraqi journalist named Samir visited several museums in Europe.

He found marvelous texts in Babylonian, heroes and gods sculpted in the hills of Nineveh, winged lions that had flown in Assyria . . .

Someone approached him, offered to help: "Shall I call a doctor?"

Squatting, Samir buried his face in his hands and swallowed his tears.

He mumbled, "No, please. I'm all right."

Later on, he explained: "It hurts to see how much they have stolen and to know how much they will steal."

Two months later, US troops launched their invasion. The National Museum in Baghdad was sacked. One hundred seventy thousand works were reported lost.

I Swear

In 2014, for the thousandth time, the United Nations solemnly promised to hold a referendum to allow the people of Western Sahara to choose between independence and remaining as booty stolen by Morocco.

For the thousandth time, the United Nations swore to respect and enforce the result.

But the vote never occurred, and for a simple reason: Morocco refused to keep the promise it had made before the eyes of the world. It carried on as owner and overlord of the land and people of the Sahara, of the mineral-rich soil and subsoil, and of the fish-endowed waters of the sea.

In vain, Saharan patriots continued proclaiming their desire for independence. Many have landed in prison or the cemetery for the unpardonable crime of wanting to be free.

Wars of the Future

In the year 2012 Brandon Bryant worked at a US airbase in the New Mexico desert.

He was a pilot without a plane. Via fourteen screens and several keyboards, he directed planes without pilots, "drones," seven thousand miles away.

On one occasion, a country house in Afghanistan appeared on his screens, outbuildings and all. Every detail was clear.

Fifteen seconds: from some far-off perch, a commander gave the order to fire.

Ten seconds: Brandon warned the commander that a child was running toward the house.

Six seconds: the order was repeated.

Five seconds: Brandon pressed a key.

Three seconds: the drone fired a missile.

Two seconds: an explosion; the house disappeared and so did the child.

Nothing but smoke.

"Where is the child?" asked Brandon.

The machine did not answer.

Brandon repeated the question.

The machine finally spoke: "It wasn't a child. It was a dog."

"A two-legged dog?"

That was when Brandon Bryant resigned from the military.

Calumnies

The saying has it that man is wolf to man.
But rarely do wolves kill other wolves.
Unlike us, wolves do not seek mutual extermination.
Wolves have a bad reputation, but they are not the ones turning the world into an immense lunatic asylum and an overcrowded cemetery.

War Against War

While the twenty-first century was being born, Bertie Felstead, at the age of 106, lay dying. His lifespan touched three centuries and he was the sole survivor of an extraordinary soccer match played on Christmas Day 1915. The match was between British and German soldiers on an improvised pitch between the trenches.

A ball appeared, who knows from where, and it started rolling, who knows how. The battlefield became a playing field. Enemies threw down their weapons and raced to control the ball.

The soldiers played on until furious officers managed to remind them they had come to kill and to die.

Once the soccer truce was quashed, the butchery began anew, but the ball had opened the door to a fleeting world where men obliged to hate each other met face to face.

Soccer Revolution

In the days when Brazil was still under military dictatorship, the players of the powerhouse team Corinthians, led by their most beloved and respected member, an extraordinary midfielder named Sócrates, managed to gain control of the club.

Unseen, unheard of. The players discussed and decided everything by majority vote: the training regime, the approach to each match, how to divvy up the money from the gate, absolutely everything. Their shirts read "Democracia Corinthiana."

After two years, the displaced directors regained the tiller and put an end to it all. But while democracy lasted, Corinthians, governed by its players, served up the flashiest, most audacious soccer in Brazil, pulling in the largest crowds and winning the São Paulo championship two years running.

Let's Have Another Cup

At the first Soccer World Cup, held in Uruguay in 1930, the hosts won the Jules Rimet trophy, a cup of pure gold studded with precious stones.

During World War II, when Italy was champion, the head of the Italian soccer federation, Ottorino Barassi, hid the trophy in a shoebox under his bed to keep it from the Nazis.

The trophy was stolen from a London display case during the 1966 World Cup in England. Scotland Yard found no clue, until a dog named Pickles discovered it, wrapped in newspaper, in a garden on the outskirts of the city. Pickles was declared a national hero.

The next robbery happened in 1983, more than a decade after three-time champion Brazil won rights to keep the Rimet Cup in perpetuity. Melted down into ingots, the trophy disappeared into the black market of Rio de Janeiro.

Ever since, the winner of each world championship receives a copy of the new trophy, while the original can be seen but not touched in a display case at FIFA headquarters in Zurich.

The Barefoot Idol

Thanks to Sailen Manna, India won the gold medal in soccer at the Asian Games in 1951.

He played his entire career for Mohun Bagan Athletic Club, without pay, and never was he tempted by the contracts offered by foreign clubs.

He played barefoot. In the opponents' end his naked feet were rabbits that could not be snared.

In his pocket he always carried an image of Kali, the goddess who knows how to go head-to-head with death.

Sailen was nearly ninety when he died.

The goddess accompanied him on his final voyage.

Barefoot, like him.

I Confess

I am going to reveal my secret.

I don't want to take it with me to the grave. I can't.

I know how Uruguay won the 1950 World Cup.

Yes, Obdulio's courage, Schiaffino's smarts, Ghiggia's speed were all essential. That's true. But there was something more.

I was nine years old and very religious, a devotee of soccer and God, in that order.

Listening to Carlos Solé broadcast the match over the radio from Maracanã Stadium, I chewed my fingernails that afternoon and my fingers, too.

Goal for Brazil.

Oooh.

I fell to my knees and pleaded in tears, "Oh God, dear God, do me this favor, I beg of you. Do not deny me this miracle."

And I made Him a promise.

God kept his part of the bargain: Uruguay won. But I never managed to recall what it was I had promised.

It could be worse.

Perhaps I saved myself from going about muttering Our Fathers day and night, for years on end, a sleepwalker lost in the streets of Montevideo.

The Ball as Tool

At the World Cups in 1934 and 1938, the Italian and German players saluted the crowds with outstretched palms. "Win or die," Mussolini ordered. "Winning a match means more to some people than capturing a city," Goebbels once noted in his diary.

At the 1970 World Cup, Brazil's military dictatorship wrapped itself in the glory of Pelé's team. "Now no one can stop this country," proclaimed the government's advertising campaign.

At the 1978 World Cup, the Argentine brass celebrated their triumph arm in arm with the unavoidable Henry Kissinger, as prisoners were being tossed alive from airplanes into the open sea.

In 1980 Uruguay hosted the "Little World Cup," a tournament among previous world champions organized to celebrate the Cup's fiftieth anniversary. The dictatorship's public relations machine trumpeted the home team's victory as if the generals themselves had played on the pitch. But that tournament was where the crowd dared to break seven years of compulsory silence. The stands roared: "It's going down, it's going down, military rule is on the ground."

Sly but Honest

On April 14, 1997, *Sports Illustrated* reported on a poll of elite athletes, most of them US Olympians or aspiring Olympians, conducted by the esteemed physician Bob Goldman.

The athletes were guaranteed anonymity so they would tell the truth without fear of consequences.

The question posed was:

"You are offered a banned performance-enhancing substance, with two guarantees: (1) You will not be caught; (2) You will win. Would you take the substance?"

Answering yes: 195 athletes.

Answering no: 3.

Depraved

A few centuries before Europe invaded South America, the high point of the fiestas of the Mapuches, the Tehuelches, and other peoples was a game that involved chasing a ball with a stick that had a curved end.

In 1764 the council of bishops, meeting in Santiago, issued a condemnation. The council president, Bishop Manuel de Alday, decried the game's "promiscuity, because it is played by men and women, all mixed together."

Today we call it "hockey" and it is no longer a sin.

Jailed

In 1572 the poet Fray Luis de León was imprisoned in Valladolid.

He spent five years in solitary confinement.

The Holy Inquisition punished him for translating into Castilian the Song of Songs, the book of the Bible that celebrates human desire and human passion:

Open to me, my sister, my love, my dove, my undefiled:
 For my head is filled with dew, and my locks with
the drops of the night . . .
 How much better is thy love than wine!

Banned

No one wanted to publish Mark Twain's ringing denunciations of the massacres perpetrated in the Philippines and elsewhere by imperial troops of the United States.

In 1905, he wrote:

"Free speech is the privilege of the dead, the monopoly of the dead. They can speak their honest minds without offending."

Beloved, Behated

Monteiro Lobato, the writer who made and continues to make Brazil's children the happiest,

the one who taught them to love the land of their birth,

the adorable spiller of Brazil's deepest secrets,

who did time for defending the country's oil and for railing against governments that conspired with the corporate behemoths of black gold and other mineral riches,

died in 1948 at the age of sixty-something, homeless and penniless.

His name could not be published in the dailies or spoken on the radio, and his books, banned from public libraries and public schools, were burned in churchyards because they did not treat religion with sufficient respect.

Bless You Laughter, Always

Darcy Ribeiro went in and out of the jungle as if it were his home, and indeed it was.

He traveled light: a single book was all he carried, an old Spanish edition of *Don Quixote*.

In his hammock, swaying under the leafy trees of the Amazon, Darcy reveled in his favorite book. On every page he let out a belly laugh, and the local children laughed with him. None of them knew how to read, but they all knew how to laugh.

The Weaver

In Remigio Mestas's workshop in Oaxaca, clothing comes alive.

Some passersby are attracted by the beauty of his blouses, shawls, and kerchiefs, but beauty is only the beginning.

A Zapotec Indian, Remigio organized a national network of indigenous weavers, who through weaving discovered their roots and recovered their pride.

"Clothing is more than cloth," Remigio says, and he explains that garments have a spirit and transmit energy when they are born of loving hands.

"Good clothing will tell you: I am your second skin."

Touch any of his creations and you'll know he's not lying.

The Hatter

The straw hats Andrés de la Cruz González weaves in a village in Chiapas take some time to come into existence. The palm leaves must be boiled, then set out to bleach for three days in the sun and another three nights under the watchful eye of the moon.

Andrés decries the preference young people have for imported caps, and he points out that his fine palm-leaf sombreros offer protection to dreams and thoughts worth remembering.

He inherited his secret art from his grandparents and will transmit it to the children of his children, so that the slender chain of time is never broken.

Textiles and Time

The Dogon people of Mali spin and weave under the bright sun.

Nourished by light, their textiles shine and laugh. The weavers call them "words."

Textiles woven at night, in contrast, would be silent and dark.

No one wants to weave after dusk. When the sun goes down, it closes the gates of heaven, and whoever continues weaving runs the risk of going blind.

The Carpenter

To illustrate a book published by the International Labour Organization, Daniel Weinberg searched high and low for a graphic of Jesus as a carpenter.

No luck: in the entire history of art, Christ seemed never to have appeared as a worker.

At long last, however, Daniel found one in Oaxaca. Painted on wood in 1960 by an anonymous artist, it portrays the entire family with the child Jesus helping his father in the workshop.

How strange.

The Discoverer

Louis Pasteur invented more than the process that bears his name and protects our food.

He also discovered several vaccines, including one for rabies.

More difficult was his struggle against another sort of rabid beast: the envy of many of his colleagues.

In the middle of the nineteenth century, Paris dailies debated which insane asylum Pasteur would be sent to. Would it be Charenton or Sainte-Anne?

The Light Rider

In 1895 when he was on the cusp of adolescence, Albert Einstein had a vision that opened doors to the unknown: he dreamed, or imagined, that he was riding through the heavens mounted on a beam of light.

Some years later those doors led to the theory of relativity and other illuminations.

The Sculptor

In May of the year 1649 Seville lost the fragrance that was its fame and consolation.

The city of orange blossoms reeked of death.

As the plague spread, people dug ditches where they could lie down and die, while the orange trees stood bare and pitiful.

The sculptor Juan Martínez Montañés, having throughout his long life made Christs and saints for Seville's temples, wanted to sculpt the missing fragrance.

He dedicated all his remaining energies to the task, day and night.

Still carving flowers, he died.

 People say Seville recovered because he sacrificed what little life he had left. They say the flowers born from his hands cleansed the air of the moribund city.

The Cook

In ancient times the king of Maní in the Yucatán handed the cook a freshly killed animal and asked to be served the best part.

The king received a plate of roast tongue and savored it.

A short while later, the king gave the cook another freshly killed beast and asked to be served the worst part.

Once again, there was tongue on his plate.

The king might have been angry, but the cook was right.

The Fireman

From the day he was born, Emilio Casablanca was a painter and an incorrigible nighthawk.

On one of his long drinking bouts, Emilio repeatedly lost his way in the labyrinth of Montevideo's Old City, until at last he stumbled upon the office of the Socialist Party, where he had a bed. Somehow he managed to climb the stairs to the attic and collapse on his mattress. A lit cigarette dangled from his fingers.

In the cold dawn, Emilio was out cold. But the cigarette was not.

When "The Pistol" Dotti arrived to perform his daily chores as janitor, he smelled something acrid in the air.

Smoke was seeping out of the attic. The Pistol leapt up the stairway, shoved open the door, and through clouds of smoke that stung his eyes, saw flames bursting from the bed where Emilio lay sound asleep.

The nearest source of water was in the bathroom or the kitchen, neither of them at hand, so The Pistol, plucking up his courage, dropped his pants in one swoop and sprayed. Thereby earning his nickname.

Artists

The anarchist bricklayer Lucio Urtubia printed travelers' checks by the thousands to sabotage the Spanish dictatorship.

Governments print money to finance speculation, but Lucio dreamed of funding revolution. What's more, while banks rob countries, in his free time Lucio robbed banks.

Another celebrated forger of that period was Adolfo Kaminsky, a dyer and draftsman. Thanks to his diligence, many of the persecuted managed to flee occupied France disguised in military uniforms, even if they were slightly off-tint. During the Nazis' reign of terror in Paris, Adolfo never slept. He spent his nights falsifying identity documents, baptismal certificates, and safe-conducts, at the pace of thirty an hour.

The Deceased

In 1976, at the age of fifteen, a farmer named Lal Bihari applied for a bank loan in the municipality of Azamgarh in the Indian state of Uttar Pradesh.

The loan was denied. According to the civil registry, Lal Bihari was dead. No matter that he was breathing, the death certificate was unambiguous. Not only was he dead, his plot of land was now owned by an uncle.

Ever since, Lal Bihari sleeps in the street, eats from garbage bins, waits night and day in interminable lines, roams from office to office filling out forms and signing letters, and beseeches churches and other charitable institutions for assistance. A lawyer once advised him to hang himself, because correcting the official registry is impossible. For how could Lal Bihari prove he was not playing a lively trick?

He has learned how difficult it is for a dead man to find a job or a wife. And he has learned he is not alone. Many are the living dead in India.

Having no union to defend him, he founded the Uttar Pradesh Association of Dead People, the world's first union for the deceased.

Papa Goes to the Stadium

During a soccer match in Seville, Sixto Martínez tells me, "There's a fan here who always brings his father along."

"So it goes," I say. "Soccer-loving dad, soccer-loving son."

Sixto takes off his glasses and fixes me with a glare. "The one I'm telling you about brings his dead father."

His eyelids close. "It was his last wish."

Week after week, the son carries the ashes of the one who gave him life and sets them down beside him on the terrace. The dying man had begged, "Take me to see my beloved Betis."

At first the father came to the stadium in a glass jar.

One afternoon the security refused to let the jar in, glass being prohibited due to violence in the stadiums.

Ever since, the father comes in a cardboard box wrapped in plastic.

Lost Steps

Every November 2nd, the dead of Mexico visit the living.

On this sacred date of nonstop partying day and night, the living and the dead meet and eat and drink and dance and sing and talk.

But many are the dead who get lost along the way, no matter how loudly the bells and prayers summon them, and no matter how simple the route marked out by flowers.

The lost ones departed long ago, fleeing hunger or bullets, and died far away.

Now the poor wandering souls roam hither and yon, seeking the land of their birth, hoping against hope to find themselves, even for a day, once again among the family awaiting them: "my people, my loved ones."

However, it turns out their people have also changed addresses and everything else. What was no longer is, and neither is it where it was, and there is no telling who is whom, or whether they are from here or from there or from nowhere.

Absent Without Leave

Mexico City, Day of the Dead, 2012.

Dolores Cemetery was thronged. Enough people to fill a town had gathered to await their dead relatives.

But the most anticipated among the deceased, Diego Rivera the painter, again failed to show.

It's said he said, "No way would I go. I've got three widows buried right there and I don't want them ruining my death."

The Offering

I once asked the journalist Fernando Benítez, who knew everything about the living and the dead, why the deceased who return to Mexico every November 2nd are always, or almost always, male, and almost never female.

He answered without answering, by telling me the sad story of Juana the deceased.

Fernando had learned of the misfortune in Cihualtepec, from the mouth of one Pafnucio. Pafnucio had been left a widower when Juana died and had married another "because I was not born for living alone."

The Day of the Dead was approaching and Pafnucio was working far, but very far, away. So he gave his new wife the task of building an altar and setting out an offering for Juana the deceased.

The new wife built the little altar and as an offering laid out a stone heated until it was red hot. "This nectar of the gods is what your beloved Pafnucio sends to you."

Juana the deceased received that fire on her tongue and her shrieks carried to the farthest reaches imaginable.

"So, picture this," Pafnucio recounted. "Here I come galloping back to set things straight. You know I've always been a man of peace. So when she confessed her evil deed, all I did was give her a few lashes."

The Other Stars

When the Day of the Dead arrives, some Mayan towns, like Sumpango and Santiago Sacatepéquez, fly the most enormous and colorful kites in the world.

These kites sow the thirteen heavens with new stars. Everyone makes them, children and grandparents included, and in the firmament they cross paths with the dead on their way down to the world, where good drink and tasty food await them.

Strong gusts playfully blow the kites about, along with the children clutching the strings. No child screams. They sing as they fly and they refuse to obey the shouts from the ground that would ruin the voyage.

Kings of the Cemetery

Enrique Antonio, born in the high mists that rise above Mérida, has seen many people arrive in no shape to depart. He even witnessed a resurrection: in the middle of the wake, a dead man got to his feet when his mourners began arguing about the cost of the funeral. "If that's the way it is, I'd rather walk," he said angrily.

Enrique does not like people to call him the burier or the gravedigger. He is the king of the cemetery, like his colleague Fortunato Martínez, who inters the dead in the town of Arenales.

Both have reigned for a number of years. "I take care of my dead, and they take care of me," each says. Every morning, bright and early, he and Fortunato right the crosses knocked over by wind or rain or age, and plant them anew in their proper places. It would be inexcusable to set a cross over the wrong body.

Last Wish

On the final morning of the year 1853, Ciriaco Cuitiño, a ranking police officer and feared throat-cutter, paid his due.

He owed for many deaths.

Never had his hand trembled, and neither did his voice now when he expressed his last wish: "Needle and thread."

Calmly, as such an important occasion demanded, he sewed his pants to his shirt stitch by stitch.

As a warning, Ciriaco was left hanging for many hours, strung up on the gallows in one of the main squares of Buenos Aires.

His pants did not fall down.

Trigger Music

In Ceará, in Brazil's Nordeste, a dry land populated by tough people, some are born marked for death.

When the owners of lands and people decided to do away with the most dangerous one around, they gave the job to an experienced and efficient *cangaceiro*, who bore the stain of a goodly number of victims.

They warned him: "It won't be easy. He's surrounded by henchmen who owe him favors."

And they asked him: "Are you ready to do what it takes? Have you got the nerve?"

The *cangaceiro* clarified: "Nerve, I couldn't say. I have the habit."

Colors

Over a thousand years, the Virgin Mary changed clothes four times.

In mourning for her murdered son, she dressed in black.

Later on, she wore blue. Then from blue she turned to gold.

Since 1854, when Pope Pius IX revealed the creed of the Immaculate Conception, the Virgin Mary has dressed in white. The color symbolizes the purity of the woman who became the mother of God without ever having been touched by the hand of man.

Bodies That Sing

In several jungles and along several rivers of the Americas, a custom that frightened the European conquistadors remains alive: Indians display themselves in colorful nudity.

Arabesques and other symbols adorn their skin from head to foot in red, black, white, or blue.

The Indians say the godly markings guide their steps and illuminate their ceremonies.

Their painted bodies are vaccinations of beauty against sadness.

The Body Is a Sin

In 1854, after six years of matrimony, the English writer John Ruskin got divorced.

His wife alleged he had never fulfilled his conjugal duties, and he swore his inaction was justified because "her person was not formed to excite passion; on the contrary, certain circumstances completely checked it."

Ruskin was the leading art critic of Victorian England.

He had seen innumerable women in the nude, painted, drawn, or sculpted, but never had he seen one with pubic hair, not on canvas or in marble and certainly not in bed.

On his wedding night, the shock of finding hair between her legs ruined his marriage. That "certain circumstance" was an indecent act of nature, not in keeping with a well-bred woman and perhaps only typical of black savages who paraded around the jungle naked, as if their entire bodies were faces.

Holy Family

Punishing father,
self-denying mother,
submissive daughter,
mute wife.
As God wills, tradition teaches, and the law dictates:
the child beaten by the father
who was beaten by the grandfather
who beat the grandmother
who was born to obey
carries on,
because yesterday is the fate of today and all that was
shall continue to be.
But on some wall, someplace, someone scrawls:

I don't want to survive.
I want to live.

First Flush of Youth

One night at a forbidden hour, not long after I started wearing long pants, I went for a stroll by myself past the bars in the port of Montevideo.

Turning a corner, I heard groans and slaps coming from Yacaré Street.

I took a deep breath, mustered my courage, and went to investigate. By the light of a streetlamp I saw a woman against a wall, arms outstretched, being smacked around. Timidly, I approached and said, or tried to say, "Listen, sir, that's not right . . . "

The man knocked me flat with one punch.

As I lay spread-eagled on the ground, he began kicking me in the ribs, while she, the woman who had been slapped, took to driving the heel of her shoe into my head, like someone hammering nails.

I don't know how much time went by before they tired of it and ceased punishing me. They moved off, he far ahead, she obediently following.

And there I lay, crumpled, until someone picked me up.

I had received a lesson.

I never managed to learn it.

Pleasure, a Masculine Privilege

What is that little button of flesh peeking out from between a woman's legs? What is it for?

Science found no answer, until it became accepted wisdom that the clitoris was a mistake of female anatomy.

In 1857 English scientist William Acton decreed: "As a general rule, a modest woman seldom desires any sexual gratification for herself. She submits to her husband, but only to please him; and, but for the desire of maternity, would far rather be relieved from his attentions."

By then it had been proven that the female orgasm was a figment of the imagination, utterly unnecessary for the sacred exercise of motherhood.

Virtuous Men

The experts dictating the norms of sexual life were clerics who had made a vow of chastity.

In the year 1215 Cardinal Robert de Courçon declared: "Feeling pleasure disgusts the devout man, but he endures his disgust in order to conceive healthy children."

The Church warned: Children conceived on any of the three hundred days of obligatory abstinence would be born "epileptics or lepers."

Punishments

In 1953 the Lisbon City Council published Bylaw No. 69,035:

Having verified the increase in acts that threaten public morals and good customs, which are daily occurrences in parks and other public places, it is hereby decided that police officers and forest wardens shall maintain permanent vigilance over those who make use of dense vegetation to practice such acts that threaten public morals and good customs, and the following fines are hereby established:

1. Hand on hand: $2.50
2. Hand on that: $15.00
3. That in hand: $30.00
4. That in that: $50.00
5. That behind that: $100.00

Sole subparagraph: Tongue in that: $150.00 fine, prison, and photograph.

Bésame Mucho

Kissologists have discovered that a passionate smooch works thirty-nine muscles in the face and other parts of the body.

They have also proven that it can transmit the flu, German measles, smallpox, tuberculosis, and other diseases.

Thanks to these scientists, we now know that a kiss can exhaust an Olympic athlete and make the healthiest of humans hopelessly ill.

And yet . . .

The Disobedient Woman

According to the most ancient of voices, Eve was not the first woman God offered to Adam.

There was another before her. Her name was Lilith and she was not bad looking, but she had one serious defect: she was not the least bit interested in spending her life serving Adam.

Images, all by anonymous male artists, depict her naked, equipped with bat's wings so she could fly about her kingdom of the night, wrapped in serpents and sporting a devilish smile on her man-hungry face, with fires burning below her belly.

Lilith is not very popular in the masculine world.

It's understandable.

Gastronomic Chronicle

Chichevache was one of several characters the French people dreamed up in the Middle Ages.

The monster fed on women who never contradicted their husbands' orders.

Submissive wives were the only dish on his menu.

But they were rather scarce, despite what some historians claim.

And poor Chichevache died of hunger.

Two Guilty Women

Aglaonike, the first woman astronomer, lived in Greece in the second or first century before Christ. She was accused of witchcraft because she could predict eclipses. People suspected she was the one who made the moon disappear.

A number of centuries later, in August of the year 1322, Jacqueline Felice de Almania was put on trial in Paris for curing the sick, a talent forbidden to women and legally reserved for doctors who were male and single.

The Cursed Woman

The most beautiful woman in Chile, Catalina de los Ríos y Lisperguer, known as La Quintrala, was accused of practicing witchcraft, poisoning her father, knifing her lovers, and torturing her serfs.

But the most horrendous of her crimes was another: she was born a redhead. Her long tresses grew from the flames of hell and her freckles were the Devil's brand.

She died in 1665, long after she used her enormous fortune of inherited lands and slaves to purchase a pardon, and thus elude the stake and bonfire the inquisitors had prepared for her.

Love Story

The orchid, beauty queen of the world's gardens, calls out for love and love appears, swearing his intentions are honest.

The orchid believes him to be her longed-for butterfly, the fly of her life, the bee of her dreams, and she sighs deeply, for at long last she will be able to start a home and raise pretty little insects who look just like their mama.

Their eternal love lasts but thirty seconds. The lover, bored with conjugal monotony, realizes the orchid's nectar is not his favorite and departs, taking her pollen with him. From flower to flower he flies, penetrates, and flees.

The orchid, no longer so foolish, does not grow discouraged.

She waits.

Charles Darwin, lover of orchids, told this sad story in strictly scientific terms, three years before publishing his famous work on the origin of species.

Fleas

In Panama I heard it said: "They're dirty. They have fleas. Indians are dirty."

In the archipelago of San Blas, sea of mirrors, islands of white sand, I found that to be true and not true: the Kuna Indians do have fleas, but they bathe so frequently and with such enthusiasm that in the few days I spent among them I was crowned king of the filthy.

Water never touches their heads. The Indians save the fleas on their scalps for their loved ones to remove.

As tradition dictates, whoever loves you has to prove their love by rescuing you from the torment of the minuscule demons.

Spiders

In the town of Sabaneta they called him Spiderman because he walked the streets selling spiders:

"Hot spiders for old women with no teeth!"

"Tasty spiders for pretty girls!"

The spiders the child was selling had no hairy legs, caught nothing in their webs, and poisoned no one. Neither did the females have the bad habit of swallowing the males after making love.

Hugo Chávez's grandmother made the treats from crushed papaya, so that her grandson could contribute to the family budget. How they came to be called "spiders," nobody knows.

That Neck

In 1967 I spent some time in Guatemala, where death squads were sowing terror. These soldiers without uniforms were waging dirty war, a technique the US Army had tried out in Vietnam and was then teaching in its first Latin American testing ground.

I met the most despised enemies of those fearmongers, the guerrillas.

To reach their mountain hideout I traveled in a car driven by a woman who astutely evaded every checkpoint. I never saw her face and never heard her voice. She was covered from head to toe and spoke not a word during the three-hour trip, even when she opened the back door and pointed to the secret path I was to take.

Years later I discovered her name was Rogelia Cruz Martínez, a guerrilla collaborator and former Miss Guatemala, who was twenty-six when she was found under a bridge after having been raped and mutilated by Colonel Máximo Zepeda and every one of his six thousand troops.

I only saw her neck.

I see it still.

Those Eyes

Cesare Pavese wrote: "Death is coming and it will have your eyes."

He met death in a hotel in Turin one summer evening in 1950.

He recognized it by its eyes.

That Blessed Sound

Every afternoon the factory siren in a town in Alicante would blare at two on the dot. And at two on the dot, Joaquín Manresa would be standing on the corner waiting.

Then she would appear, pedaling, face to the wind, hair flying, a singular figure among the many women leaving work. Joaquín was blind to the others.

He never missed that date arranged with no one, and her bicycle never stopped.

Joaquín never knew her name.

Many years later he was walking the streets of Oporto, far from his home in Alicante, a different map, a different language, a different country, when he heard once again that unmistakable factory siren, the ugly screech that thirty-two years before had announced the grandest moment of every day.

He stood on the corner and waited.

No one came by.

No one was there.

The siren got it wrong.

It was May Day.

Marriage Problems

Once upon a time the moon and the sun lived to-gether, getting along quite well, until the sun caught the moon kissing the morning star in a passionate embrace.

The sun slapped the moon. According to the Mapu-che Indians, the scars of that blow are still visible on her face. What's more, her silver tears gave birth to the art of silversmithing.

The sun and the moon never lived together again. When the sun comes out, the moon sets. When the moon appears, the sun hides.

Family Problems

Roberto Bouton, a rural physician, collected many voices in the countryside of Uruguay.

Here is the goodbye to life of a woodcutter, shepherd, and handyman named Canuto:

Look, doctor. It just so happens that I married a widow with a grown daughter, and my father went and fell in love with that daughter and married her, and so my father became my son-in-law and my daughter through marriage became my stepmother.

And my wife and I had a son, who was the brother-in-law of my father and therefore my uncle. And later on my daughter had a son who became my brother and also my grandson.

Are you following me, doctor? All this is a little complicated, I know, but to sum it up I ended up being both the husband and the grandson of my wife. And so it went, doctor, until one awful day when I realized: I am my own grandfather!

You see? An insufferable state of affairs. I'm telling you because you're a doctor and you'll understand.

The Revelation

The telephone rang.

The accent was unmistakable, but I did not recognize the voice.

A long time had passed. I knew nothing of this friend who had remained in Montevideo when I went into exile.

"Come," I said, and I told him the times the trains ran along the Catalan coast to Calella de la Costa.

Walking to the station, I brought to mind a few of the adventures we had shared.

My friend had not changed much. His frank laugh was the same, and so was he.

We went for a stroll down a few of the town's streets.

He said nothing, then grimaced and said, "What an ugly place!"

We walked on in silence.

It was the first time I had heard anyone say that. It may have also been the first time I realized it was true.

That hurt.

And because it hurt, I discovered that I loved the town where I lived.

The Taxi Driver

Some years back I was in Stockholm for the first time. And for the first time I took a Swedish taxi.

When we arrived at our destination, the driver got out of the car the way one might descend from a horse-drawn carriage, opened the door for me, charged me for the trip and, with every possible courtesy, gave me my change and bid me farewell with a brief salute.

It was very cold, as it usually is there, and I confess that such useless self-sacrifice seemed unjust.

That night I mentioned it to my friends.

Isn't there a socialist government in Sweden? What's with these servant-like customs from the days of lords and lackeys?

They fell silent.

Then, with saintly patience, they explained that the taxi driver was obeying a law passed by the socialists to protect the workers.

To collect his fare, the driver must get out of his car. Thus, without realizing it, he gets some exercise. Those few steps in the street help improve circulation, stretch muscles, and activate the lungs.

Since the law came into effect, health problems among taxi drivers had declined drastically.

The Newborn

On the last day of April of the year 2013, Galulú Guagnini was born in Caracas.

Her father, Rodofo, explained: "She came to teach us everything anew."

Aphrodite

Not long ago Catalina and Felipe discovered the sea, and nobody could wrest them from the water. They spent their days playing in the waves, their toys, shovels, and pails abandoned on the sand.

One night I told them: "Once upon a time there was a woman named Aphrodite. She was born from the foam. It seems to me you were too."

The following morning, I heard screams coming from the waves.

It was them, shouting at the foam: "Mama!"

Lilossary

Things said by Miss Lila Rodríguez when she was between six and seven years old:

"Why can't you see Martians in the sky?"

"Does a baby have toys when he's in his mother's belly?"

"I'm in danger! Two ants are watching me!"

"Of all the letters, my favorite is U, because it laughs."

"Why did you turn on the light, Mommy? Why did you turn out the darkness?"

"I want to chew on my earlobe, but I can't!"

"Know what? I always want to be where I'm not."

"When I grow up, I'm not going to have children because they bust your balls."

"Do I want those cookies for tomorrow? Of course. The future's hungry."

"Santa Claus exists because I want him to exist."

The Inventor

Manuel Rosaldo started school not long before he invented his injection.

It stuck you in the rear but worked on your head. A single injection was sufficient to stuff your brain with all the knowledge humanity has accumulated in thousands upon thousands of years of discovering the world's secrets.

The invention was great for the child inventor, since it meant he could spend his life on vacation, and it also turned out to be undeniably useful for parents and teachers, since they did not have to waste time teaching students who had already learned everything via injection.

As occurred with humanity's other great inventions, no one took this pedagogical revolution seriously.

A Children's Dictionary

Here are the voices of children defining words in the schools of Antioquia, Colombia, as collected by Javier Naranjo and other teachers:

Mouth: "God made it for chewing, but we use it for talking."

Rain: "It's Jesus, when he pees."

Devil: "He's the biggest double-talker."

Distance: "It's when somebody leaves someone."

Spirit: "It's the second body, which lives on after death."

War: "When people kill for a piece of land or a piece of peace."

Church: "Where people go to forgive God."

Moon: "It's the one that gives us night."

Universe: "House of the stars."

Back in My Childhood

It was January 5th, eve of Epiphany.

I left a letter in my shoe and next to it a few handfuls of grass and glasses of water for the camels, who were going to be exhausted when they arrived from the Orient.

All night long I did not shut my eyes. Every so often I heard the hooves of the camels loaded down with enormous bundles, and caught sight of the shadows of the three kings.

As soon as the sun peeked above the horizon, I leapt up and ran to find the toys the kings had left for me.

A few months later I started school for the first time.

At recess one of my classmates was kind enough to inform me, "Dummy. Don't you know the three kings are your parents?"

I had trouble responding. When I came to my senses, I was blind with fury. I pushed him up against the wall and punched him until he cried.

The principal sent me home.

After I was pardoned and could return, no one ever raised that dangerous topic with me again.

The Vocation

His name is Rama and he works in Tenali, a village in the south of India.

He was a small child when he discovered his vocation.

It happened in the temple of the goddess Kali.

Bowing at the goddess's feet, little Rama sang the hymn to her but could not keep from laughing.

The goddess was not pleased.

She has a thousand faces, and from her thousand mouths she demanded an explanation.

The child confessed: "I have only one nose. It's complicated enough to blow it when I get a cold. How do you manage with a thousand?"

The goddess condemned him to eternal laughter. And that is how he makes his living.

That Question

The Uruguayan dictatorship had the Majfud family cornered. They suffered prison and torture and humiliations, and were dispossessed of everything they had.

One morning the children were playing in an old cart when a gunshot rang out. They were some distance away, but the sound traveled across the fields of Tacuarembó and they knew, who knows how or why, that the report came from the bed of their most beloved aunt, Marta.

Ever since that morning, Nolo, the youngest in the family, has wondered out loud: "Why be born, if we have to die?"

Jorge, his older brother, tries to help him.

He searches for an answer.

The years flow on, the way trees slide past the windows of a train, and Jorge is still searching for the answer.

Rain

Among all the world's music and all heaven's too, my favorite is the concerto for solo rain.

Every time it plays on the skylight of my house, I listen as if I were at Mass.

Clouds

At night, when no one sees them, clouds descend to the river.

They lean against it and pick up the water that later on they will spread on the land.

Sometimes, in the midst of this task, a few clouds fall in and the river carries them off.

When morning comes, you can see the fallen clouds go by.

They drift on the waters, slow boats made of cotton, staring at the sky.

The Strange River

They were children from far upcountry, who had never been to the beach at Piriápolis or any other beach, and had never seen the sea.

The most they dared was to get their feet wet, and none went into the waves.

To conquer his fear, the smartest among them explained: "It's a river with only one bank."

Paths of Fire

In the most ancient of ancient times, flowers had no petals and the pampa was filled not with gauchos but with dinosaurs.

A long time later came fire.

Ever since, fire saves us from darkness and cold. And while it fulfills its earthly duties, it sends smoke up to the sky, to the home of the gods.

As I was told in Michoacán, smoke is the food of the gods.

Or could it be that the gods smoke?

The Moon

The moon was dying to visit the earth.

After much hesitation, she let herself float down.

She intended to stay for only a short while, but when she began her ascent she got caught in the crown of a tree.

Convinced she would never free herself from that prison of branches, she felt horribly alone. Lucky for her, a wolf turned up from the depths of the forest and spent the night playing with her, caressing her with his snout, tickling her on her white belly, telling her jokes that were not all bad.

Just before dawn, the wolf helped free her from the branches and the moon took off for the sky.

But she did not go alone: she stole the wolf's shadow, so he would never forget the night they shared.

That's why the wolf howls.

He's begging the moon to return his stolen shadow.

The moon plays deaf.

The Sea

For hours or maybe years, Helena had been sitting by the sea that began at her feet and penetrated her eyes and lungs.

To leave it made her sad.

To never have to leave it, she put little wheels on the sea and took it with her, as if it were her shadow. Because the sea, like her, was made of sun and salt.

Stories Tell the Tale

CARLOS BONAVITA ALWAYS TOLD ME, "IF what they say about making the road as you walk is true, then you must be the Minister of Public Works."

My feet like to drift down Montevideo's waterfront on the banks of the River Plate. In 1656 Antonio de León Pinelo wrote from Madrid that this was one of the four rivers of Eden. I think he exaggerated a little, truth be told, though back in my childhood, or at least in my memory, its waters were transparent.

Years have passed and the waters of this river as wide as the sea are limpid no more, but I continue walking its shores, while inside me walks the land as it was when I was born, what you might call the walked walker.

I walk and inside me words also walk, seeking out other words to tell the stories they want to tell. These words travel without haste, like the wandering souls that flit about the world and like the shooting stars that sometimes drift slowly down in the heavens of the South.

The words beat a steady rhythm as they walk. By coincidence the other day I heard that in Turkish "to walk" (*yürümek*) and "heart" (*yürek*) come from the same root.

Quite a few years ago now, during my time in exile on the coast of Catalonia, I got an encouraging nudge from a girl eight or nine years old, who, unless I'm remembering wrong, was named Soledad.

I was having a few drinks with her parents, also exiles, when she called me over and asked, "So, what do you do?"

"Me? I write books."

"You write books?"

"Well . . . yes."

"I don't like books," she declared.

And since she had me against the ropes, she hit me again: "Books sit still. I like songs because songs fly."

Ever since my encounter with that angel sent by God, I have attempted to sing. It's never worked, not even in the shower. Every time, the neighbors scream, "Get that dog to stop barking!"

I do not know Jorge Ventocilla. Rather, I should say I do not know him personally, but my books are his friends and, through them, I am too.

When *Mirrors* was published, Jorge decided that the book, unknown in Panama, should circulate from hand to hand.

His savings did not amount to much, but in a fit of insanity he spent them all on copies of *Mirrors*, and he set the books loose in cafés, stores, barbershops, kiosks, wherever, each inscribed with a warning:

"This free book is a traveling book. You read it and pass it on to someone else."

And on they go.

I DID NOT HAVE THE GOOD LUCK TO MEET Scheherazade, and neither did I learn the art of storytelling in the palaces of Baghdad.

My universities were the old cafés of Montevideo.

Nameless storytellers taught me all I know.

During the little formal schooling I had, since I did not get past the first year of high school, I was terrible at history. But in those cafés I discovered that the past could become the present, and that memories could be recounted in such a way that they would stop being yesterday and become right now.

My teachers were exemplary liars who met in cafés to recover the times they had lost.

At these friendly get-togethers, where I snuck a place for myself, I heard one of the best stories that's ever come my way. It happened at the beginning of the twentieth century during the cowboy war on the plains of my country, but the teller told the story so grippingly we were all exactly where he said he had been.

Following a battle, he had walked through a field sowed with dead bodies.

Among the dead was a beautiful young man who was, or at least appeared to be, an angel.

On his forehead he wore a white band stained red with blood.

On it was written: "For the fatherland and for her."

The bullet had pierced the word "her."

 ONE OF MY TEACHERS IN THE ART OF NARRA-tion was named Rolendio Martínez.

I don't think he knew how to read or write.

When I met him, he was nearly a hundred years old, and he liked to say: "I'm beyond age. I don't have birthdays anymore and I don't wear a watch."

He recalled his friends from times long past, affectionately but without any gloss: "Yes, that one was good. Good. But no more than good."

And to speak of the war, he began by clarifying: "I'm not some old widower walking around with his head on backward. I see it clear as could be."

The images were burned into him in childhood.

A few horsemen had passed like wind before his eyes, child's eyes. One had his throat slit, the wound from ear to ear, the spurt of blood an endless gush: "The poor guy had lost his horse and he was throwing punches, stumbling along, with no idea he was dead."

I wrote Soccer in Sun and Shadow to convert the pagans. I wanted to help fans of reading lose their fear of soccer, and fans of soccer lose their fear of books. I never imagined anything else.

But according to Víctor Quintana, a congressman in Mexico, the book saved his life. In the middle of 1997, he was kidnapped by professional assassins, hired to punish him for exposing dirty deals.

They had him tied up, face down on the ground, and were kicking him to death, when there was a pause before the final bullet. The murderers got caught up in an argument about soccer. That was when Víctor, more dead than alive, put in his two cents. He began telling stories from my book, trading minutes of life for every story from those pages, the way Scheherazade traded a story for every one of her thousand-and-one nights.

Hours and stories slowly unfolded.

At last the murderers left him, tied up and trampled, but alive.

They said, "You're a good guy," and they took their bullets elsewhere.

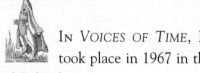 IN *VOICES OF TIME*, I TOLD A STORY THAT took place in 1967 in the main soccer stadium of Colombia.

Not a pin would fit; the stadium was raging. It was the annual classic between the two teams from Bogotá, Millonarios and Santa Fe.

Santa Fe striker Omar Devanni fell in the penalty area in the final minute of that super match-up, and the referee whistled a penalty.

Devanni had tripped. No one had hit him or even brushed against him. The referee was wrong, but no way could he change his mind in front of that roaring crowd.

So Devanni took the kick for a foul that never occurred. He executed it serenely, sending the ball wide, nowhere near the net.

His act of courage may have sealed his ruin, but it gave him the right to look himself in the eye when he faced the mirror every morning.

A few years later, I received a letter from someone I did not know named Alejandro Amorín. He had found Devanni nowhere near soccer, running a bar somewhere in the Caribbean, and asked him about the incident. Devanni first said he couldn't remember. Then he said it could be, who knows—maybe it just went wrong. "It came out like that, I made a lousy kick, it was by accident, these things happen in soccer . . . "

As if excusing himself for acting with such dignity.

ANOTHER STORY FROM *VOICES OF TIME*. Every year on a certain day in October, the telephone rings in Mirta Colángelo's house. "Hi, Mirta. It's Jorge Pérez. You can guess why I'm calling. Today marks sixteen years since I found that bottle. Like every year, I'm calling to celebrate."

Jorge had lost his job and his desire to live. He was walking off his misfortune, along the rocky shore of Puerto Rosales, when he found one of the vessels from the fleet that Mirta's students tossed into the open sea every year. Inside each bottle was a letter.

The one Jorge found was wet but still legible. It said: "My name is Martín. I'm eight years old. I'm looking for a friend on the paths of the water."

Jorge read the letter and it gave him back his life.

MY BOOK *DAYS AND NIGHTS OF LOVE AND War* opens with a quote from Karl Marx: "In history, as in nature, rot is the source of life."

When the book was translated into German, the translator, who knew Marx's work from A to Z, asked me where I found that sentence, because he did not recall it and could not locate it in any book.

I searched as well, but in vain. Still, I was certain my memory had not betrayed me on that perfect synthesis of dialectical thinking. So, I told the translator: "The sentence is from Marx, but he forgot to write it down."

IN 1970, I SUBMITTED *OPEN VEINS OF LATIN America* for the Casa de las Américas prize in Cuba. I lost. According to the jury, the book was not serious. Back then, the left still thought serious works had to be boring.

But I found a publisher and the book had the good fortune of earning high praise from several military dictatorships, which banned it. The truth is, that's what gave the book prestige. Up to then no copies had been sold, not even to my relatives.

The attention the book garnered from the censors gave it a boost everywhere except in my country, Uruguay, where *Open Veins* was allowed to circulate freely in the military's prisons during the first six months of the dictatorship. Strange, because at that time the dictatorships of several South American countries were coordinated under the Condor Plan and had very similar, if not identical, characteristics. They banned the same things.

The Uruguayan censors, reading the title, must have thought it was a book on anatomy, and medical texts were not forbidden.

The error did not last long.

JAMES CANTERO, A URUGUAYAN LIKE ME, A SOC-
cer player like I dreamed of being, wrote me a letter
in the year 2009.

I had never met him.

He told me he had something for me.

And he gave it to me.

It was a book of mine, an old edition of *Open Veins*.

A captain from the Salvadoran army had given it to
him some years before.

The book then traveled half the world, accompanying
James in his soccer wanderings.

"It sought you out," he told me when he handed it
over. "It was hoping to find you."

The book was mortally wounded: a bullet hole went
from the front cover right through the back.

The captain had found the book in the knapsack of a
dead guerrilla, one among many who died in the battle of
Chalatenango at the end of 1984.

Nothing else was in the knapsack.

The captain could not say why he took the book or
why he saved it. Neither could James explain, even to
himself, why he carried it around from country to country.

The fact is, after wandering for a quarter of a century,
the book reached my hands.

And in my hands it sits.

Nothing else remains of that boy without a name.

This book shot through is his body.

IN *MIRRORS*, I RECOUNTED STORIES THAT were little known or entirely unknown.

One of them took place in Spain in 1942. Francisco Franco's military putsch, known as the National Uprising though it was no more than a vulgar coup d'état, had annihilated the Spanish Republic.

The dictatorship triumphantly announced that a prisoner, Matilde Landa, was to publicly repudiate her satanic ideas and would receive the holy sacrament of baptism in prison.

The ceremony could not begin without the guest of honor, but Matilde had disappeared.

The dignitaries, gathered in the prison yard, realized she was on the roof when she threw herself off. Her body hit the ground and exploded like a bomb.

The show went on. The bishop baptized the bits of her that remained.

Mirrors was at the printers when I received a letter from the publisher's copy editor, who had finished her hunt for errors.

She wanted to know where I had found the information for that story. All of it was correct, but she only knew about it from what her relatives had told her.

Matilde Landa was her aunt.

My granddaughter Catalina was ten.

We were walking along a street in Buenos Aires when someone came up and asked me to sign a book. I can't remember which one.

We continued on, the two of us, quietly arm in arm, until Catalina shook her head and offered this encouraging remark: "I don't know why they make such a fuss. Not even I read you."

Some time ago I was in a school in Salta, in the north of Argentina, reading stories to the children.

Afterward, the teacher asked them to write me letters about the reading.

One of the letters counseled: "Keep writing. You'll improve."

The story that opens *The Book of Embraces* tells of a man from the town of Neguá, on the coast of Colombia, who managed to travel up to the heavens.

Upon his return he said he had contemplated human life from on high, and that we are a sea of flames. There are big flames, little flames, flames of all colors. There are people who burn serenely, never feeling the wind, and people who burn crazily, filling the air with sparks. Some silly flames give off neither light nor heat, but others burn with so much yearning for life that you cannot look at them without averting your eyes, and whoever goes near them catches fire.

That story is often read in the schools of my country.

One afternoon I was taking a walk in Rodó Park, at the edge of the river-sea of Montevideo, when suddenly I found myself surrounded by an uproarious crowd of children, dressed in their school uniforms, the girls with big blue ribbons in their hair.

The children screamed, "It's the lord of the flames! The lord of the flames!"

That afternoon, that gang of kids gave me the only title of nobility I've ever received.

 MAY DAY IS THE MOST WIDELY CELEBRATED OF all holidays.

The entire world stands still to pay homage to the workers hanged long ago in Chicago for the crime of refusing to work more than eight hours a day.

On my first trip to the United States, I was surprised to learn that May 1st was a day like any other. Not even the city of Chicago, where the tragedy occurred, seemed to notice. In *The Book of Embraces* I confessed that such willful forgetting pained me.

Much later I received a letter from Diana Berek and Lew Rosenbaum of Chicago.

They had never celebrated the holiday, but in the year 2006, along with the largest crowd they had ever witnessed, they paid homage to the workers sent to the gallows long ago for their bravery.

In the letter, Diana and Lew told me they finally understood the discomfort I described in *The Book of Embraces*.

"Chicago embraces you," the letter said.

 MARIE-DOMINIQUE PERROT TAUGHT AT A high school in Geneva.

She wrote to me that in the middle of 1995 a fire razed the school, leaving nothing but a pile of smoking ruins. The next day one of the teachers defied the order to stay clear and returned from the skeleton of the building with a half-burned book. It was badly singed, but the title was legible, more or less: *Mémoire du feu*.

The French edition of the first volume of *Memory of Fire* was the only object that survived the flames.

In her letter, the teacher remarked, "It is as if the fire wanted to sign its work." She added, "This reminds me of what Jean Cocteau said when asked what he would save if his house were burning. He answered, 'The fire.'"

IN THE DIFFICULT TASK OF SAYING A LOT WITH a little, two people have helped me enormously and mercilessly: Helena Villagra and Fernando Rodríguez.

Fernando was like a wild plant, having grown up poor with little or no formal education, but his nose for superfluous words was first-rate.

When I wrote the second volume of *Memory of Fire*, I faced the challenge of telling in a few words the story of Camila O'Gorman and the priest Ladislao Gutiérrez, protagonists of a scandal that swept the city of Buenos Aires off its feet in the middle of the nineteenth century and culminated in their both being shot by a firing squad for the crime of love.

It is not easy to write of love without clouding it in words.

Fernando, who was living in my house at the time, rejected everything. "There are still a lot of stones in the lentils," he said and said again, as he continued crossing out stones until only a single line remained.

Then, at last, Fernando gave in.

The line said: "They were two by an error that the night corrected."

MY TRILOGY *MEMORY OF FIRE* WAS BORN from a poem by Constantine Cavafy. Reading the great Greek poet of Alexandria, I took his challenge to heart: Why not see the universe through a keyhole? Why not write the big story of the past by telling the little one? In Cavafy's poem, the victory of Mark Antony in Greece is told from the point of view of a poor merchant on his donkey, trying to sell something, and no one pays him any mind.

IN MY WANDERINGS AS A STORYTELLER, I WAS giving a reading in the Galician city of Ourense one night.

A man in the back row glared at me, brow furrowed, eyes unblinking: a farmer's face, tanned by long days of labor, angry enough to want to kiss.

After the reading, he approached slowly, eyes fixed, as if he intended to kill me. But he did not kill me.

He said, "It must be so hard to write so simply."

Having delivered the most insightful review I ever received, he turned on his heel and left without saying goodbye.

I WROTE MIRRORS FROM A DREAM.

    Usually my dreams are embarrassingly mediocre: missing a flight, waiting in line, unfamiliar cities, falling from the tenth floor . . .

My wife Helena has prodigious dreams. Breakfast time is truly painful because the dreams she recounts contrast so starkly with my own, in which I argue with an official who does not speak a language I understand, or I simply miss yet another flight.

She says, "Oh, so you missed the plane. . . . I dreamed about an airplane last night too. I dreamed the two of us were waiting in an incredibly long line to board. Every passenger had a pillow under his arm. The pillows had to go through a machine that read their dreams from the night before. The dreams were in the pillows, and the machine was a detector of dangerous dreams."

Modestly, she adds, "I believe it had something to do with public security."

I take a sip of *café con leche*, exile myself to the bathroom for half an hour, try to rouse my spirits and hold my head high, but it isn't easy.

However, one night I had a pretty good dream, the one that gave rise to *Mirrors*. In the dream I got into a taxi and said, "Take me to the French Revolution, take me to where Olympe de Gouges is on her way to the guillotine."

The driver took me. I wanted to see Olympe at the very moment she stood under the blade, to hear her say these lovely words: "If we women are good enough to be on the scaffold, we're good enough to be on the judge's bench."

I was still with the taxi driver, so I said, "Now take me to Brazil, to Congonhas do Campo. I want to see Aleijadinho sculpting his prophets."

And off we went. By the way, what a fabulous paradox: Aleijadinho, the least attractive man in Brazil, created the loveliest colonial art in the Americas. The ugliest guy crafted the finest beauty.

I wanted to see all of it, to witness it personally. The taxi driver obeyed my every instruction and in the dream I continued traveling all over a world without borders in time or space. From that dream came my book. I knew I could write it because I had already dreamed it.

ON ANOTHER STORYTELLING NIGHT I READ to a roomful of Mexican university students.

A passage in *Voices of Time* is about the Spanish poet Federico García Lorca, shot by firing squad and his works banned during Franco's long dictatorship. It recounts how a troupe from Uruguay dared to put on one of his plays in Madrid, the first after many years of involuntary silence. At the end of the play, the Spanish audience did not applaud. Or, better put, they applauded with their feet, stamping on the floor. The actors were stunned; they had no clue what it meant.

Had they done such a bad job? Did they deserve such a protest?

A long time later in Montevideo, when China Zorrilla, a member of that subversive troupe, told me about it, I thought it couldn't have happened like that. But then it occurred to me that the stamping might have been for the author, executed for being red and gay and peculiar. Maybe it was a way of saying to him, "You should know, Federico, just how alive you are."

When I retold this story at the university in Mexico, something occurred that had never happened in my many other retellings across Andalusia and elsewhere: the students applauded with their feet, six thousand feet stamping on the floor with all their heart and soul. They extended both my story and what my story told, as if we were all in a theater in Madrid some years before. The same thundering on the earth, the same way of saying, "You should know, Federico, just how alive you are."

AT ANOTHER READING IN ATHENS, TO STUdents at the Polytech, I was accompanied by a dog named Kanelos.

He curled up at my feet onstage. I did not know him, but somehow he found the patience to listen, eyes alert, from beginning to end. Kanelos was a dog's dog, a street dog, rude, wild, who never missed a student demonstration and was always on the front lines facing off with the police.

Seven years later, in 2010, the fury of the Greeks exploded. Students led the protests against the exterminators who were forcing Greece to pay for the sins of Wall Street. In pictures, at the head of the clamor, amid tear gas and smoke, was a dog I recognized. It was Kanelos. But my Greek friends told me Kanelos had died a year and a half before.

I told them they were mistaken. That dog looking for a fight, that unpresentable tramp, was indeed Kanelos. If now he was named Lukanikos, it was to fool the enemy.

A FEW YEARS BEFORE SALVADOR ALLENDE became president of Chile, I had the good fortune to accompany him on a trip south.

I had never seen snow. Drinking good wine, we made one toast after another while the snow fell softly, in slow cotton balls, on the other side of the window.

That night, in Punta Arenas, Allende showed me the speech he was going to give at a campaign rally.

The following day, between cheers from the crowd, he used a sentence that was not in the version I had read.

Maybe it was an involuntary prophecy.

Who knows?

Allende said: "It is worth dying for all the things without which it is not worth living."

MANY YEARS AGO, I LEARNED A LOT FROM working with Carlos Quijano at the weekly *Marcha*.

I will never forget the afternoon, in the middle of an election campaign, when we were listening to political speeches on the radio.

They promised a lot, said little, meant practically nothing.

Don Carlos listened and remained silent. Then he murmured, "The only sin that cannot be forgiven is the sin against hope."

 CHILDREN OF THE DAYS TAKES THE FORM OF a calendar. A story sprouts from every page. Or put another way, each day has a story to tell.

Sonia Breccia read it looking for her true birthday: not the day she was born, but the day she wished to be born.

Now Sonia celebrates every May 13th, even though her birth certificate says something else.

Sonia chose it because she liked the story that day tells.

It tells what a wise elder taught me years ago in the jungle where the Orinoco River is born:

To see the worlds of the world, shift your eyes.
To have the birds hear your song, shift your throat.

IN *CHILDREN OF THE DAYS*, I ALSO TOLD THE story of an exceptional African, the King of Dahomey, Agaja Trudo, who refused to sell slaves and rose up against the traffickers in human flesh.

Shortly after publication, I received a letter from Carlos Feo. He had visited the museum in the royal palace in Dahomey's capital and saw no trace of that king. Agaja Trudo had been erased from history because he had sinned against the most profitable trade of the European powers of his time.

Carlos also told me that the worst enemy of the rebellious king was his father's wife, who coveted the throne and was the slave trade's most fervent defender. When Agaja Trudo outlawed the slave trade, he made one exception: he sold her.

AMONG THE STORIES COLLECTED IN *WALKING Words*, there is one that tells of the adventures of a boy and his shadow.

The story ends with the boy having left his childhood far behind and feeling sorry that he will die and leave his shadow alone.

One reader, Daidie Donnelle, wrote to tell me not to worry: the shadow would not be left alone because the shadow of the shadow would keep it company.

IN THE FINAL VOLUME OF *MEMORY OF FIRE*, I told a story about the daughter of a Uruguayan political prisoner, a five-year-old girl who was named Mylai in homage to a Vietnamese village wiped off the map by the US military.

After that I received several letters from parents of newborn girls who wanted to name their daughters Mylai but the bureaucracy would not allow it. From the city of Rosario in Argentina, Nélida Gómez told me of her misadventures: "My daughter is still undocumented," she wrote in March of 1999.

The unusual name did not appear on the calendar of saints, nor was it on the list of the National Registry of Names. So Mylai had no right to call herself Mylai.

 IN THE YEAR 2012 I WAS SIGNING BOOKS AT the Casa del Libro in Barcelona.

"Who is it for?"

Told the name, I would·then write it and sign my own.

Sometimes I would add something, a sketch, a comment, anything to help me feel less like a robot with an artificial hand.

On it went, book after book.

Then a young man who had been in line for a long time stood before me. "Who is it for?"

"For the Paraná River."

I had never dedicated a book to a river.

That was a first.

MANY YEARS AGO, VISITING THE CAVES AT Altamira, I was astounded by the delicacy of the paintings. I thought, but dared not ask, "These marvels, wouldn't they be the work of women, not of men?"

The question had simply popped into my astonished head. When I included it in one of my books, there was no lack of people accusing me of being a dogmatic feminist.

Years went by and in 2013 an American professor, Dean Snow, completed his lengthy research in several prehistoric caves and concluded that most of the paintings were done by women, not by men.

He backed up his assertion.

My question was born of my imagination. Now it had found someone to keep it company.

For the Record

An Utterly Complete Autobiography

I was born on September 3rd, 1940, while Hitler was devouring half of Europe and the world was expecting nothing good.

From a very young age, I demonstrated a real aptitude for making mistakes. So often did I put my foot in my mouth, it was evident I would make my mark on the world.

With the healthy desire to deepen my mark, I became a writer, or at least I tried to.

My most successful works have been three articles that circulate on the Internet under my name. In the street people stop me to offer congratulations, and every time I start pulling petals off a daisy: "I kill myself, I do not, I kill myself . . . "

None of the articles was written by me.

A Few Things About the Author

I could be the world champion of absentmindedness, if such a championship existed. Frequently I mix up days, times, places. I have trouble telling night from day, and I miss appointments because I sleep in.

My birth confirmed that God is not infallible. But I'm not always wrong when it comes to choosing the people I love and the ideas I believe in.

I detest the contrite, hate complainers, admire those who wordlessly roll with the punches. Luckily there is always some friend telling me to keep on writing, telling me that age helps and that baldness comes from thinking too much and is a risk of the profession.

Writing is tiring, but it consoles me.

Why I Write/1

I want to tell you the story of my first real challenge as a storyteller, the first time I feared I might not be up to the task.

It occurred in the Bolivian town of Llallagua, near the mine where the San Juan massacre had taken place. The dictator Barrientos had ordered his troops to open fire from the heights of the surrounding hills on the drinking, dancing miners celebrating Saint John's Eve.

I arrived about a year later, in 1968, and stayed on thanks to my abilities as an artist. You see, I had always felt an urge to draw, though my sketches never managed to close the gap between myself and the world.

The bigger abyss was between my skills and my aspirations, though some of my portraits turned out all right and I was good at lettering. In Llallagua I drew portraits of the children of the miners and I painted posters for the carnival, for public events, whatever was needed. So the town adopted me, and the fact is I had a great time in that miserable frozen world, where the cold intensifies the poverty.

The night of my departure arrived. The miners were my friends and they gave me a goodbye party with lots of drink. We downed chicha and *singani*, a sort of tasty but somehow terrible Bolivian grappa. We were celebrating, singing, telling jokes, each worse than the one before, and all the while I knew that at five or six in the morning, I don't remember which, the siren would blast, summoning them to work in the mine, and there it would all end. We would say goodbye.

When the moment approached, they surrounded me as if about to accuse me of something. It wasn't to accuse me of anything, rather to ask, "Now, tell us about the sea."

I was speechless. The miners were condemned to an early death from silicosis in the bowels of the earth. In those days life expectancy in the shafts was thirty or thirty-five, no more. They would never visit the sea, would die with no chance of laying eyes on it, were fated by poverty to remain in that stricken little town of Llallagua. My duty was to bring the sea to them, and find words capable of soaking them through.

That was my first test as a storyteller, and it convinced me that the pursuit is worth something.

God's Little Angel

I was once a child, one of "God's little angels."

At school, the teacher taught us that Balboa, the Spanish conquistador, standing on a hill in Panama, had seen the Pacific Ocean on one side and the Atlantic on the other. He was, the teacher said, the first man to see both oceans at once.

I raised my hand: "Miss, miss."

And I asked, "Were the Indians blind?"

That was the first time I got kicked out.

Why I Write/2

If I'm not mistaken, it was Jean-Paul Sartre who said, "Man is a useless passion." I would add that so is writing.

You write without really knowing why or what for, but I suppose it has to do with your most deeply held beliefs, the things that won't let you sleep.

Those few articles of faith provide a basis for writing, but they are not always convincing. In my case, my capacity to believe fluctuates according to the time of day.

Normally until about noon, I feel rather optimistic. Then from noon to four, my soul plummets. Toward dusk, it nestles back into place. At night, my soul falls and rises a few times more. And on it goes.

I don't trust full-time optimists. In fact, I think they come from a mistake of the gods.

According to the Maya, we were all made from corn, which is why, like corn, we come in so many colors. Before that, the gods idiotically tried out other recipes and the results were atrocious. Once they made man and woman out of wood.

These wooden people were just like us but with nothing to say or even a way to say it, since they had no breath, no courage. The gods grew terribly bored. I have always suspected that it was their lack of courage that kept the wooden people from getting *dis*couraged. Discouragement is proof you have courage, you have the breath. So, it's not so bad if your soul plummets. It is one more indication of being human, nothing but a puny human being.

And as a puny human, twisted around by courage and discouragement according to the time of day, I continue writing, practicing that useless passion.

Silence, Please

I learned a lot from the Uruguayan novelist Juan Carlos Onetti when I was starting out.

He taught me flat on his back, smoking. He taught me with silences or lies, because he loved to add some luster to the few words he spoke by attributing them to ancient civilizations.

On one of those nights of silences and cigarettes and wine that caused instantaneous cirrhosis, the master was lying down, as always, and I was seated by his side. Time passed without us noticing in the least.

That was when Onetti told me a Chinese proverb: "The only worthwhile words are ones that improve upon silence."

I suspect the proverb was not Chinese, but I never forgot it.

Neither did I forget what I was told by one of Gandhi's granddaughters, who years later visited Montevideo.

We met up at my café, El Brasilero. Recalling her childhood, she told me about her grandfather's word-fasts: for one day a week Gandhi neither listened nor spoke. Not at all.

The next day, words sounded different.

Silence, which speaks without a sound, teaches us to speak.

The Craft of Writing

From Onetti I also learned the pleasure of writing by hand.

By hand, I work and rework every page, who knows how many times, word after word, only typing it up on a computer when I have the final version, which always turns out not to be the final version after all.

Why I Write/3

A confession, to begin with. As long as I can remember, I wanted to be a soccer player. I was good, the best of the best, number one, but only in my dreams. Once I woke up and took a few steps, I kicked some pebble and discovered I wasn't made for soccer. It was obvious I would have to seek some other profession. After trying my hand at several unsuccessfully, I began to write, to see if something would come of it.

I tried, I still try, to learn how to fly in the dark like a bat in these somber times.

I tried, I still try, to accept that I cannot be neutral or objective, because I refuse to turn myself into an object, indifferent to human passion.

I tried, I still try, to write about women and men who have a will for justice and an urge for beauty, unbound by the borders of maps and time, for they are my compatriots and my contemporaries, no matter where they were born or when they lived.

I tried, I still try, to be stubborn enough to continue believing, in spite of all evidence, that we humans may be poorly made but we are as yet unfinished. And I continue believing that the human rainbow has more color and sparkle than the rainbow in the sky, but that we are blind, or rather blinded by traditions that have mutilated us.

In sum, I would say that I write hoping to make us all stronger than our fear of failure or of punishment when it comes to choosing sides in the eternal battle of indignation against indignity.

I Crave, I Covet, I Yearn

Living Out of Curiosity

The word "enthusiasm" comes from ancient Greece, where it meant "having the gods inside."

Whenever a gypsy woman grabs my hand to read my fortune, I always pay her double to leave me alone. I do not know my future, nor do I wish to.

I live and survive out of curiosity.

It's that simple. I don't want to know what awaits me. The best thing about my future is that it's unknown.

Last Door

After he lay down for the last time, Guma Muñoz had no wish to get up again.

He did not even open his eyes.

In one of his rare moments awake, Guma recognized his daughter, who was holding his hand to give his sleep some peace.

Then he spoke, or rather murmured, "Strange, isn't it? I used to be afraid of death. Not anymore. Now it makes me curious. What will it be like?"

Wondering how it would be, he let himself go, into the heart of death.

Nightmare

The mountain told a friend and he told me.

A man was climbing, driven by who knows what yearning and hunger. On he pressed, more and more determined, though with every step the hill grew longer and his legs weaker.

"No slacking allowed," he muttered, giving himself orders so inaudibly he appeared tight-lipped. On he went. The nearer he got to the summit, the greater his fear of the afterward calling to him from the distant depths.

Finally, he let himself fall; he let himself go.

The steep mountainside was endless.

Everything receded, his world, his people, and though it was a matter of fate he could not stop blaming himself: "chickenshit," "coward." Now at the end of the final voyage, his hands, torn to shreds by rocks and thorns, lost their last grip and he was carried off, off toward the void, with no chance to say goodbye.

At the End of Each Day

The sun always offers an astonishing goodbye. Today's sunset is never a repetition of yesterday's or a harbinger of tomorrow's.

The sun is the only one who departs in such an extraordinary way.

It would be so unfair to die and see it no longer.

At the End of Each Night

A Maya god greets the rising sun.

Hoisting it onto his back, he takes it home to the Lacandón jungle and feeds it beans, tortillas, fish, and squash seeds, and he pours it coffee.

When it is time to say goodbye, the god carries it to the other horizon, which is the hammock where the sun goes to sleep.

To Live, to Die

"I am sending you this photo of me, for my daughter who is so far away. I want her to come see me, and when she gets here I want to die in her presence.

"I am old and sick, already walking with the wind."

—Collected by David Acebey from a Guaraní Indian in Bolivia

I Crave, I Covet, I Yearn

In beauty may I walk.
May I find beauty before me
And beauty behind
And below
And above
And around me more beauty
Beauty the entire length of the trail
That comes to an end in beauty.

—From "Night Song of the Navajo"

EDUARDO GALEANO (1940–2015) was one of Latin America's most distinguished writers. A Uruguayan journalist, writer, and novelist, he was considered, among other things, "a literary giant of the Latin American left" and "global soccer's preeminent man of letters." His works published in English include the three-volume *Memory of Fire, Open Veins of Latin America, Soccer in Sun and Shadow, Days and Nights of Love and War, The Book of Embraces, Walking Words, Upside Down, Voices of Time,* and *Children of the Days.* Born in Montevideo in 1940, he lived in exile in Argentina and Spain for eleven years before returning to Uruguay in 1984. His work has been translated into twenty-eight languages. He is the recipient of many international honors, including the first Lannan Prize for Cultural Freedom, the Casa de las Américas Prize, and the Most Illustrious Citizen of the countries of Mercosur. Galeano once described himself as "a writer obsessed with remembering, with remembering the past of America and above all that of Latin America, intimate land condemned to amnesia." Isabel Allende, who said her copy of Galeano's book was one of the few items with which she fled Chile in 1973 after the military coup, called *Open Veins of Latin America* "a mixture of meticulous detail, political conviction, poetic flair, and good storytelling."

 # The Nation Institute

NATION
BOOKS

Founded in 2000, **Nation Books** has become a leading voice in American independent publishing. The imprint's mission is to tell stories that inform and empower just as they inspire or entertain readers. We publish award-winning and bestselling journalists, thought leaders, whistle-blowers, and truthtellers, and we are also committed to seeking out a new generation of emerging writers, particularly voices from underrepresented communities and writers from diverse backgrounds. As a publisher with a focused list, we work closely with all our authors to ensure that their books have broad and lasting impact. With each of our books we aim to constructively affect and amplify cultural and political discourse and to engender positive social change.

Nation Books is a project of The Nation Institute, a nonprofit media center established to extend the reach of democratic ideals and strengthen the independent press. The Nation Institute is home to a dynamic range of programs: the award-winning Investigative Fund, which supports groundbreaking investigative journalism; the widely read and syndicated website TomDispatch; journalism fellowships that support and cultivate over twenty-five emerging and high-profile reporters each year; and the Victor S. Navasky Internship Program.

For more information on Nation Books and The Nation Institute, please visit:

www.nationbooks.org
www.nationinstitute.org
www.facebook.com/nationbooks.ny
Twitter: @nationbooks

FIRE

FIRE

Hazel Rossotti

Fellow and Tutor in Chemistry
St Anne's College
Oxford

Oxford New York Tokyo
Oxford University Press
1993

Oxford University Press, Walton Street, Oxford OX2 6DP

Oxford   New York   Toronto
Delhi   Bombay   Calcutta   Madras   Karachi
Kuala Lumpur   Singapore   Hong Kong   Tokyo
Nairobi   Dar es Salaam   Cape Town
Melbourne   Auckland   Madrid

and associated companies in
Berlin   Ibadan

Oxford is a trade mark of Oxford University Press

Published in the United States
by Oxford University Press Inc., New York

A catalogue record for this book is available from the British Library

Library of Congress Cataloging in Publication Data
Rossotti, Hazel.
Fire / Hazel Rossotti.
Includes index.
1. Fire.   I. Title.
GN416.R67   1993   398'.364–dc20   92–22005
ISBN 0–19–855722–1 (hardback)

Typeset by Footnote Graphics, Warminster, Wilts
Printed in Hong Kong

Preface

There must be few, if any, of those who open this book who have never kindled fire. Even in this era of electricity, we take matches and cigarette lighters for granted. Some of us are smokers. Others cook over flames or embers, burn rubbish, use firearms, light candles, make camp-fires, pull crackers, drive cars, let off fireworks, or heat chemicals over a bunsen burner. A small proportion of fire-users are the experts who work with fire: tending it in furnaces, extinguishing it in town or forest, exploiting it in such a way that it does minimal harm to our surroundings, learning how better to tame and contain it, and studying its multitudinous steps so that we understand it more fully. Some of us, happily a still smaller proportion, are direct victims of fire which may claim not only property but also eyesight, mental health, limbs, and even life itself. And all of us are at risk from any change which it may bring to our planet.

This book aims to tease out the common thread which runs through the immensely varied phenomena which we call Fire. Woven into the warp and woof of the physics and chemistry of combustion are other strands: mankind's developing exploitation of fire and his progress in controlling it; the effect of fire on the rest of the natural world; and humanity's intellectual and spiritual relationship to it. The background canvas of science has been kept largely verbal, so that those who are familiar with only few aspects of fire (or with none) may enjoy ready access to its other facets.

Many people have helped me with this book and in a large number of ways. My husband, Francis, has been particularly productive of ideas; and our offspring Ian and Heather, together with Oxford colleagues, pupils, and other friends have been most generous with their knowledge, their suggestions, and their time. St Anne's granted me two terms' paid leave, during which kind colleagues took over

my teaching and other jobs; and the college's librarians gave me invaluable help. Both lab and college have provided facilities for the
diverse chores of authorship. I have been very lucky to receive much
whenever I sought it, in as varied circumstances as foraging around
for unlikely books in many of Oxford's libraries; seeking advice on
botany and on bonfires from college gardeners; telephoning art galleries, defence establishments, and museums; or visiting the village of
Agia Elena in Northern Greece to watch the fire-walking ceremony.
The book owes much also to all those owners and copyright holders
who have kindly sent us permission to reproduce illustrations (see
p. 271), often together with valuable information and material. Since
some of those to whom I am particularly grateful defy classification, I
hope it would not be invidious to record a few names: Peter Patrick,
formerly Fire Officer of Oxford University; Bernard Rudden, whose
knowledge of fire in the humanities extends far beyond the law
he professes; Mercia Macdermott, folk-historian, formerly of the
University of Sophia; Keith Waters, who took the photos for Plates
2, 3, and 16; Jenny Harrington, who fed me with much good advice
as well as with an immaculate typescript; the OUP editorial team
who made the serious business of book production so enjoyable; and
Ed Tenner for his unwavering encouragement. It is a pity that the
publishers' advisers must remain anonymous; I owe them so much
that I should have liked to thank them personally. It seems that the
only parts of the book for which I am solely responsible are those
containing any residual errors. A very warm thank-you to the named
and the un-named alike; I am indeed extremely grateful to you all.

St Anne's College   H. S. R.
and   January 1992
Inorganic Chemistry Laboratory
Oxford

Contents

___

List of plates

Plates 1 and 2 appear between pp. 22–3, Plates 3–4 between pp. 38–9, Plates 5–6 between pp. 54–5, Plates 7–8 between pp. 70–1, Plates 9–10 between pp. 86–7, Plates 11–12 between pp. 102–3, Plates 13–14 between pp. 118–19, Plates 15–16 between pp. 134–5, Plates 17–18 between pp. 150–1, Plates 19–20 between pp. 166–7, Plates 21–22 between pp. 182–3, Plates 23–24 between pp. 198–9, Plates 25–26 between pp. 214–15, Plates 27–28 between pp. 230–1, Plates 29–30 between pp. 246–7, Plates 31–32 between pp. 262–3.

I

Fire, the phenomenon

... it might almost be true to say that we know more about processes in some stellar atmospheres than we do about processes in a bunsen burner!

Gaydon and Wolfhard (1979) *(Ref. 7, p. 6.)*

1

What is fire?

Fire fascinates. From nightlight to forest fire, from icon lamp to blazing factory, from sparkler to incendiary blitz, flames draw the eye, be they leaping, twinkling, flickering or inexorably steady. With its power to warm, to light, to comfort, and to destroy utterly, it is little wonder that fire was worshipped as well as used, and that, even today, fire has many religious and social, as well as utilitarian, applications.

If the impact of a physical phenomenon on human affairs can be judged by its assimilation into everyday metaphor, then fire must surely have pride of place. We are afire with enthusiasm, burning with fever from inflamed tonsils, fired by ambition, or lit up by passion for an old flame. Smouldering resentment can flare up into anger and lead to a blazing row. Do we consign our enemies to Hell fire or do we heap coals of fire upon their heads? We kindle an idea, fan the flames, add fuel to the fire, and have several irons in it. There is a rumour that a director is under fire, and may be fired; it spreads like wildfire, and now the fat is in the fire. (No smoke without a fire.) Next time he'll be more careful; a burnt child fears the fire. His successor will have a baptism of fire; his mettle will be tried in the fire, and he may be reduced to ashes. He's no fireball, but does he have any spark at all? Will he ever set the Thames on fire?

Although each of these clichés illustrates some aspect of the received wisdom on fire, none totally encapsulates its nature. We learn of fire's need for air, fuel, and an initiating hot-spot; its production of heat, light, smoke, and ashes; and its power as a driving force, both for technology and for destruction. But they do not tell us what fire actually is, nor why one flame can look so different from another. What then is the essential similarity between a candle and a rescue flare, or a bonfire and a gas stove?

Turning for enlightenment to a dictionary, we find that

'flame'   = ignited gas
'ignited'   = set on fire, burning
'fire'   = the active principle operative in combustion, popularly conceived as a substance in the form of a flame or of a ruddy glow or incandescence
'combustion' = burning
'burn'   = to be in the state of activity characteristic of fires; to be in a process of combustion so as to give light; to be reduced to ashes, cinders, etc. by fire

From these interdependent definitions, we can distil the idea that fire involves gases, consumes materials, and usually emits light; the associated release of heat seems to be taken for granted.

Many of us learned at school that burning or 'combustion' involves a chemical reaction between fuel and atmospheric oxygen; the fuel contains a store of chemical energy which on burning is released as heat and light. Most fuels contain carbon and hydrogen and so burn in air to give mainly carbon dioxide and water, which together contain less energy than was present in the initial mixtures of fuel and air. Chemical mixtures will if possible undergo any change which relieves them of energy and so makes them more stable, in the same way that a football will roll down a hill. However, if the ball is lodged behind a stone or hummock, it may need a push to get it going. Similarly, an unlit bonfire will not catch fire spontaneously; it needs a lighted match to give it the small push or input of energy needed to initiate the change. Once the burning has started, enough heat is released to activate and ignite adjacent fuel. In favourable circumstances, combustion is therefore self-sustaining for so long as both fuel and oxygen are available.

Although we must extend these ideas about fire, we do not need to unlearn them. Almost all combustion does indeed involve reaction between fuel and gaseous oxygen, usually in the form of air (but see Chapters 11 and 12 for exceptions). Not only does it release heat, often in dramatic amounts, but it nearly always increases the number of particles present. For example, when octane burns, thirty-four molecules of products are produced from two of fuel and twenty-five of oxygen. The resulting increase in the disorder or 'entropy' of the system reinforces the (dominant) effect of heat release in boosting the stability of the products relative to the initial flammable mixture.

So we can define fire as a self-sustaining, high-temperature oxidation reaction which releases heat and light; and which usually needs a small input of heat to get it going; but we may feel that this pedestrian statement denies fire its true nature by excluding any aesthetic consideration. The descriptive arts have had limited success in the depiction of fire. William Sansom, one of the many men of letters amongst the fire-fighters of the London blitz, bemoaned the inadequacy of pigment to portray emitted light, despite the attempts of many generations of painters, cf. Plate 1. In our time, colour photography, and in particular cinema and television, can capture something of the blaze and flicker, and, despite the lowering of impact by reduction in scale, films such as *Gone with the Wind* and *The Towering Inferno* have brought to viewers something of the awesomeness of a large fire. Music has offered some convincing impressions of fire, ranging from the flickers of the final consuming flames of Wagner's *Parsifal* to the evocation of an Australian bush fire in Barry McKimm's *Ash Wednesday*. For the novelist, fire provides dramatic incidents on which to peg his plot: for the death of Grace Poole in *Jane Eyre*; the demonstrations of bravery and gratitude in *I am David*; for material destruction in *Fahrenheit 451*; and for the evolution from play to arson in *Eroïca* from 1930s Greece. But the main gift of fire to the arts is that of symbolism, which covers much of human experience, evoking desire, passion, sexuality, romance, vitality, curiosity, knowledge, anger, punishment, evil, destruction, purity, domesticity, and comfort.

The diverse role of fire in both metaphor and symbolism is based on the immense variety of chemical reactions which fall within the definition of combustion. Much of this book is concerned with this diversity and in particular with the way in which mankind has succeeded in increasing the number of contexts in which fire can be exploited and controlled; and the final section explores the appeal of fire to the human spirit and intellect. First, however, we must take a closer look at some combustion reactions so that we can get a clearer idea of what is happening when something burns. Here the scope for variety is an embarrassment; what, apart from our tentative definition, relates the tiny, controlled pilot flame of a gas burner to ravaging wildfire? Do we understand either well enough to predict its quantitative behaviour? In the next chapter, we shall discuss what is happening inside some simple flames, and see how far we can extend the ideas to more complicated fires.

2

Fire and flames

'High-temperature self-sustaining oxidation', less pompously known as Fire, usually manifests itself as a hot, visible flame; but here the generalization ends. Flames vary enormously in structure, colour, shape, size, and temperature, according to the exact changes which are taking place within them. These in turn depend on the fuel, the supply of air (or of other substances which provide oxygen, such as those discussed in Chapter 11), and the exact physical conditions. There are, moreover, exceptions. Some fires smoulder without flaming, while some flames are barely visible and others only slightly warm. The simplest type of flame is that which is fed by a premixed supply of gaseous fuel and air, as in the central parts of the flames of a gas cooker or bunsen burner. Such flames have been studied in great detail and some are so well understood that we can predict their behaviour mathematically. They are, however, less familiar and less appealing than the humble candle, which was used by Faraday to illustrate the principles of combustion in one of the most lucid expositions of science yet written: his famous *Chemical history of a candle*, based on six lectures to 12-year old boys, and first given in London in 1849. We shall therefore give the romantic precedence over the classical and look first at a candle flame, which many of us will have lit, watched, run a finger through, pinched, and blown out on countless ritualistic, and often happy, occasions.

An unlit candle can, of course, persist almost indefinitely in contact with air, even though it is less stable than its combustion products; but the situation changes dramatically the moment we put a burning match to the wick. Solid candle wax consists of molecules arranged in a fixed three-dimensional pattern, not totally still, but moving only little round an average position. Every molecule of wax contains a puckered backbone, sometimes branched, of eighteen to twenty carbon atoms, each carrying two (or for end positions three) hydrogen atoms. Each atom is linked to its neighbours by sharing a pair of electrons, to form a so-called chemical bond. When a lighted match is brought near to the wick, some of its heat is transferred to the wax near the tip of the candle. The molecules move more vigorously as the temperature increases and may break loose from their ordered positions. When the temperature reaches 400 °C, the wax round the base of the wick melts to a liquid which is soaked up the open-weave cotton wick. The outside of the candle is cooled by the air, and it remains solid, acting as a rim which retains the small pool of molten wax. The heat from the match flame speeds up the wax molecules in the liquid, and some of those near the surface break away completely from their neighbours to become vapour. These gaseous molecules also absorb heat from the flame of the match and move still faster, both from place to place and internally, by rotation, stretching, and bending. Some vibrate so violently that one of the electron pairs may be severed. If one or more of the chemical bonds is broken, 'pyrolysis' occurs: the heat shakes the molecule into fragments.

The pyrolysis products are much more reactive than the original molecules of wax; many contain an odd number of electrons and readily take part in further changes which may eventually result in the formation of pairs of electrons and hence in other chemical bonds. Indeed many species which contain a single, unpaired electron are so reactive that they exist for only a fraction of a second. They may attack another molecule in the vapour, chipping a fragment off it, or causing it to break in half. In this way, one fragment loses energy, while one or more others are generated through a chain reaction. Alternatively, two reactive fragments may combine to produce a more stable molecule. The 'cracking' process takes place faster than the recombination, and the size of the fragments decreases until the vapour around the tip and the wick contains appreciable amounts of the very small and very reactive groups CH_2, CH, and C_2. This cloud of reactive vapour is also very hot, and pushes outwards from the wick, lowering the pressure (particularly round the bottom of the flame). The air which diffuses in to replace it contains about 20 per cent oxygen, which reacts with some of the unstable fragments in the fuel-rich vapour. Many of the hydrogen atoms in the small reactive groups are converted into water vapour which can be detected if a piece of cold, shiny metal is held above the flame. (Faraday's demonstration that the condensate was indeed water must have delighted his young audience: he treated it with metallic potassium (see p. 28) and watched it catch fire.) Much heat is given out when oxygen converts atomic hydrogen to water, and this further heats up the gases around the wick. More fuel vapour is decomposed or 'cracked'. Some fragments such as CH and C_2 emit part of their energy as light, which gives the blue colour around the base of the flame, showing the edge of the zone where the primary reaction is occurring (see Plate 2a).

Some of the carbon atoms may also combine with oxygen to form carbon monoxide, or even carbon dioxide; but many of the unstable C_2 groups combine with small molecules, such as acetylene (or ethyne, C_2H_2), which are formed during cracking. The resulting aggregates react with oxygen. They lose much of their hydrogen to form water, evolving much energy and leaving roughly spherical masses which are composed mainly of carbon. The shapes of these aggregates resemble those which can be formed by winding a sheet of chicken wire irregularly around itself; but a few particles may have a

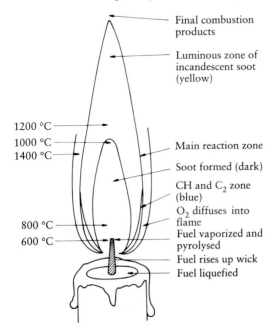

Final combustion products

Luminous zone of incandescent soot (yellow)

1200 °C

1000 °C
1400 °C — Main reaction zone

Soot formed (dark)

CH and C_2 zone (blue)

O_2 diffuses into flame

800 °C

600 °C — Fuel vaporized and pyrolysed

Fuel rises up wick

Fuel liquefied

Candle flame

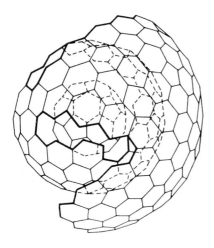

Soot. Small particles may resemble a coil
of hexagonal-mesh chicken wire

regular 'football' structure such as that of the spherical buckminster-
fullerene, which contains sixty carbon atoms. The temperature of
these soot particles is about 1200 °C, i.e. between 'red heat' and
'white heat', so they glow with an orangish-yellow light which produces the useful light of a candle and gives it its characteristically
'soft' colour. A piece of cold metal placed in this part of the flame
is rapidly blackened by soot. As the glowing soot particles travel
outwards and upwards, they meet the oxygen-laden air travelling
inwards, and are converted first to carbon monoxide and then to
carbon dioxide, and yet more heat is given out. Much of this energy
which is liberated can be attributed to the formation of the strong
bonds which join carbon to oxygen, and which, in carbon dioxide,
are largely responsible for the 'greenhouse effect', see p. 166.

By no means all the energy is emitted as light. Some is conducted
into the solid or liquid wax, thereby ensuring a small pool of molten
wax to replace that sucked out of the wick as vapour. Some is lost to
the atmosphere when the hot products, carbon dioxide and steam,
escape by diffusion and convection into the surroundings. Much heat
is radiated from within the main reaction zone. Radiation occurs in
all directions, including back into the dark central fuel-rich region
around the wick, where the temperature can be kept high enough to
vaporize and pyrolyse the fuel, and to give it enough energy to react
with the incoming air, so as to keep the combustion going. Given an
ample supply of fuel and air, the maintenance or spread of any form
of fire depends on the extent to which the heat generated by the
burning is ploughed back into the complex combustion process or is

dissipated into the surroundings. If the hot gases are blown, or pinched, away from the fuel-supplying wick, they become mixed with the much cooler surrounding air and their temperature falls below that needed to vaporize and pyrolyse the wax: the flame is extinguished. We, like Faraday, can show that the resulting wisp of smoke contains unburned wax vapour by holding a lighted match a little distance from the wick and seeing how the smoke ignites an instant before the flame jumps back to the wick.

Although we now understand many of the changes which occur in a candle flame, it is very difficult to give a full mathematical description of them because we have no control over the mixing of fuel vapour and air. These intermingle by both diffusion and convection, the concentration of fuel decreasing and the concentration of oxygen increasing outwards from the wick. The movement of gases and the reactions which occur depend on the temperature, which itself depends on heat evolved by the reaction, on the loss of useful energy by movement of gases and outward radiation, and on the retention of heat by radiation back to the reactive zone. Similar diffusion flames are formed when a stream of gaseous fuel, such as methane, burns in an atmosphere of air; and, analogously, when a jet of air is burned in

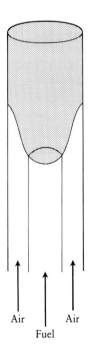

Tulip-shaped under-ventilated flame

an atmosphere of methane to form a so-called 'inverse flame'. The shape of the flame depends on the ratio of fuel to air. A jet of fuel gas burns in a restricted supply of air with an inverted tulip-shaped flame.

It is less difficult (although still not easy) to understand the changes which take place during the combustion of a pre-mixed gas containing both fuel and oxygen, familiar to many of us from gas cooking stoves and bunsen burners. Suppose we put a lighted match to one end of a long tube which contains a mixture of fuel gas and air. The heat of the match flame decomposes some of the fuel in the same way as it breaks down vaporized candle wax, and if the ratio of fuel to air is suitable, the mixture will ignite. Since the molecules in the gaseous fuel are much smaller than those in wax (each having up to only about five carbon atoms), they are pyrolysed more easily; a single spark is often sufficient to ignite the mixture. Once formed, the flame will travel rapidly back down the tube at a speed which depends both on the type of fuel and on the fuel to air ratio. If the pre-mixed gas is supplied to the tube in the opposite direction to that in which the flame front travels, it will oppose its progress; and if the speed of the gas supply is equal and opposite to that of the flame front, the mixture, if ignited, will burn with a steady flame near the mouth of the tube. The tube itself acts as a heat sink and, by conducting away some of the energy which is generated, cools the gas just inside the tube and so helps to prevent the flame from entering.

The design of a bunsen burner is very simple. Fuel gas enters an upright tube through an inner nozzle in its base. At the lower end of the upright tube is an adjustable hole, open to the air. When the gas supply is turned on, the gas flows upwards, sucking air into the tube with it. The two streams of gas intermingle as they move. The flow is streamlined and 'laminar', parallel to the tube but somewhat slower at the circumference than at the centre; and so the bunsen flame is conical. At the edge of the tube, the gases burn just above the rim, while nearer the centre the flame front is pushed upwards by the faster-moving stream of gas. The products of combustion are carried away, both by the gas stream and by diffusion, warming up the surrounding atmosphere into which they escape.

Despite the apparent simplicity of pre-mixed flames compared with the 'diffusion' flame of the candle, there is much scope for variety. We can change the nature of the fuel and the ratio of fuel to oxygen, either by adjusting the amount of air mixed with the fuel (see

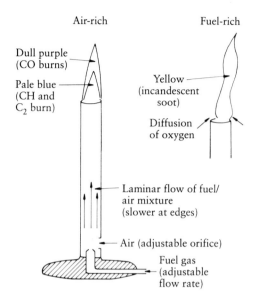

Air-rich   Fuel-rich

Dull purple
(CO burns)

Pale blue
(CH and
C_2 burn)

Yellow
(incandescent
soot)

Diffusion
of oxygen

Laminar flow of fuel/
air mixture
(slower at edges)

Air (adjustable orifice)

Fuel gas
(adjustable
flow rate)

Bunsen burner flames

Plate 3), or by replacing air with pure oxygen. Mixtures are flammable only within certain limits, which may be quite narrow (for example from 2.2 to 9.5 per cent fuel by volume, for propane–air mixtures), or very wide (from 4 to 94 per cent for hydrogen–oxygen mixtures). Different fuel mixtures naturally burn at different rates, and give flames of different temperatures, often between 2000 °C and 3000 °C. The oxygen–acetylene flame used in welding can reach 3400 °C. The higher the flame temperature, the more effective is the fragmentation of the molecules, which may lose (negatively charged) electrons and become positively charged ions; and since these electrically charged particles are free to move, these ionized flames can conduct electricity.

The design of a bunsen burner allows us to adjust both the flow rate of the fuel and the ratio of fuel gas to air. When the air intake hole is closed, or nearly so, the fuel to air ratio is too high for flammability of the pre-mixed gas. Combustion can occur only when oxygen diffuses into the gas stream as it emerges from the tube. The resultant flame then resembles the diffusion flame of a candle and is yellow from incandescent soot. If the gas flows rather slowly or if the burner is placed in a stream of air, a fuel-rich diffusion flame may be blown sideways from the end of the tube. Much more of the heat generated by the burning gases will then be lost to the surrounding air, and such heat as returns to the reaction mixture may be insufficient to keep the combustion going. The burner may then 'blow out', leaving unchanged fuel gas to escape into the air. At high flow rates of fuel-rich mixture, the flame may lose its previously regular conical shape and become ragged, with a surface which is dented and crumpled, more like a sponge than smooth skin, and with a larger area of contact between fuel and air (see Plate 3c–f). Turbulence can therefore increase both the rate of burning and the difficulty of predicting it. In larger turbulent flames, the combustion products may escape in a series of vortices, which cause irregularities in pressure and momentarily prevent oxygen from reaching the hot fuel. The dark, non-burning region then elongates, expels the blanket of products, meets more oxygen, ignites, and contracts again; the flame flickers. If the same flame is enclosed in a glass chimney, air is sucked vertically upwards as the hot combustion products escape. This constant upward draught discourages turbulence, and so steadies the flame.

When we gradually open the air intake at the base of the tube, the flame shortens, and becomes both steadier and less yellow. With the hole about half-open, the barely-visible flame glows a dull, purplish blue (see Plate 3b). A further increase in the air supply produces a short, steady, bright-blue hollow cone inside the purplish region, and the burner may hiss on account of turbulence in the air which is sucked into the bottom of the tube by the hot gases escaping from the top. The combustion of air-rich mixtures proceeds apace, consuming all the fuel without intermediate formation of specks of carbon, and so there are no solid particles which can incandesce to give a yellow luminous flame. In the earlier stages of combustion, carbon monoxide is formed, together with the reactive fragments CH and C_2, all of which have acquired considerable excess energy from neighbouring particles in the hot flame. They can become more stable by radiating some of this energy as light, but unlike the relatively large soot particles, they cannot emit light over a wide range of energies. Small groups of atoms can give out light of only a few energies, as characteristic as a fingerprint of the emitting species. The human eye cannot analyse this light, but senses only the mixture of energies, which we perceive as a particular colour. The light which we see as the pale bright-blue inner cone of the bunsen flame (see Plate 3a) is radiated by the fragments CH and C_2. Outside this region, the carbon monoxide itself burns to carbon dioxide, probably using oxygen both from the original mixture and from the air diffusing into the flame, here coloured purplish blue.

These air-rich pre-mixed flames have a much more stable shape than the flickering diffusion flames into which oxygen penetrates only if the gas is emerging at a suitable speed. But if the gas-flow is decreased, the burner may 'light-back' because the flame front travels back down the tube and ignites the gas which is coming out of the inner nozzle. At too high a flow of gas, the flame may also be dislodged from the neck of the tube, but in this case it moves upwards. After such a 'blow-off', there is a space between the rim of the tube and the combustion zone; rarely, the flame settles uneasily in mid-air over the burner, usually it goes out. The flow of combustion products from both pre-mixed and diffusion flames destroys the laminar flow of the unburned gases and gives rise to vortices and irregular differences in pressure; but in pre-mixed flames this 'turbulence' occurs well outside the zone which emits light, so the visible flame is of constant shape. Burners of other designs produce stable flames of quite different shapes, such as a flat layer, an inverted cone, two separate cones one above the other, or a pimpled layer.

The behaviour of a premixed flame above a cylindrical tube naturally depends on the diameter of the burner. For each fuel, there is a complex relationship between those values of the fuel to oxygen ratio, the burner diameter, and the flow rate, which together will give a steady flame without danger of either 'flash-back' or 'blow-off'. A narrow-bore burner favours the required non-turbulent and 'laminar' flow of gas but the smaller the rim, the larger is the ratio of circumference to cross-sectional area, and the larger the proportion of heat which is lost from the flame. If the tube is too narrow, the heat loss is such that combustion cannot take place and the flame is 'quenched'. For this reason, wire mesh, or a series of fine tubes, can be used in a device called a flame trap, to prevent flame propagation. An example is the miner's safety lamp developed by Humphry Davy. The flame is surrounded by a fine metal gauze, which offers little resistance to gases, but which leads heat away from them so effectively that the flame cannot cross it, and may also deactivate some of the short-lived fragments in the vapour.

One of the difficulties of studying flames is the variety and the great reactivity of the pyrolysis products. Analysis of the light emitted, and of the mass of the species formed when methane, CH_4, burns in air, shows that the flame contains free atoms of hydrogen and oxygen

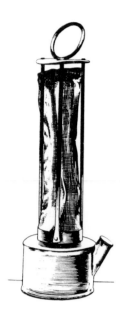

Davy safety-lamp for miners, 1816

together with very short-lived fragments, such as CH, CH_2, CH_3, OH, and C_2, and with more stable intermediate molecules such as ethene C_2H_4, carbon monoxide CO, and formaldehyde HCHO, which themselves react with oxygen. The many diverse mechanisms by which this melée of fragments exchanges components, and energy, has yet to be completely described. But despite the quip (p. 1) that we know more about distant stars than about the bunsen burner, the flames of some very simple fuels, such as hydrogen, are now fairly well understood.

Some mixtures of air and fuel gas burn faster with increased turbulence, which may be induced during the burning. At certain pressures and temperatures, combustion may be so rapid as to cause a sudden very large increase in pressure, i.e. an explosion, perhaps preceded by one or more transient 'cool' flames (see Chapter 12). Even if a gas appears to burn with a more or less steady flame, combustion may be occurring by a regular series of very small explosions, and in this case the flame emits a continuous popping sound, quite different from the hiss caused by entrainment of air. If a tube of the right acoustic properties surrounds the flame, the frequency of the explosion can resonate with it, producing a note of fixed pitch, as in an organ pipe. Research on these gentle 'singing flames', about which there was much speculation in the nineteenth century, has helped to lessen noise pollution from their more vigorous descendants in jet aero-engines.

As we cannot yet fully describe what happens when a gas burns, we should guess that the changes which take place in a wood fire pose an even greater challenge to understanding. Why can we easily ignite a matchstick but not a log? Why do three logs burn better than one? Should you remove the ashes daily or let them accumulate?

Since vaporized candle wax has larger molecules than fuel gas and so is pyrolysed less readily, it is not surprising that a still higher temperature is needed for the decomposition of the lengthy lignin molecules in wood. Heat is, of course, also needed to vaporize the decomposition products of wood, while fuels such as propane are gases at room temperatures. Moreover, wood heats up less easily; if we want to achieve the same rise in temperature throughout two samples of the same volume, we should need about 723 times as much heat for oak as for propane. When we supply heat to a small part of a large sample, we might guess that the difference between the two samples is even more marked, since wood conducts the heat away from the hot-spot over seven times faster than a gas does. However, gases become less dense when heated and so rise, carrying their heat with them by 'convection', which is the most important route for heat loss from small solid-fuel fires. When the diameter of the fire is larger than about one-third of a metre, radiation of heat becomes increasingly important, although heat loss by convection continues to occur. Moreover, the strong buoyant force of hot gases has serious implications for the spread and control of accidental fire (see Chapters 18 and 19).

However, if the wood is supplied with enough heat it too will be pyrolysed. Some of the decomposition products are gaseous and force their way to the surface, causing cracking and maybe hissing. Here they may be further decomposed and eventually ignite, to burn with a luminous, sooty diffusion flame. The heat which is given out may pyrolyse another small region of the wood and so sustain the combustion. Or it may not. The burning will continue and spread only if the wood becomes hot enough; a goodly amount of the released heat must therefore be transferred back into the fuel. A little energy passes from hotter to cooler regions of the wood by conduction, but longer-range heat transfer is responsible for most of the feedback. Hot materials, such as flames, other burning logs, hot ashes, the fireplace itself, and even the wall opposite all radiate energy. Skilful grate-design and fire-laying can ensure that a generous fraction of this energy is returned to the unburned fuel. Three logs in contact therefore burn better than the same logs at a distance: each can reradiate heat to the other two. Ashes are best left under the fire, as they absorb the heat that radiates downwards and return some of it to the fuel. Spatial factors are also very important in the transfer of heat by convection. It is important that hot spent combustion gases escape so that fresh supplies of fuel and oxygen can be sucked into the flame; but they should have ample chance to heat up the unburned fuel before they be allowed to lose all their heat up the chimney. It may be that there is enough feedback of heat to pyrolyse the wood, but insufficient to ignite the gaseous products. The wood may then smoulder to become a charcoal skeleton, red-hot only in the small region where it is being slowly oxidized in air. The pyrolysis products remain as fairly large fragments which condense on cool surfaces as a tarry oil. The ancient craft of 'charcoal burning' is in fact the conversion of wood into charcoal by allowing it to smoulder for several days in tightly packed mounds to which air has limited access (see also page 132).

As Chandler and his colleagues suggest (Ref. 46), the importance of radiative and convective heat transfer can be elegantly demonstrated by striking three identical ordinary wood-splint matches (see Plate 2b). The first is held vertically, head upwards: it burns with a small flame which soon goes out. The second is held horizontally and burns steadily with a bigger flame, while the third which is held (with tweezers!) vertically, head downwards, is consumed extremely rapidly. In the first case, the match-stick receives little radiation from the flame or charred head and is cooled by the upward flow of air which is sucked towards the flame by the escape of the combustion products. The second match-stick, at right angles to the flame, receives much more radiation, and has some contact with hot gases at the base of the flame; while the third stick is totally surrounded by the flame and hot gases and so becomes hot enough to catch fire almost immediately.

The early stages of a coal fire are similar to those of a log fire, except for the fact that the flammable vapours issuing from the hot fuel are not decomposition products of the bulk material, but are formed by the vaporization of pockets of tarry deposits. The vapours may escape with enough vigour to hiss, split the lump of coal, and maybe hurl out a small, red-hot ember. Luminous yellow diffusion

Sticks laid in preparation for charcoal burning (Dodecanese, 1991)

flames again appear and the combustion is sustained by an interplay of heat-feedback and ventilation which resembles that of a log fire.

The similarity decreases, however, when the tarry deposits have been consumed. At this stage the coal has become coke, a porous material, of the same shape as the original coal but, like the charcoal produced from smouldering wood, composed entirely of carbon. The coke itself burns, combining with oxygen both at the surface of the lump and inside the pores, to form first carbon monoxide, and then carbon dioxide. The hot carbon dioxide, passing upwards through the hot coke, combines with it, to regenerate carbon monoxide. When this meets air at the surface of the fire, it burns and again forms carbon dioxide, producing a flame with the same dull bluish purple as we see in the flames of a candle and a bunsen burner.

So, despite the increase in complexity between the combustion which occurs at a bunsen burner, a candle, a log fire and a coal fire, they have a common basis. They all produce a visible flame. The changes which occur give out enough heat to perpetuate the combustion, during which oxygen combines with pyrolysis fragments of the fuel. All these reactions, however, must first be initiated by some hot-spot, which generates the first decomposition fragments of the fuel; that is, the fire must first be ignited. In the next chapter we shall discuss the various ways which have been developed for kindling fire.

3

Ignition

It seems difficult to reconcile the difficulties and frustrations of attempts to light camp-fires and coal fires with the alarming ease with which an unwanted fire can start accidentally (see Chapter 19). If we wish to ignite a solid or liquid, we must supply it with enough energy first to vaporize the fuel and then to pyrolyse the vapour. Ignition of a gaseous fuel needs added energy only for the second process, and, for some mixtures of fuel gas and air, the energy required for initiation is low. A few reactions need almost no added energy, and for these ignition occurs spontaneously when the reactants are mixed (see p. 28 and Chapters 11 and 18). Here, however, we shall discuss mainly ways of supplying heat in order to initiate combustion. Since ready flammability constitutes a fire hazard, a balance must be struck between safety and ease of ignition; one should not light a bonfire by

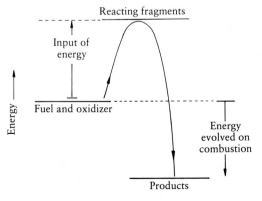

Ignition by input of energy

first dousing it in lighter fuel, and then striking a spark from the flint of a cigarette lighter.

Ignition of solids is generally carried out in stages; little would be achieved by sparking a flint at the end of a cigarette, or by holding a lighted match to a large lump of coal. The spark from a lighter flint does, however, supply enough energy to ignite the mixture of air and vaporized lighter fuel which surrounds the wick of the lighter. The heat from the flame is sufficient to pyrolyse a little tobacco, to vaporize some of the volatile flammable components, and to ignite the mixture of vapour and air at the tip of the cigarette. There is a brief flame, and the heat generated starts a smouldering zone, which then travels slowly through the tobacco.

By far the simplest way to supply heat to kindling is to light it from some fire which already exists. This method must have been the only one available to the earliest fire-users, who could either have moved hot embers or used a dead, leafy branch as a torch. As our primitive forbears were nomadic, they would also have needed to preserve fire in some portable form for both land journeys and voyages. Consider-able skill must have been needed to prevent the combustible material either from burning too fast, or from cooling and 'going out'. In the Greek myth, Prometheus used a dried fennel stalk to bring the gods' fire to men. The tiny packets of air enclosed by dry cellulose are pro-tected from the atmosphere by the tough outer casing over the circumference of the cylinder, allowing the stalk to smoulder ex-tremely slowly. The rate of burning can be even further reduced by applying wax or clay to one or both ends of the stalk. This method of fire preservation was used on some Greek islands right up to the twentieth century. 'Slow matches' made of twisted bark, and doubt-less of other plant fibres, smoulder in a similar way, and as recently as the 1980s, pedlars in Piraeus were selling slow matches of plaited (and presumably very oily) wool, dyed bright red and smouldering acridly. A small increase in the oxygen supply, achieved by blow-ing, or by sucking through a cigarette, can coax a flame from the smouldering fuel.

Another way of transporting fire is to carry the burning material at a higher temperature in a separate, non-combustible container, such as a horn, shell, coconut, or later a clay or metal pot. Larger con-tainers were used by later, less nomadic communities. A fire inside a hollowed tree-trunk stays alight under the ashes, much as a domestic open fire can be preserved by a generous covering layer of coal dust, or slabs of peat. Cherokee Indians even buried a smouldering log

1 Fire at the Houses of Parliament, Westminster, 1834

(a)

(b)

2 (a) Candle flame; (b) match held vertically upwards, horizontally, and vertically downwards

under their community meeting house, and could dig it up and fan it to start another fire.

If there is no fire already available, we must produce a hot-spot of high enough temperature to ignite the tinder. There are many possible techniques. Since almost all forest fires in uninhabited regions are caused by lightning, electrical ignition can claim the longest history; but the oldest of mankind's technological methods is certainly friction, generated by his own muscle power. The devices for kindling fire by 'rubbing two sticks together' vary considerably with the type of wood available, but usually involve a stationary part, the 'hearth', of soft wood. When a piece of harder wood (or, in China, porcelain) is moved vigorously over, or into, the hearth, its outer surface is heated. Some pyrolysis occurs, as does some mechanical damage, with the result that small charred particles of the softer wood are rubbed off. The friction heats them up to incandescence and when the sparks (together with air) are blown on to some readily ignitable

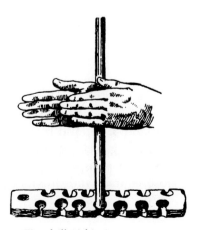

Fire-saw (Australia)

Fire-plough (Oceania)

Fire-drill (Africa)

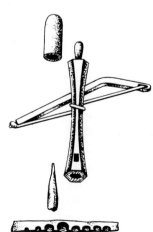

Bow-drill (Egypt)

tinder, this catches fire. In the hands of skilled tribesmen of so-called non-technological communities, ignition can be achieved in one or two minutes; visitors from technologically more advanced cultures usually need rather longer. The frictional motion may be along the grain of the hearth (ploughing), across it (sawing), or it may be into the wood with a rotary movement (drilling), or with an up-and-down movement (pumping). The fire-drill may be rotated between the palms or with the aid of a thong with handles, or a bow.

Similar frictional methods involving minerals may have been learned by observing the sparks produced by rocks rolling in an avalanche. Tiny pieces chip off the rocks and are heated by friction, which may produce local red-hot areas in such rocks as flint and pyrites, which fracture easily and conduct heat badly. With skill and patience, the sparks can kindle a good tinder when air is also blown on it. This method was used from early times up to the nineteenth century. The spark was produced by rubbing pyrites on itself or on flint, or by striking flint on steel. These sparks are not very hot (they cannot ignite petrol), and so a highly inflammable tinder was needed. Many elaborate and beautiful devices were made, for holding tinder, for use as steels, and for producing the friction. The pistol was a common design and in some the spark first ignited a small charge of gunpowder, which then ignited the tinder. One pistol from eighteenth century Vienna was coupled to a clock; at a pre-set time the trigger-held flint was released on to a steel, to ignite a charge positioned to light a sunken candle, which then sprang up out of the container. Nowadays, the cerium alloys used for cigarette lighters produce white hot sparks which can ignite the air–vapour mixture around a wick carrying 'lighter fuel'.

We also use friction to produce a hot-spot every time we strike a match, but very high temperatures are not needed because the combustion starts very easily, providing enough heat to pyrolyse the matchstick tinder and to ignite that, too. The match industry is based on the element phosphorus, which was first isolated in Hamburg in 1669; the white form, which is highly toxic, sometimes ignites spontaneously in air. Only 11 years later, Robert Boyle* found that he could ignite sticks, tipped with sulphur, by pulling them through a coarse folded paper which had been coated with phosphorus; this action both brought the reactants into close contact and provided

---

* Formulator of Boyle's Law and author of *The sceptical chymist*.

enough energy to start the reaction. A similar frictional technique is still used in pull-wire fuses.

The next few generations of matches could be struck on any rough surface, since all the components were present on the match head. The first type contained only white phosphorus and often ignited spontaneously when removed from its sealed case. The matches were less toxic and less dangerous to transport if the phosphorus was replaced by a mixture of a substance, such as potassium chlorate, which produces oxygen if heated, and some fuel such as sulphur, which is readily combustible without igniting spontaneously in air. Matches of this type were difficult to ignite and produced showers of sparks and, in the case of the sulphur-containing 'lucifers', choking fumes of sulphur dioxide. Similar matches, called 'light-bearing slaves' were probably used in China as early as the tenth century.

The safety match, patented in Sweden in 1852, was a great improvement in that it used red phosphorus which is more stable and less toxic than the white form. The combustible materials, kept separate on the match-head and the striking strip, came into contact only on striking. In 1898, a 'strike-anywhere' match, which contained a relatively harmless sulphide of phosphorus instead of the vicious white form of the free element, was patented in France. The manufacturers immediately made the details available to their competitors, free of charge. Matches made from white phosphorus were soon widely banned.

Present-day matches differ little from those developed in the nineteenth century; the head end of the (usually wooden) shaft is impregnated with paraffin wax to increase flammability, while the handle may contain a fire-retardant (see Chapter 19). Wood may be replaced by cardboard (for book-matches) or by dangerously flammable waxed paper or cotton. Although safety matches predominate, strike-anywhere matches have been made safer by restricting the ignitable portion to a small patch on the top of a globular combustible match-head, and so preventing chance contact between the ignitable parts of nearby matches in a box.

Attempts to make matches for all-weather use have resulted in 'windproof' matches in which the wax is replaced by a more flammable substance which makes the wood a better tinder so that, once ignited, the flame can survive some wind and spray. However, since both the ignitable and combustible materials absorb moisture, it is very difficult to ignite a match which is already damp (see p. 30).

Matches described as waterproof have been developed using substances which are less prone to take up water, but as these are expensive and difficult to ignite, they are not widely available.

Mechanical energy also initiates combustion of the explosive devices discussed in Chapter 12, which are set off, not by friction but by percussion, or even by a footfall. The shock of impact ignites a small amount of very sensitive 'primer', giving out enough heat to set off the main explosive charge. Some substances are too unstable even for this use; a filter paper contaminated with silver azide AgN_3 is said to explode if a fly alights on it. Nowadays, these salts of heavy metals have been largely replaced by the cheaper, less toxic, and better hexanitromannitol, which likewise explodes on impact to give simple gaseous products. A mixture of lead styphnate and an oxidizer also ignites on being stabbed or hit and is used as a 'primer' in the first stage of setting off an explosive charge.

A quite different device for producing heat from movement is the fire-piston, which originated in primitive South-East Asia, but was reinvented in France and Britain early in the nineteenth century. When you pump air into a bicycle tyre, the nozzle of the pump gets warm; and if you compress air suddenly to one fifth of its original volume, the high temperature produced is enough to ignite a little tinder on the underside of the piston. In Munich, about 1888, a lecturer on heat-transfer lit his cigar by this method; in the audience was one Herr Diesel, who later said that the demonstration was a major inspiration for his new engine, in which ignition is achieved by compression alone (see Chapter 10).

It has long been known that the sun's rays can be concentrated to produce a hot-spot of sufficiently high temperature to ignite tinder. In the ancient world, concave mirrors of brass or bronze were used because fire, which was lit directly from the sun, without the intervention of muscle-power, was sometimes thought to be particularly holy (see Chapter 23). The fire tended by the Vestal Virgins in Rome about the seventh century BC was lit by this method, as is the Olympic flame to this day (see Plate 4). The legend of Archimedes defending Syracuse by using a mirror to set fire to enemy warships could well be based on fact; Buffon reproduced the effect in 1747, using a mirror constructed from 168 planar pieces. Present-day solar furnaces, like that at Mont Louis, France, use a planar mirror to reflect sunlight into a roughly parabolic concentrator, about 10 metres across and made of numerous curved mirrors. The parallel

rays of sunlight are brought to a focus by the concentrator to produce a temperature of around 3500 °C. The author has seen even
an apparently innocent brass buckle concentrate the Aegean sun
sufficiently to ignite a beach-bag.

We can also use a lens to focus sunlight; many of us will have used
a magnifying glass on a sunny day to char paper, or even to produce
a flame. Lenses were used by chemists such as Priestley and Lavoisier
to set fire to gases in closed containers (see Chapter 24). In Paris,
sunlight was focused to ignite the fuse of a toy cannon, which fired at
noon on every sunny day for about 130 years, up to 1914. The
Chinese used 'fire-pearls', which were transparent spheres probably
of glass or rock-crystal, but possibly of ice. Hooke certainly used an
ice-lens to produce fire in the early days of the Royal Society of
London. Lenses, like mirrors, may also kindle fire by accident. Thick
pieces of broken glass can start a forest fire, and a flask of liquid left
all day in a sunny laboratory can produce a charred arc on the
surface of the bench, or if flammable materials are around, something much worse.

The kindling of forest fires by lightning must date from the colonization of land by plants; but only recently has mankind learned to
generate electricity and to use it intentionally for kindling. Lightning
strikes the earth about one hundred thousand times each day and
when it discharges it produces a region of very high temperature,
unless the first object it encounters is a good electrical conductor,
which allows the electric charges to flow rapidly down to the ground.
Smaller scale discharges of electrostatic charge also produce hot-
spots and can set off both accidental fires, in dust-laden or other
highly flammable atmospheres (see Chapter 19), and intentional
ignition of gasoline–air mixtures in the internal combustion engine
(see Chapter 10). An electrically operated cigarette lighter produces a
small electric spark, sufficient to ignite the air–fuel mixture when
pressure is applied to certain types of 'piezoelectric' crystal.

Heat can also be generated electrically when a current is passed
through a metal wire, as in an electric heating element. A red-hot
electric element can ignite a mixture of air and gas, as in a battery-
operated gas-lighter, used for bunsen burners and cooking rings
alike. Photographic flash bulbs produced their intense light by the
combustion of fine magnesium wire heated electrically in an atmosphere containing oxygen (see Plate 6a).

Fire may sometimes be started by chemical energy alone. If a small piece of the metal potassium is put into water, it reacts violently with it, generating hydrogen gas and enough heat both to melt the potassium and to ignite the resulting air–hydrogen mixture. A mauve flame dances on the surface of the water. Naturally, potassium is far too reactive, e.g. with damp air, for use as an initiator of combustion, but the use of water to initiate violent, and incendiary, reactions has long been known. It has been suggested that in classical Greece, quicklime (CaO), mixed with some readily combustible substance such as sulphur or crude oil, was smeared on enemy buildings during some dry summer nights. Come the autumn rains, the quicklime reacted vigorously with water (to give $Ca(OH)_2$) and the heat evolved ignited the fuel, which in its turn produced enough heat to set fire to the building. The Royal Air Force tried similar tactics during the Second World War and dropped small sheets of white phosphorus and nitrocellulose over German forests. In tests, the devices had ignited spontaneously when it rained. But the weather after the raid was too cold for the reaction to occur, and the sheets oxidized slowly and harmlessly in air. Calcium phosphide (Ca_3P_2) is also used as an initiator because heat is evolved when it reacts with water; but in the more humanitarian context of rescue flares at sea. Like phosphorus itself, it reacts to give hydrides, mainly PH_3, with some P_2H_4; the latter is very unstable in air and ignites spontaneously, setting fire to the PH_3 as well. A similar ignition has been invoked to account for the 'will-o'-the-wisp' (but see Chapter 24). It is not only 'chemicals' which react violently with water or air; it has been claimed that very dry cellulose fibres can react with the air, generating enough heat to ignite them, so that a pile of hot, ultra-dry washing might in exceptional circumstances ignite spontaneously when it is removed from the drier. Although extremely unusual, spontaneous combustion of dried-out cloth seems less improbable than that of living flesh, which is also discussed in Chapter 24.

A well-known and violent reaction which generates much heat is that between concentrated sulphuric acid ('oil of vitriol') and water. So great is the affinity of the anhydrous acid for water that it also reacts very vigorously with many sugar and starch-like substances, extracting the atoms of hydrogen and oxygen from them, and again generates much heat. In 1805, Chancel in Paris discovered that a splint, tipped with a mixture of sugar, glue, and the oxygen-rich potassium chlorate, ignited if dipped into concentrated sulphuric acid. The acid is, of course, a particularly hazardous material and uninviting for general use. But the reaction was tamed somewhat in a device known as the Promethean match which was patented in 1828. The acid was contained in a small glass ampoule, coated on the outside with the combustible solid mixture and wrapped in paper; when the glass was crushed with pliers (or between the teeth!), the paper caught fire. The same reaction is the basis of a delayed ignition mechanism used by saboteurs and terrorists. The acid is initially separated from the combustible solids by a barrier which it slowly corrodes. When it has eaten its way through, it reacts with and ignites the mixture of sugar and chlorate, producing enough heat to set off an explosion.

Another group of self-igniting reactions comprises porous materials which can combine with oxygen. Heat generated by slow internal fermentation (e.g. of damp hay) may be sufficient to cause smouldering combustion, which creeps to the surface. On contact with a more generous supply of air, the material catches fire spontaneously. Much industrial waste behaves in this way, and so constitutes a serious fire hazard. Culprits are oil-soaked rag, fish scrap, peanut meal, resinous shavings of fibre board, and many dusts such as from coal, metals, plastics, and starch products. Many metals, such as nickel, are similarly 'pyrophoric' when they are finely divided, even though they are quite stable in bulk quantities: not only do the small particles have greater access to oxygen, but the large area of metal surface gives rise to a large number of unpaired electrons which, somewhat like those in the intermediates found in flames (see Chapter 2), make the metal very reactive. Some pyrophoric mixtures were used in the nineteenth century for starting combustion. Hare's pyrophor was made by roasting Prussian blue to give finely divided iron which was sprinkled on top of the tobacco in an unlit pipe; the smoker could light his pipe merely by sucking air through it.

Spontaneous ignition can also occur when two gases are mixed, as in the self-lighting welding torch, powered by chlorine trifluoride and hydrogen. The gases react vigorously together to give hydrogen fluoride and hydrogen chloride; this mixture is so much more stable than the initial one that the heat generated is sufficient to produce a flame. Some pairs of liquids which ignite on mixing are used as rocket propellants (see Chapter 11).

We have frequently been referring to 'tinder' and other easily combustible materials; but what sort of substances are they? Much tinder is finely divided vegetable matter, such as rotten wood, fungus, thistledown, and moss, all of which have been used by the most primitive of fire users. As any of us who has tried to light a camp-fire in even slightly damp conditions will know, the tinder must be exceedingly dry; otherwise the heat which we have managed to generate will be squandered both by heating up and by vaporizing any water in the tinder. Moreover, since water is a better thermal conductor than dry plant material, heat escapes from the hot-spot more quickly if the tinder is damp. For its weight, tinder has a vast surface area which allows ready access of hot combustion gases and oxygen. Since only little heat is needed to heat up the low mass of material, pyrolysis occurs easily and widely, to be quickly followed by ignition. Finely divided material of vegetable origin is used also in urban societies. Tinder boxes often contained charred rag; charcoal ignites at about 300 °C, compared with about 120 °C for sawdust from softwoods. And newsprint is still a standby for the lighting of a solid-fuel fire, although some newspapers are more flammable than others. More exotic tinders are dusts of sulphur or of magnesium, which is used for kindling camp fires. A block of magnesium is rubbed with a piece of harder metal, dislodging hot chips which ignite in air, because magnesium, like aluminium, forms a very stable oxide. Powders of these metals are widely used for fireworks, flares, and other devices which require ease of ignition and a high release of energy (see Chapter 13).

It is often necessary to increase the oxygen supply in order to achieve a flame. The earliest method, still current, is to blow on smouldering tinder with pursed lips. The blast is better directed by using a pipe (e.g. of bamboo) and can be made stronger and steadier with bellows, operated by hand or foot, or with a piston pump.

Instead of increasing the air-flow, we can use tinder which contains

Egyptian goldsmiths using blowpipes (about 2400 BC)

its own oxygen supply. The widely-used amadou was a dried fungus impregnated with saltpetre; a hot spark both pyrolyses the vegetable matter and liberates oxygen from the saltpetre. The tinder, or 'first fire', used in pyrotechnics (see Chapter 13) and in the highly combustible contents of incendiary bombs and document destroyers (see Chapter 7) also contain oxygen-rich compounds, and in such a quantity that the combustion is independent of the supply of air.

Liquid fuels are of course readily combustible, but it is surprisingly difficult to set fire to a pool of some liquid fuels. If a lighted match is in contact with molten candle wax, the hot liquid near the flame is dragged away from the hot-spot by the stronger surface tension of the cooler liquid and so cannot be heated sufficiently for vaporization, pyrolysis, and ignition unless it is absorbed in a wick which restrains its escape. Although more volatile flammable liquids can be ignited easily in a pool, they are not to be recommended as tinder, being both dangerous and ineffective. A lighted match applied to, say, coal doused in paraffin, would vaporize the liquid over a large area, igniting any readily flammable material within range, but not sustaining the high temperature long enough to pyrolyse and ignite the coal. If the liquid can be restrained from flow, e.g. by absorption into some porous material such as brick, it can safely be used as an effective fire-lighter. One ingenious device for lighting a coal-fire consisted of vegetable fibres sodden with liquid fuel and attached to a clockwork fan which blew air on to the flames. During the twentieth century, paraffin and petrol have been thickened into solids or very viscous liquids by coagulation, originally on aluminium salts of naphthenic and palmitic acids. Blocks of such materials are convenient fire-lighters, while thickened liquid fuels, such as the notorious Napalm (named after its constituent acids), have been used in incendiary warfare (see Chapter 7). Other thickeners have since been developed. The most general is probably pyrogenic silica, which with particles of diameter about 0.02 millimetres will form a gel with many liquids, while smaller silica particles, of diameter 0.007 millimetres will gel even liquid hydrogen. Recalcitrant fuels, such as coke, may be ignited by the fairly prolonged application of a flame from burning fuel gas as the 'gas poker' which was widely used in the UK during its coal gas era.

The thrust of all these efforts to kindle fire is to produce a hot-spot at a point where there is a suitable mixture of oxygen and flammable vapour, so that the initiation energy hump can be surmounted in

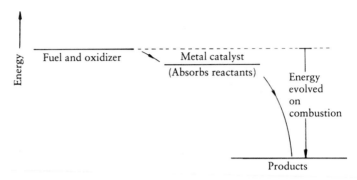

Spontaneous ignition in the presence of a catalyst

a small portion of it. Sustained combustion should then follow (see p. 22). An alternative approach would be to try to lower the hump so that combustion would occur spontaneously at room temperature. It is difficult to see how this could be done for solid or liquid fuels which need a high temperature for pyrolysis. A flammable mixture of gases, however, ignites much more readily. If a few of the participating molecules could be brought into close proximity, the probability of their reacting with each other would be greatly increased and so the energy hump would be lowered. This can be achieved by introducing various finely divided metals in which the surface acts as an anchorage for small gas molecules. The adjacent molecules react together very readily when absorbed on the surface and no extra energy is needed to initiate the combustion. Catalytic lighters for domestic gas appliances work in this way. Ignition takes place immediately a small patch of finely divided metal is waved near the gas outlet. Ignition by catalysis has a history almost as long as the fuel gases themselves. In the Döbereiner lamp (1823) a stream of hydrogen was ignited in air by being passed over a piece of spongy platinum.

We shall see in Chapter 19 how our knowledge of methods of intentional ignition can be harnessed to help us to prevent unintentional ignition. In the two following sections, however, we shall survey some of the many tasks for which mankind has, intentionally, kindled or harnessed fire.

II

Fire for comfort

Praisèd be my Lord for our brother fire, through whom thou givest us light in the darkness: and he is bright and pleasant and very mighty and strong.

St. Francis of Assissi
from *The song of the creatures* (1225)
Trans. Matthew Arnold

4

Fire for heating

The history of fire-tending is longer than that of *Homo sapiens* himself. Remains of fossilized charred bones in southern Africa and northern Greece strongly suggest that fire was tamed over one million years ago, when hominoids walked upright but were not yet wise. The first fire user was probably our direct ancestor, *Homo erectus*, but bones of the more ape-like *Australopithecus robustus* were also associated with some of the African finds. Peking man, previously thought to have been the first fire-user, lived about half a million years later. There is no evidence that any of these early users of fire were able to kindle it but they would have had problems enough in capturing, tending, controlling, and preserving it. It is probable that hot embers, remaining from the ravages of a passing wildfire, were fed with the dry charred sticks found nearby. Several such speculations survive from classical times, but the most famous account of this momentous step is given by the Roman author Vitruvius, writing about two thousand years ago on the origins of architecture:

In the olden days men were born like wild beasts in woods and caves and groves, and kept alive by eating raw food. Somewhere, meanwhile, the close-grown trees, tossed by storms and winds, and rubbing their branches together, caught fire. Terrified by the flames, those who were near the spot fled. When the storm subsided, they drew near, and, since they noticed how pleasant to their bodies was the warmth of the fire, they laid on wood; and thus keeping it alive, they brought up some of their fellows, and, indicating the fire with gestures, they showed them the use which they might make of it.

A print from 1547, illustrating Vitruvius' idea of the taming of fire. In the background, people flee with animals from a forest fire, but in the foreground, others tend a fire they have isolated.

Vitruvius attributes to the discovery of fire the development of language, upright gait, wonder at nature, manual skills, and, finally, house-building. This passage was widely circulated during the Renaissance, often illustrated with a woodcut. It probably served as an inspiration also to the artist Piero di Cosimo (1461–1521) for his oil painting now called *The Forest Fire*.

We can only speculate as to how much our ancestors learned by observing wildfire and how much by trial and error on a fire already tamed. Both would allow him to observe the wind enlivening the flames and blowing them sideways; the crackle and blaze of dry twigs falling on glowing embers; and the hissing and smoking of green leaves pitched onto a hot fire. One wonders how quickly they learned, with what sense of satisfaction, and with what sense of awe. Smouldering fire must have been the first natural phenomenon which mankind learned to control reversibly, to quicken and to dampen, at will. Considering how many supposedly sophisticated members of Western technological societies still stare as if hypnotized at a simple bonfire, it would be difficult to appreciate fully the feelings of those early fire-tenders, even if we had any insight into their cognitive processes or their emotional make-up.

In primitive societies fire would have served a variety of functions before it was put to any culinary or technological use. A nearby source of heat and light must have been a great comfort, as well as being a protection from wild beasts and noxious insects, and would have been the natural social focus of the group. A camp-fire still performs these functions, both for small family units and for larger communal gatherings such as youth camps (see Plate 5). Until mankind learned to kindle fire, it was of paramount importance that fire, once captured, should be assiduously preserved (see Chapter 3). The early fire tenders used a variety of fuel such as charcoal, dung, and small bones and branches. Larger branches and, where available, coal, lignite, and bitumen, had to await the development of cutting tools.

The camp-fire, although of immense significance in the development of technology, is a very inefficient way of generating heat. As the smoke and hot gases drift upwards, much energy is lost into the air. If the fire is built on grass or damp earth, yet more energy is dissipated in heating up and eventually vaporizing the water they contain. These losses appreciably reduce the amount of energy which can be put to good use, either externally, or to sustain combustion. Camp-fires are therefore difficult to ignite, and, particularly in the initial stages, the sluggish combustion may not provide enough draught to suck in sufficient oxygen.

Although the development of our modern heaters and burners from the primitive camp-fire has been partly in response to new requirements and new fuels, much progress is due to the quest for the ideal balance between the oxygen supply, the escape of combustion products, and the transfer of heat in order to make the most efficient use of the energy released. The supply of oxygen to an existing fire can be improved by increasing the access (by poking) or the pressure (by fanning and blowing). Present-day blowers include the electric hairdrier (seen by the author in use in a Greek taverna to encourage the charcoal grill) and the tuyère, which directs jets of air into a furnace. Design is crucial if the fire is to be effectively ventilated. An early modification was to build the camp-fire on stick or stone slabs laid over a small depression in the ground. These both allowed air to enter from below and reradiated heat to the fuel.

Whilst a good draught is a prerequisite for a lively fire, too much should be avoided. The fuel must not be consumed too fast, nor should the fire become hotter than needed. Gusts of wind may sweep out hot gases so that a very small fire may be 'blown out', while a large one may spread to any nearby flammable material. A fire could be protected from the prevailing wind by erecting a shield to one side of it; or from any wind by building it inside a circular windshield. A small fire could be contained in a stone trough (with holes for access of air), and a slab of stone across the top would give a prototype stove. Alternatively, the fire could be protected from the weather, and maybe exploited more effectively, if it were surrounded by the dwelling area.

The small step of moving a fire from the outside to the inside of a cave produces important changes in the transfer of both matter and heat. Modern cave-dwelling members of mountain fighting units know the importance of a ventilation fissure to allow for the (preferably unobtrusive) escape of smoke. If the fire is near to a wall of the cave, the rock will reradiate heat, even long after the fire has gone out. Fires in mankind's first constructed dwellings such as tepees, tents, Lapland kotas, and igloos, were usually placed in the centre, to prevent the walls from igniting (or melting). A central hole or chimney in the roof allowed the escape of smoke and hot burned gases, together with a lot of warmed air which would have been more useful if it had been able to circulate in the dwelling.

The convective escape of hot gases is very wasteful of heat, since the air it sucks into the fire is not only cold, but is in excess of that needed for combustion. Moreover, as anyone who has tended a fire in an old hillside cottage will know, a gust of wind can produce a high enough pressure at the mouth of the chimney to prevent all the smoke from escaping; some may be forced back down the chimney

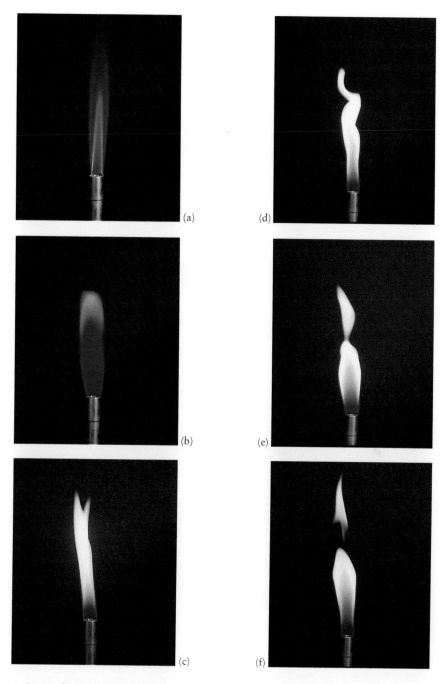

3 Gas-air flames of bunsen burner, with air-hole (a) almost fully open; (b) half open; (c), (d), (e), and (f) almost closed, to give turbulent flames

4 Olympic flame, kindled from sun with parabolic mirror, Greece

and into the fireplace. There are several ways of trying to prevent chimneys from smoking in this way. The upper part of the fireplace may be closed off, in order to produce a strong draught up the chimney. This sweeps all the smoke upwards, but makes the fire burn fast and wastefully. The escape of heat, and the return of smoke, may be lessened if the chimney is fitted with a moveable door or 'registers' to reduce the opening or with a primitive valve to prevent the smoke from returning to the room. If the neck of the chimney, just above the fire, is partially closed by a diagonally placed sheet of metal, most of the smoke which is blown back down the chimney will hit this 'smoke shelf' and be redirected upwards. All the hot combustion products will escape through the remaining opening, sweeping with them any smoke particles in their path. Downdraught may also be reduced by cowls fitted on top of the chimney. In regions where there is a strong prevailing wind, the chimney may be totally covered except for a side opening in the opposite direction. A turbulent wind, as on the lee on a hill, is more difficult to deal with. One approach is to break up the wind by having a large number of very small holes in the mouth of the chimney. The ornate chimney pots which fulfil this function in the Algarve region of Portugal are reminiscent of fine lace. A less picturesque solution is a vaned metal cowl which rotates in the wind in such a way that the openings are always on its leeward side.

The raised camp-fire developed into the grate with free entry of air from below. The logs in domestic wood fires were often supported on metal firedogs. Coal, however, needs a higher temperature for

Chimney pots from the Algarve region of Portugal

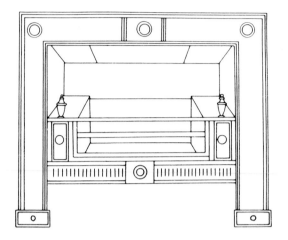

Grate with register to adjust
chimney opening, 1795

Grate with register, angled
sides, and perforated inner
back, about 1830

pyrolysis, and so coal fires have to be more compact. The fuel is
supported by an iron trivet or basket, either above a hollow in the
floor or in a raised grate, often with a closed front. In either case, the
air enters through a series of slots, which may be partially closed by a
moveable damper. The upward escape of hot combustion products
up the chimney then sucks the fresh oxygen-rich air over the combustion regions. The same principle is used in the dangerous but often
highly effective method of 'drawing-up' a newly lit coal fire by

holding a piece of newspaper in front of it so that air enters only from below; but a metal sheet with an insulated handle does the same job much more safely. The air supply may also be controlled, and smoking reduced, by a damper in the neck of the chimney, perhaps incorporated into the smoke shelf.

The rate of air flow varies greatly with type and size of fuel used. A wood fire can be left unattended for many hours if the logs are first allowed to become very hot, and then covered with overlapping slabs of peat turf. The barely porous peat burns slowly, giving out little heat and air is drawn up only sluggishly between the slabs. A coal fire can be preserved in a similar way if 'damped down' with a generous covering of coal dust, which may seem to smother it, but allows the passage of just enough air to maintain the smouldering. Much heat is preserved, and some of the inner hotter coal dust is doubtless pyrolysed. When a more lively fire is needed, a few upheavals with the poker will admit enough air to reactivate the fire and produce immediate flames.

Fireplace design must also take into account the fate of the radiant heat from the fire; it is indeed largely this heat which warms the room, since air is a poor thermal conductor. When we stand in front of a fire and enjoy its warmth, we feel mainly that heat which is radiated from the front of the fire. If the fire is centrally placed in the room, the radiant heat is absorbed by the furniture and walls, which gradually increase in temperature. Some of the heat taken up by the walls is conducted through them and is lost to the colder air outside the house. The thinner the wall, the more quickly it will be warmed up, but the more easily it will lose heat to the surroundings, particularly if the air outside is much colder than the wall. Some of the heat absorbed by the walls is, however, reradiated into the room, and so once the fabric of the house has reached a temperature higher than the air indoors, it will help to warm this air, even after the fire is no longer alight.

More often, the fireplace is placed along one of the walls, or in a corner. The heat radiated from the back and sides of the fire is again absorbed by the wall, and as this is so near to the fire, it may become quite hot. The difference in temperature between the back of the fireplace and the outside air will be so great that much heat will be lost to the outside. Some heat will, of course, be reradiated from the inner walls of the fireplace. If the fireplace has upright walls, at right angles to each other, heat from one side wall will merely be reradiated back to the other side wall, and much of the heat from the back wall will be returned to the fire. However, if the side walls are slanted outwards towards the room, and the top of the back wall is tilted inwards, much more heat is radiated back into the room. As Count Rumford pointed out, firebrick is preferable to iron for the sides of fireplaces, as it radiates more effectively. In some medieval castles, an especially thick stone wall was built *opposite* the fireplace in order that it should absorb, and so reradiate, as much heat as possible. The same principle was used in the USA in the early nineteenth century, the brick wall opposite the fireplace sometimes being as thick as 0.7 m.

Heat can also be radiated from hot surfaces under the fire. Wood ash should be removed only when it hinders the flow of air to the fire. Rumford advocated that grates should be lowered in order to heat the floor and also to prevent excessive draught. Heat loss from hot air and combustion gases can be lessened both by controlling the air-flow and by absorbing some of the heat from the gases. If the fire is lit inside a fireproof container, adjustable openings for intake and exit of gases can limit the air-flow to that needed to support combustion. The first such stove appears to have been built of brick and tile in France at the end of the fifteenth century. Much of the heat from the combustion gases was absorbed by the flue, which was of the same material. An iron flue, used later in Scandinavia, contained baffles which slowed down the escape of the hot gases and so enhanced the exchange of the heat. The Russian stove, used around the North Sea coasts, had masonry flues, several to a stove. These stoves were often built in the middle of a house, at the point of intersection of a number of rooms, so that each received some of its warmth.

The first stove built completely of iron was cast in the USA in 1642, but this was a mere fire-container, without even a grate. About a century later, a greatly improved stove was designed by Benjamin Franklin. In front there was a door, which could be fully opened to allow the flames to be seen. The other sides of the stove were encased in a larger box, containing only air. A lower opening allowed cold air from the room to enter the air-box where it became warmed by the fire, rose by convection, and returned to the room through an upper exit hole. The idea of warming room air by circulating it round an open fire had been used in Paris as early as 1624 to heat the Louvre. Cold air was drawn in under the hearth, and warm air was returned to the room through slits in the mantelpiece. The Franklin stove was

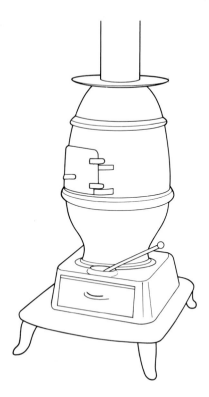

Pot-bellied stove, nineteenth century
USA

located in the fireplace, replacing the open fire. But if the stove is moved out into the room, no separate air box is needed; all the surfaces of the stove itself are exposed and radiate heat into the room, and also warm the surrounding air by convection. Some stoves, such as the commonly installed iron 'pot-bellied' stoves, were placed in the middle of the room. The chimney-pipe, which led up to the ceiling, absorbed heat from the escaping combustion gases and so helped to heat the room. Brick and stone stoves, often tiled, were usually built against a wall, but standing out into the room, again for effective radiation from a large surface. The flue gases were led through a convoluted path at the back of the stove, in order to exchange as much heat as possible with the masonry before escaping from the chimney.

Enclosed stoves use fuel much more efficiently than open fires, however well designed their fireplaces and chimneys may be. They are also safer, in that there is no possibility of glowing coals being ejected from the fire by a spurt of escaping gas. Psychologically, however, there is no comparison. There is much pleasure to be gained by gazing into an open fire, watching the moving flames, and seeing partially burned lumps of coal turn into glowing embers of ever-changing shape: 'seeing dragons in the fire' it used to be called. Some stove designers appreciated the importance of visible flames and fitted fireproof windows into the door of the stove. But this praiseworthy concession to romanticism is no substitute for an open fire; you cannot see dragons through small pieces of mica. Modern stoves and screened fireplaces have much larger panels of a special glass, which is both much more transparent than normal glass to radiant heat, and much more resistant to heat damage.

Until about a century ago, domestic room heaters were fuelled only by solids: in Western countries usually either by wood or coal. More recently, however, both paraffin and gas have been used in stoves or 'open' fires. In the paraffin stove, the fuel was burned as a diffusion flame from a ring-shaped wick low in the casing. Holes in the base and the lid allowed ventilation and transport, from the body of the stove, of air heated by radiation. At the end of the last century highly decorated oil stoves were made in cast iron or ceramic. The flames could be seen through leaded stained-glass windows or through a sphere of ruby glass in the shape of a huge lamp. The tops could sometimes be used as cookers, convertible by a wire table to a hot plate for tea and muffins. Less elegant portable paraffin stoves consisted of a metal cylinder with a perforated top. These stoves were smelly, not very effective, and exceedingly unsafe; if accidentally knocked over, they spilled burning paraffin over the floor. But they took the edge off the cold of an unheated bedroom and, in the dark, threw intricate geometrical patterns of soft light onto the ceiling. Present-day paraffin heaters are (slightly) less hazardous, but also cast less interesting shadows.

Domestic gas heaters were widely introduced in the early part of the twentieth century, although the prototypes had been made at least one hundred years earlier. The traditional design involved a row of premixed flames from the combustion of a mixture of coal gas and air, covered by a line of non-combustible 'elements' which became red-hot and radiated heat to the room. Some elements were made of tufted asbestos but most were openwork ceramic tubes. More recently, there have appeared models in which the radiative material simulates coal and when the gas has been lit, the heater gives a plausible but unchanging imitation of a coal fire.

A fire or stove can be used not only to heat the room in which it is situated, but also to provide hot water, and to heat some fluid which will carry heat to other rooms (or even to other buildings). These additional uses are by no means new. Roman baths were heated by an open fire housed directly under the water cistern. The hot water was piped to a fountain leading to a hot pool, from which the water was fed to a second tepid pool, and was finally led to a third cool one. In some Roman houses, the hot water plumbing system also had taps. The hot air and combustion gases from the fire circulated through the hypocaust cavities under the floors and inside the walls, thus providing the first central, and underfloor, heating. Rudimentary central heating seems to have been reinvented in England at the end of the eighteenth century; hot air from a stove passed through channels to warm remote rooms. In Northern Asia hot smoke was similarly led under stone seats in order to heat them.

Open fireplaces may readily incorporate pipes in which water can be heated for domestic use. Central heating, however, normally needs a special burner located away from the living area. The psychological comfort of what grate-manufacturers' advertisements call a 'living fire' has been sacrificed to the increase in thermal efficiency and ease of running, which is indisputable, regardless of either the fuel or the heat-carrier. The first heat carrier, air, was commonly used in fan driven central heating until the Second World War. Hot-water heating, first used in the eighteenth century for French greenhouses and chickenhouses, and for the Bank of England, is at present

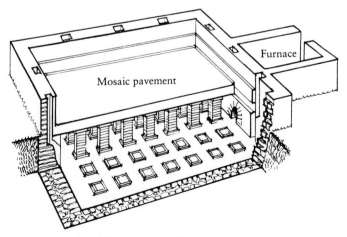

Roman hypocaust at Silchester, Hampshire, second century AD

favoured for houses. Steam heating, which also dates from the late eighteenth century, was first used for industrial heating. It is now used in large buildings such as office and apartment blocks, for example in New York, where steam may sometimes be seen coming out of vents in the sidewalk.

Before the Second World War, most central heating was fired by coal products and some installations which were self-stoking and self-riddling required very little attention. Oil, however, is suited to totally automatic and thermostatic control, and has the great advantage that it produces neither dust nor ashes. The oil may be vaporized for combustion either by thermal evaporation or by first 'atomizing' the oil by breaking it up under pressure into tiny droplets, and then spraying this mist into a stream of air. Gas burners for central heating may also be fully automated, and are simpler, and so more

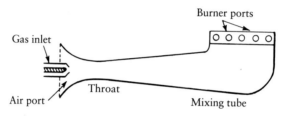

A typical domestic gas burner

trouble-free, than oil burners. If a direct supply of either coal gas or natural gas is available, there is no storage problem and gas may therefore be preferable to oil for central-heating plants. Both fuels started to replace coal products in the 1920s, and the choice between the two is now governed largely by consideration of price, supply, and convenience.

Some burners are constructed so that they may be adapted merely by use of a few controls, to burn either gas or oil, or possibly also pulverized coal which now fuels many large boilers of varying design. In some, an airborne stream of very fine coal-dust particles (of diameter about 1/25 of a millimetre) enter the hot combustion chamber, where the volatile products burn off. A second blast of air is admitted to burn the resulting coke. But large chambers are needed for complete combustion, and the powdery ash which is formed may clog the flues. If the fuel is injected tangentially at high speed into a cyclone furnace, combustion is completed more readily and the slag

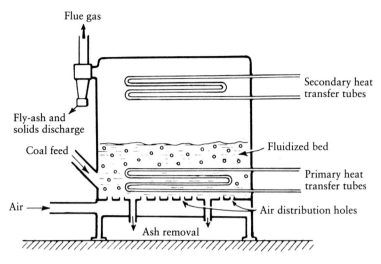

A fluidized-bed combuster

collects at the furnace walls, where it can be tapped off. An alternative method for burning small solid particles is to use a fluidized bed combustor in which air is forced upwards through the fuel bed at such a speed that the particles become buoyant, and the suspension behaves like a liquid, agitated by bubbles of excess air. The coal dust can be quite coarse (about 1 millimetre diameter). Heat exchange is very efficient and the relatively low temperatures needed reduce atmospheric pollution by oxides of nitrogen (see Chapter 17). Sulphur can be removed with limestone and incompletely burned ash can be recycled. However, we do not yet fully understand several of the processes involved, in particular the transfer of heat between the air in the suspension and that in the bubbles.

Central heating is nowadays so widespread in industrialized societies that some readers of this book may have had little experience of houses without it and may find it difficult to imagine a house which is heated only by an open fire in one room, and the dramatic temperature gradient from the fireplace to the edge of the room. Portable stoves, however, could be used as a supplement. Of the many predecessors of the hazardous paraffin stove (p. 44), some were mere bowls, which burned charcoal without draught, and were used not for heating rooms, but as personal heaters for bodily extremities. In many parts of the world, such basins were made of metal (such as the polished copper pans used in Sicilian villages to this day) but

Charcoal heater, South
Spain, 1991

some fire bowls from Kashmir are made of plates of mica, covered
with plaited osier. In Japan portable fire bowls were also used for
belly-warming and for the convenience of smokers. Some were
covered by perforated lids. In Europe, hot coals were put into metal
pans on long wooden handles and used to warm beds; some of these,
too, had intricately perforated lids. Warming pans were superseded
by using materials that could contain as much heat as glowing
embers, but at a lower, safer temperature: water near its boiling
point, or, in Switzerland, a bag of cherry stones, heated in the oven.
Mini-stoves have been devised as internal heating for irons. A model
which contained burning charcoal and had an opening to take
bellows dates from about 1850 and is still in use in regions without
electricity. Later irons with their own fires were heated by alcohol,
petrol, paraffin, and gas (including a rotary iron for valeting top hats
at the turn of the century). Meta-fuel pellets were used for heating
curling tongs and goffering irons. The ingenuity of those who have
over the centuries adapted fire for bodily comfort makes it the more
an indictment of our society as a whole that there are so many deaths
from hypothermia, not of ill-fated outdoor adventurers, but of elderly
people in their own homes.

Warming pan, 1662 (Ashmolean Museum, Oxford)

Even out of doors, fire, often in the form of portable coke braziers, provides both comfort to those who have to live and work in the cold (see Plate 7), and an appetizing way of roasting chestnuts and sweetcorn in city streets. More sophisticated cooking, however, requires more advanced technology, as do the many other tasks outlined in Section III; and mankind has been enabled to carry out such work through his increasingly competent taming of fire, either directly or by using it to generate electricity.

5

Fire for lighting

———

It must have seemed an obvious step to our early ancestors, familiar with the blaze of wildfire or camp-fires, to use a burning branch or a glowing ember to lighten some corner of cave or forest. Inflammable branches, charred at one end, were found in an early Stone Age settlement in France. Thought to be the earliest torches known, they indicate that mankind has been using artificial lighting for at least one hundred thousand years.

We saw in Chapter 2 that many of the small chemical species formed during combustion are so overloaded with energy that they re-emit it, not only as heat, but also as light, often of different colours in distinct parts of the flame. As each fragment can give out light of only a limited number of energies, it produces a flame of a definite, characteristic colour: CO and C_2, for example, emit clear blue light. Anyone who has dropped table salt (sodium chloride) into a gas flame will have seen the flame turn bright yellow, a colour characteristic of the element sodium (and familiar from low-pressure sodium street-lighting). Salt was indeed added to lamp-oil in ancient times to produce a brighter clear yellow light. Since solid particles are much larger than gaseous fragments, and can absorb and re-emit light of a wider range of energy, a flame laden with incandescent soot emits a mixture of yellow, orange, and red light. As the temperature of the glowing solid increases, green light is also emitted, and finally blue and violet light are added. Since a mixture of light of all visible colours looks white, we say the solid is then white hot.

Not all substances can survive the high temperature required for white-hot incandescence. Soot particles in contact with air are burned to oxides of carbon at high flame temperatures. Combustion, however, is not always complete: we know from Shakespeare that smoky, ill-smelling lamps were familiar images in Elizabethan England. We shall see (pp. 57 and 61) that the heat of the flame can be used to produce useful incandescence of other, non-combustible, solids. Until about two hundred years ago, however, flames containing glowing carbon provided almost all artificial lighting. The soot was often collected for use as the pigment 'lamp black'.

Many of the materials used for torches were of vegetable origin such as birch bark (in North America), coconut bark (in Malaya), resinous pine splinters (in Greece), split fat-pine knots (in Virginia), and candlenuts (in Polynesia) which were threaded on a string to provide light for a long period. Bodies of small birds and fish have also been used as torches in cold regions, where many such creatures have a rich layer of fat for insulation. In the far south, penguins were used, and in Orkney, the stormy petrel. Alaska provided the candlefish. These bodies were sometimes pierced with an absorbent dry stick, or threaded on a cord; the torch thus acquired a wick and evolved into a candle. In Europe during the Middle Ages, a wick of rope or peeled rush was soaked in resin, fat or beeswax. Although in the modern candle the fuel supply surrounds the wick, the positions may be reversed. In Africa and Asia vegetable fibres were wrapped round a central store of resin or fat. Candles and tapers, like torches, are solid except in the small region where the fuel has been melted by the flame; but a candle flame is small and generates rather little heat. Even a gentle gust can remove the hot gases far enough from the wick to blow out the flame. Indoors, or in a sheltered spot, however, a candle burns much more steadily than a torch, and often for much longer periods.

The candle has a long ancestry, dating from at least Minoan times. Although it was a major fire-hazard (see Chapter 19), its other shortcomings were not too serious. The smoke from the soot-laden flame could be prevented from dirtying the ceiling by use of a shield or 'smoke bell'. The wick, which was consumed more slowly than the wax, could be trimmed, a chore which was unnecessary for the rushlight, where pith and grease burned down together. The modern wicks are made so that they are consumed at the same rate as the candle and so need no trimming. New fuels have been used: in Japan insect waxes have been scraped off trees, while in the USA candles have been made from bayberry wax.

Minoan candlestick (Crete) before 1600 BC

A candle and tapers (Egypt), about 1300 BC

The candle, however, is unlikely to be the oldest form of steady artificial light. The lamp, basically a reservoir for liquid fuel into which usually dips a wick, has a history of possibly as much as thirty thousand years. Primitive, probably wickless, lamps have been found associated with the late Stone-Age cave-paintings in Spain and in Central France, thought to have been executed between 30 000 and 10 000 BC. As no daylight penetrates the caves, the work would have required a sustained source of artificial light. The containers were stones with natural concavities, and the fuel appears to have been animal fat, which would have been largely melted in the heat of the flame. Other later societies used different natural containers such as sea-shells and skulls (stone and shell lamps of this type were still in use in some of the Scottish Isles in the late nineteenth century). Later, hollowed-out containers were made by hand from clay or soft stone such as chalk; lamps of this type were used for flint mining about 2000 BC. Fuel varied according to availability: whale blubber for the Eskimos, olive oil in Ancient Greece, mineral oil in Sumaria, naphtha in Egypt, and liquid asphalt in Sicily. By 1000 BC, fibrous wicks were in common use. They were usually of vegetable origin, such as

Shell lamp (Ur, Mesopotamia) about 2500 BC

twisted moss, linen, papyrus, or oakum, but the mineral fibre, asbestos, was also used. The use of a side trough, or spout, to lead the wick away from the oil supply allowed more light from the flame to reach the surroundings without being blocked by the container, and so reduced the shadows cast by the lamp. A saucer-shaped base was often incorporated to catch the oil which dripped from the wick. Only in the later glass containers, such as those used in mosques and in eastern churches, could the wick be floated on the oil (which itself often floated on a reservoir of water).

The excavations at Ur revealed that shell-shaped lamps were made nearly five thousand years ago in copper, gold, and alabaster; terracotta had already been in use in Mesopotamia for two or three thousand years. Some lamps were designed for hanging. All Mesopotamian lamps seem, however, to have had open tops. The covered pottery lamp became widespread in the Graeco-Roman era. The top contained two or more holes, one through which the lamp was filled with oil, while each of the others, often at the end of a spout, carried a wick. In the first century AD, the Romans had factories which turned out many lamps of identical design for use in Spain, North Africa, and Britain. Hough has pointed out that in lighting the Romans were far behind their sophisticated technology in other fields such as heating (see Chapter 4), and that the only advance in design over the lamps used by Stone-Age cave-painters was the lid, because in Roman times this often carried obscene designs. The comment is perhaps unfair, as later Roman lamps were made with a large number of wick-spouts and must have been very much brighter than the Stone-Age lamps.

There were two main improvements in oil lamps during the first eighteen centuries of the Christian era. Hero of Alexandria (probably in the first century AD), designed a system in which pressure of a salt solution, acting on a column of air, raised the oil to the wick. The second improvement, in 1490, was from Leonardo da Vinci, who needed a lamp good enough for study. He fitted a cylindrical chimney

Gold lamp (Ur, Mesopotamia) about 2500 BC

Calcite lamp (Ur, Mesopotamia) about 2500 BC

Phoenician pottery lamp

round the flame, thereby producing a regular draught and decreasing the turbulence. The chimney was surrounded by a glass globe, filled with water, which acted as a lens to focus the bright steady light on the work surface. New fuels included whale sperm oil and colza (rapeseed), and later oils from cotton seed, grape pips, and linseed. Nearly three hundred years after da Vinci, Argand used a tubular wick and a similar cylindrical chimney. Since the now popular colza oil was dense and did not rise easily up the wick, it was necessary to add a device for raising the oil; this was powered either by a clockwork spring or by a gravity feed. The new Argand lamp, incorporating the old ideas of Hero and da Vinci, was so successful in its production of a bright steady flame that it was accepted as a photometric standard.

The period from the end of the seventeenth to the beginning of the nineteenth century saw major experiments with a new class of fuel: flammable gases. Natural gas, from marshes and coal mines, was

5 Campfire on beach

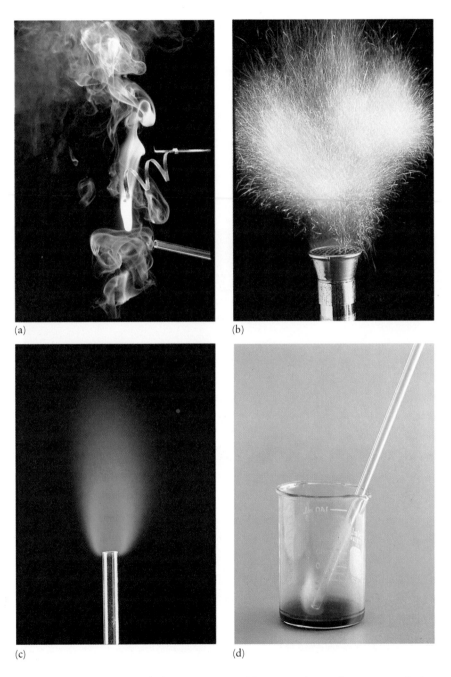

(a)

(b)

(c)

(d)

6 Burning of some inorganic fuels; (a) magnesium ribbon in air; (b) iron filings in air; (c) hydrogen in air; (d) hydrogen in bromine. (From *General chemistry*, by P. W. Atkins. Copyright © 1989 by W. H. Freeman. Reprinted by permission)

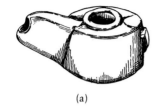

(a)

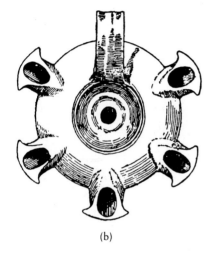

(b)

Graeco-Roman lamps: (a) stone (Egypt);
(b) earthenware (Asia Minor)

collected and ignited as a demonstration. Coal gas was at first prepared by heating coal or sawdust in a kettle fitted with a long spout, and igniting the gas issuing from the end. The first extensive use of coal gas for lighting is attributed to the Englishman, William Murdock, who used it in 1792 for lighting his house in Redruth, Cornwall, and a few years later for a factory and several shops in Birmingham. Gas lighting was later to become popular with English mill owners: partly because it was safer than candles or oil lamps (and so carried a lower insurance premium) and partly because both tallow and whale oil were obtained from Russia and became scarce and expensive during the Crimean War.

Lighting by natural gas has a very much longer history. It was used for illuminating homes and salt mines in Szechwan, China, centuries before the Christian era. The gas was brought to the surface through about 500 metres of rock salt, and piped through bamboo tubes sealed with clay. In Europe, there was rapid development in gas-lighting in the early nineteenth century. Flames became more

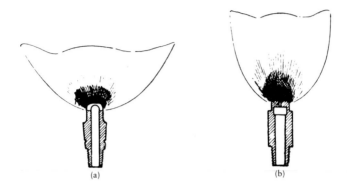

Flat-flamed gas burners: (a) batswing, 1816; (b) fishtail, 1820

complex, and so of higher area and greater power, as the single 'ratstail' hole was superseded by multiple holes and slits to give fish-tails, bats-wings, and stars. The 'town gas' then in use burned very incompletely, with a soot-laden, luminous flame. The orifices, which at first had been mere openings in an iron pipe, were now made of steatite, which did not corrode and which conducted less heat away from the flame. The flame from the later coal gas was less luminous, but a brighter light could be obtained by using either two gas jets impinging on each other or two closely spaced concentric rings of flames. Early gas lights were smoky, smelly, and stupefying; and in 1833 there was a suggestion that rooms should be lit by gas lights placed *outside* the window. Both the purity of the gas and the efficiency of the ventilation had to be much improved. The gas supply was made steadier by adding a 'governor' so that the inlet valve closed somewhat if the external pressure should increase, and the air flow was carefully controlled to suit it. In the 'atmospheric' burner, intake for air was included just below the gas exit, thereby anticipating the bunsen burner. In some gas burners, the incoming gases were pre-heated by the flame. In others, hydrocarbons were added to the gas supply in order to increase the luminosity. One lamp had a reservoir for camphor balls which gradually evaporated in the heat from the flame.

The threat of competition from the new electric lighting stimulated research. Perhaps some material other than soot, either within the flame or surrounding it, would produce a brighter incandescence. Mantles of various materials, including platinum wire, glowed satisfactorily but were expensive and deteriorated rapidly. More success-

Advertisement for gas lamp, 1887

ful was a cotton mantle, supporting a skeleton of oxides of cerium and thorium. The cotton burned off in the flame and the oxides glowed a brilliant greenish white. The various forms which were patented between 1885 and 1895 represented a decrease in price, greater robustness, and easier fitting, together with choice in the whiteness of the light produced and the direction in which it shone. The incandescent gas mantle was widely used, and is said to have made a significant contribution to the spread of literacy. In earlier eras, oil-lamps were used mainly at meals and in communal rooms, and only occasionally for study. Some oil lamps were specially made for searching for fleas.

The incandescent mantle was not restricted to gas lighting: it could be heated equally well in an oil lamp. Indeed, many of the improvements in oil lighting during the nineteenth century are parallel to those in the evolution of gas lighting. Cheaper and purer supplies of fuel followed the distillation of coal and the discovery of oil in Pennsylvania in the 1850s. Paraffin was a satisfactory lamp fuel in that it did not deteriorate, nor was it a very severe fire hazard. It rose easily up the wick, and gave a moderately non-smoky flame of good colour. Oil lamps, like gas lamps with two rows of burners, gave better light if the flames were very close together. Some lamps, suitable for cooking as well as for lighting, dispensed with the fragile glass chimney and had a clockwork fan to drive the air towards the wick. Others, like the analogous oil cooking stove, dispensed with the wick: the fuel was supplied to the combustion orifices by a simple pump and was initially vaporized from a ring-shaped trough of burning 'primer', usually methylated spirit. Once the oil vapour had ignited, its supply to the flame was self-sustaining. In the twentieth century, electric lighting has completely displaced lighting by combustion wherever a supply of electricity is available. But in the many parts of the world still without electricity, lighting by oil or gas is both effective and versatile.

The lights which we have discussed so far have been largely for indoor use. Out of doors, all but the strongest of flames would be 'blown out' unless protected from the wind, because the hot products of combustion would be removed from the unburned mixture of fuel and air too rapidly to sustain the combustion. An exception was the medieval torch known as a flambeau, which was made of several thick wicks impregnated with wax and was carried by pedestrians at night. Presumably when the fuel vaporized from the lighted torch it vaporized over quite a large region, so that, even if the flame were blown somewhat sideways, the hot products would still come into contact with some combustible gases.

The lantern, known from antiquity, is a far more satisfactory form of outdoor lighting. A lamp or candle is enclosed, usually by a transparent or translucent material, such as horn, bladder, parchment or glass (or, in the East, paper). Vents in the lid and base allow convective flow. The 'dark' lanterns used by malefactors such as Guy Fawkes had metal walls, with a small moveable opening which supposedly allowed vision without detection. Lanterns could be carried by hand or suspended on buildings or moving carriages. Some unprotected flames, distant cousins of the medieval flambeau, were also used. The 'slush light', somewhat resembling a coffee-pot, had a fat wick issuing from the spout and produced a persistent, if smoky, flame when filled with any type of oil. Naphtha flares, burning 'coal tar naphtha' were used by street traders, who lit their stalls by the bright bats-wing type flame. During the last one hundred years, paraffin lamps, enclosed in robust glass and metal containers ('hurricane' lamps), have been widely used for portable outdoor use. Up to 1939, gas lamps burning acetylene (now called 'ethyne' and prepared by dropping water on calcium carbide) were used for cycles, cars, and boats. They were understandably considered a status symbol by early cyclists, since they were beautifully made and could cost as much as the bicycle. Nowadays, bottled butane gas provides light for camping, caravanning, and for many other outdoor uses.

Public lighting, whether for indoors or out, needed a much higher intensity than most of the personal or domestic lamps described above. In Europe, public lighting was first used for processions, the torch bearers being usually human. Caesar's Gallic triumph, however, was lit by forty elephants each bearing torches on both flanks. Torches were also used in Roman theatres and gladiatorial shows, while lamps provided interior lighting for public buildings. Niches for lamps were built into the walls of the escape tunnel and water conduit of Evpaulios on Samos (Dodecanese). Over 1000 lamps were found in one of the smaller thermae at Pompeii. The town hall at Tarentum was lit by multispouted lamps, some having as many as 350 wicks.

Street-lighting was apparently well developed in ancient Egypt: it is claimed better so than during any later period until AD 1500. One method of lighting streets was to have brightly lit rooms in the adjacent houses. Judging from the many lamps found in the shops, the shopping streets of Pompeii must have been quite bright. In 1415 every London householder was required to show one lighted window during the winter months, an arrangement which persisted for nearly three centuries. Small towns in the USA relied on lighted windows until the end of the eighteenth century.

External street-lighting was used in the fourth century AD in Antioch, where lamps were suspended from ropes, and also in Caesarea. Figurines of lamp-lighters found in Rome and Alexandria suggest that these cities had even earlier street-lighting; but the frequent written references to the need for flambeaux and lanterns when walking in cities at night indicate that adequate street-lighting was not general.

The first compulsory street-lighting seems to have been in 1367 in Paris, where lights were required to be hung at stated intervals in order to lessen crime. Similar schemes followed in London and, in 1769, in North America; but as late as 1662 groups of lantern bearers could be hired after dark in Paris to accompany travellers home. Carriages were sometimes preceded by a group of runners carrying flambeaux.

External street lighting employed stationary torches, thick-wicked oil-lamps (see p. 58) and lanterns. Coal or wood fires were also used; suspended in baskets, there were six thousand such 'cressets' in the streets of Paris as late as 1739. A pillar supporting a metal fire-basket (said to be an exact replica of the original) still surmounts the medieval pump house at Walsingham, Norfolk. In the first half of the eighteenth century improved oil lamps gave much brighter lighting, and when a metal reflector was fitted, there were complaints about glare. A modified design gave more subdued illumination which was widely used to light major cities and, later, country highways; the first was the road from Paris to Versailles, which was lit in 1777.

Gas was used for outdoor public lighting in the second decade of the nineteenth century (see Plate 8). In London, Westminster Bridge was gas lit in 1813, and the façade of the Soho gas works was illuminated to celebrate the Peace of Paris in June 1814. Indoor gas lighting was installed in the New Theater in Philadelphia in 1816. Wherever gas was available it competed with the new paraffin lighting and gradually replaced it. Gas provided street-lighting in Baltimore, Maryland, in 1821; and in 1871 it lit New York, being supplied in wooden log pipes. As the motor car became more common, faster, and more dangerous, good lighting on roads became more important in an attempt to reduce accidents. Although gas was giving way to electricity for all forms of lighting, gas lighting continued to be installed on some US highways up to 1922. In late nineteenth-century London, some gas street-lamps were connected to the water main and used as vending machines. The heat from the flame kept a small reservoir charged with superheated steam which, when a halfpenny was put in a slot, supplied a gallon of hot water. Insertion of a further penny released a slab of tea or cocoa, together with condensed milk and sugar. But the machines were not commercially successful as they were frequently forced open and their takings stolen.

Large-scale illumination was also needed for theatrical performances in roofed buildings. (Early theatres were either open-air or roofless; performances took place during daylight and if torches or lanterns were used on the stage, they were not to provide illumination, but to show the audience that the action was supposedly occurring after dark.) The Elizabethan theatres in Britain, although roofed, were lit by large windows. These were, however, covered for the portrayal of gloomy scenes, which were then illuminated by candles or cressets. During the Renaissance the foundations of stage-lighting were developed in Italy and elsewhere. The lights (candles, cressets, or lamps) were hidden from the audience and their beams directed onto the actors' faces by a variety of shades and reflectors. Flood-lights were introduced, although, with the lamps at floor level, both smoke and smell were a problem, and some theatres preferred bright overhead lighting from chandeliers, or the more dramatic side-lighting. Special effects flourished. Coloured light was produced by using flasks of coloured liquid as filters. Moonrise, sunrise, and sunset were simulated in this way. 'Lightning' could be made by blowing lycopodium spores into an almost colourless alcohol flame. The fine particles ignited, incandesced, and were consumed in one brief flash. Other powders produced 'fog', 'smoke', and in the hands of Garrick's scenic designer, de Loutherbourg (1740–1812), 'the ever-popular conflagrations'. Gas was used for theatre lighting in the second decade of the nineteenth century, very soon after it was first used for outdoor illumination; but some theatres which installed it found the lighting too bright and went back to using candles or oil lamps. Despite the glare and the greatly increased fire-risk (see Chapter 21), gas became widely used; in 1881, the Paris Opera House had 960 jets, 28 miles of piping, and 88 taps, all controlled by one operator with an electrical re-lighter button.

The nineteenth century also saw an important new form of lighting which, although short-lived, has left its mark on our language. In 1826 'limelight' was made possible by the newly available current electricity, which provided enough energy to split water into hydrogen and oxygen. If these two gases are burned together and reconverted into water, much energy is given out and the flame temperature reaches about 2880 °C. Drummond used the oxygen–hydrogen flame to heat up a block of calcium oxide ('quicklime') to incandesc-ence. First used in surveying, the light is so bright that it was claimed that a source of area about 13 square centimetres could be seen 107 kilometres away. But the light is also soft, and the lamps could be designed to produce a directional beam which was ideal for theatrical work. Limelight was also used in the first magic lanterns, the fore-runners of our slide and cinema projectors. Flame lighting for the theatre, as for other uses, was superseded by electricity; and as the theatre was in the vanguard for the introduction of gas lighting, so was it for its demise. The Savoy Theatre in London was lit electrically as early as 1881.

The use of fire as a source of light is not limited to the production of artificial illumination so that we can see at night, or in places where sunlight cannot reach. The light of the flame has also been used to convey warnings and other simple pieces of information. Large woodfire beacons on hilltops have long been lit to send pre-arranged messages, such as call-up of military volunteers, or the announcement of a victory, when the beginning or the end of a war is imminent. In Babylon and Jerusalem, beacons were lit to signal a new moon when its appearance was not clearly visible. In ancient Greece, fire was used for signalling up to about ten prearranged messages such as 'send more ... infantry (or corn, or ships)'. Since the meaning of the signal was conveyed by its duration, both the sender and the reader had identically calibrated water clocks. Around 150 BC a code based on up to ten torches was used to represent individual letters, and Polybius exhorted the signaller to send messages using as few letters as possible. Later, Scipio used lights to identify different types of naval craft: a warship carried one lamp, a transport ship two, and the commander's vessel three.

Perhaps the most important use of fire to convey information was the lighthouse and similar but unattended devices such as buoys and lightships, which warned ships of coastal hazards. The earliest lighthouses seem to have been towers in which fires were intermittently lit and tended by priests. The first purpose-built lighthouse was probably the Pharos of Alexandria (third century BC), in which the light of a fire in a tower was focused by bronze mirrors into a beam visible 56 kilometres away. The Romans built over thirty lighthouses in similar stalwart towers, but in Scandinavia simple cressets were slung from an oblique pole. In the latter part of the eighteenth century the rapidly evolving oil lamp replaced the solid fuel fire. Cheap mineral oil, burned in a multiple wick burner, was widely used from 1868 until the end of the century. Chandeliers holding many tallow candles were also used at that time, although it was not unknown for the lighthouse keepers to eat the candles instead of burning them.

Gas lighting was never used as commonly in offshore lighthouses as on the mainland, because of the problem of supply. Instead, the incandescent mantle was used in conjunction with a gas lamp supplied with petroleum vapour, bottled natural gas, or a solution of acetylene in acetone, absorbed in some porous medium. Acetylene was widely used for lighting buoys long after most lighthouses had changed to electricity. Dungeness Lighthouse in Southern England was the first to be powered by electricity as early as 1862. Even in unattended devices, however, flame lighting has now been replaced by electric lighting wherever possible, although petroleum and gas lamps are often available as a standby.

Warning lights have wide use on vehicles moving at night. Candle lanterns were used not only on carriages, but also on the Panhard 1894 car. Oil lamps were more generally used for cars, and also for trains and railway signals, until ousted by electricity in the 1920s. Use was made of coloured lights for signals and to denote the front and rear of vehicles, and port and starboard of vessels. The first traffic signals were installed in London in 1868; lit by gas on 6 metre columns, they blew up almost immediately.

Most illumination generates light over an appreciable period, and indeed if an object is lit for a very brief time (less than 1/25 second), our eyes will not react in time for us to see it. A photographic emulsion will, however, record much shorter bursts of light. A photoflash can therefore be used to freeze high-speed movement as well as to correct the deficiencies of the ambient lighting. Photographic flash is now generated electronically; but the earliest form, first used in 1864, was a paper bag, containing magnesium wire and some oxygen-rich substance such as potassium chlorate. When the bag was ignited the metal burned with an intense flash. A contemporary observer reported that 'this quite unsafe device seems to have done nothing worse than engulf the room in dense smoke and lead to pictures of dubious quality and odd poses'. Evolution of the photoflash was slow; flash bulbs, containing fine wire of a combustible metal, such as magnesium or aluminium, in an atmosphere of pure oxygen at low pressure, were introduced only in the 1920s. In the earliest type, the metal was separated from the oxygen by a thin glass bulb. The flash was fired by piercing the bulb and allowing the oxygen to come into contact with the metal, which ignited spontaneously. Later bulbs were fired by an electric battery which heated the wire by passing a small current through it. Other combinations of oxidizing agents and readily oxidizable metals, such as oxygen difluoride with zirconium, have also been used. In each case enough energy is given out to heat the oxide momentarily to white hot incandescence. The smoke particles are so small that they cool rapidly; but since they are white, they contribute to the brilliance by reflecting the light from their still-incandescent neighbours. A slightly more substantial form of the metal will burn for longer.

Many of us will remember with pleasure the intense white light we saw when, in our childhood, we set fire to magnesium ribbon (see Plate 6a). It burned quickly, but by no means instantaneously; it was a flare, rather than a flash. Applications of flares and other fireworks are discussed (see Chapter 13) in the next section of this book which explores the many ways in which we have used fire to extend our power over the environment.

III

Fire for use

... So, here's the whole truth in one word:
All human skill and science was Prometheus' gift.
Aeschylus from *Prometheus bound* (about 463 BC)
Trans. Philip Vellacott

As when that diuelish yron Engin wrought
   In deepest Hell, and framd by *Furies* skill,
   With windy Nitre and quick Sulphur fraught,
   And ramd with bullet round, ordaind to kill,
   Conceiueth fire, the heauens it doth fill
   With thundring noyse, and all the ayre doth choke
   That none can breath, nor see, nor heare at will,
   Through smouldry cloud of duskish stincking smoke,
That th'onely breath him daunts, who hath escapt the stroke.
Edmund Spenser
from 'The Faerie Queene'

6

Fire for cooking

Man is not the only creature who is attracted to fire, nor is he the only maker of tools. He is, however, the only animal who tends fire, and who uses fire itself as a tool to enable him to perform other tasks. The first of these tasks was most probably cooking. In the fire-origin myths of the South American Indians, the stealing of fire (usually by an animal) was almost always followed by the eating of cooked meat. Claude Lévi-Strauss, who analysed many myths from this region, gave his famous structuralist commentary on them the title *The raw and the cooked* in order to highlight the antithesis between the untamed and the civilized. Whilst cooking indisputably distinguishes man from beast, and represents the crucial first step in his use of fire as a tool, it also had the more practical consequence of greatly extending the range and palatability of his diet. The point has been elegantly made in Charles Lamb's *A dissertation on roast pig* which tells of a son who allowed his hovel and adjacent pigsty to burn down in his father's absence. The hovel was of little significance but he feared his father's rage at the loss of a litter of piglets. He squeezed one of the charred corpses in the hope of finding some sign of remaining life, burned his hands, licked his fingers, and ... discovered roast pork. His father was quickly placated by the exquisite taste of crackling. Pig-keeping became popular in the community and even the grandest dwellings burned down with remarkable frequency. Lamb's delightful essay was published in 1828, and the modern reader's mouth waters still.

Although it is almost impossible to trace the evolution of primitive culinary techniques, it seems likely that the first cooks placed food directly in the fire, in much the same way as we might today cook sweet chestnuts in a coke brazier or a coal fire, or put flour and water 'dampers', twisted round a green stick, into a campfire. But the high temperature of the interior of the fire soon chars the outside of the food, probably long before the inside is cooked. Slower and more thorough cooking is achieved if the food is held over the fire, where it is heated both by the escaping gases and by radiant heat from the fire itself. As the surface nearest to the fire receives the most heat, the food has to be turned frequently if it is to be evenly cooked. To this day, the rotating-spit is one of the best ways for producing tender, succulent, and tasty roast meat. Someone must have noticed that if fish or meat was held too high above a fire it became somewhat dried rather than cooked; and, particularly if the fire was smoky, it did not putrefy as quickly as other food did. So fire was also used for the preservation of food (cf. Chapter 14) as well as for cooking, and the results may well have been more palatable than those obtained by drying in the wind and sun alone. (Many of us today surely prefer smoked mackerel to the wind-dried and subsequently soaked Scandinavian 'lutfisk'.)

Not all food is improved by drying and smoking, any more than it is improved by an outer casing of charcoal. Techniques emerged for trying to separate the food from the smoke, and for trying to cook it at a roughly even temperature. In ancient Egypt, the food was placed on stone slabs which were laid on top of the fire, while in India the food was enclosed in a casing of clay, the forerunner of the tandoori oven. Food was steamed by covering it with wet leaves before cooking it on hot stones, or in a hot pit where a fire had been. Boiling requires a container which will hold the water, but this need not be fireproof. Water can be boiled in a finely woven wicker basket by adding stones which have been heated in the fire. When ceramic pots became available, however, food could be boiled by placing the vessel directly on the fire. Later developments included suspending vessels from a hook over the fire, or standing them on a trivet. The first ovens, such as those used at Ur about five thousand years ago, were heated by a fire which was lit inside them. When the surroundings were hot enough, the fire and ashes were removed and replaced by the food, which was cooked by reradiated heat. This was the usual method of baking until about three centuries ago. Small villages often had (and some still have) one communal beehive-shaped baking oven

External oven of monastery (Dodecanese), 1991

of this type, usually on the outskirts, to reduce the risk of fire to dwellings. Many larger European households often had their own indoor baking oven. This was probably adjacent to the main fireplace and shared its chimney. The fireplaces were often large enough to walk into and contained hooks for smoking hams, a spit, and trivets to support pans and kettles over the grate.

The cooking range evolved in parallel with the fireplace stove, and was dependent on the availability of iron. The earlier European open cooking ranges, dating from the eighteenth century, were fixed cradle-shaped grates on iron legs, and with a slatted iron base. The width of the fire could sometimes be adjusted with a moveable side wall (or 'cheek') and the height of the fire could be reduced by swinging down the top (or 'fall') bar in front of the grate. The lowered fall bar was level with the second bar and together they formed a platform for simmering in front of the fire. Sheet iron hobs were built over the fire and circular trivets could swing out from the cheek, or the fixed side, of the fire. If the range was fitted into a low

Smoke-jack for turning spit, 1662

chimney, there would be a strong draught, and the chimney could be
fitted with 'smokejack' vanes which turned a horizontal spit in front
of the fire (cf. Chapter 9). It also contained hooks for suspending
kettles and pots over the fire.

The introduction of sheet iron allowed the construction of ovens
which could be heated from outside for as long as there was a fire
in the range. Such 'perpetual' ovens were heated by flue gases from
the adjacent fire. Not only did they do away with the tedious work
of pre-heating and raking out which was needed for the previous
ceramic ovens, but they kept a much more constant temperature.
Soon the oven formed an integral part of the range itself, replacing
one of the side supports, but still covered by a hob. The support on
the other side was also replaced: by a boiler for hot water.

During the late eighteenth and early nineteenth centuries, both
coal and iron became more readily available. The kitchen range

7 Street brazier in China

8 Street lighting by gas

became smaller as coal replaced wood as the favoured fuel, and as the price of the ranges fell sufficiently for them to be used in humbler and smaller homes. As the fire became narrower, the roasting spit became vertical rather than horizontal; and the hot water boiler became L-shaped, so that there could be heat-exchange at the back of the fire, even when the cheek was pushed across, narrowing the grate and creating a gap between the side of the fire and the boiler.

A major problem with open ranges, as with all open fires, was the loss of heat up the chimney. Count Rumford is credited with complaining, at the end of the eighteenth century, that 'more fuel is frequently consumed in a kitchen range to boil a tea kettle than with proper management would be sufficient to cook a dinner for fifty men'.

The closed range appeared early in the nineteenth century. The range was enclosed in iron sheeting, under which the flue gases circulated, exchanging heat with the oven, the boiler, and the iron itself before escaping. The top of the range was used as a hob for slow cooking, while removable lids in the iron allowed pots to be

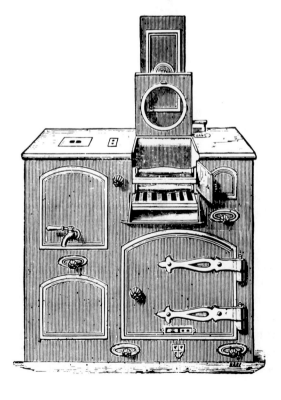

Kitchen range for cottage, 1881

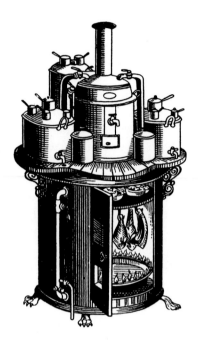

Gas cooker, designed to cook for a hundred
people, about 1850

placed directly over the fire for fast cooking. Naturally, the closed
range was much cleaner than its open predecessor. At first the fuel
savings were not so great as had been hoped, as the fire burned very
fast, but improvements in damper design reduced both the draughts
and the running costs. Modern versions of the closed solid fuel
cooking range are still in use, and nowadays also supply water for
central heating.

A further advance came at the beginning of the nineteenth century
with the introduction of heating gas. In 1802, a gas-cooked meal was
served in a dining-room heated with gas; and as the gas burned
smokelessly, the food could share an oven with the flames without
acquiring any smoky smell. Nowadays, with the swing of fashion
and the increased popularity of barbecue cooking directly over glowing charcoal, a mild taste of smoke is much valued by gastronomes.
Gas cookers, although in competition now with electrical ones, are
still in wide use, their design having changed but little, except for
improved methods of ignition.

Several traditional methods of heating are still used, particularly if
only little heat is needed. Small squat candles are burned under a
trivet for keeping food or coffee hot. A simple spirit lamp, consisting

of a wick dipping into methylated spirit in a closed flask, formed part of an early coffee percolator, and is used for heating food such as fondue which is cooked at table. Charcoal is used not only for grills, but also in the Russian samovar. The burner is at the base of the water urn. A flue passes up the centre of the urn and the hot gases issuing from it heat the tea pot on the top of the samovar, so there is always a supply of hot concentrated tea in the pot, and of hot water which can be tapped off from the urn to dilute it. A primitive form found at Pompeii has the fuel chamber totally enclosed in the urn except for a small exit flue, through which burning charcoal must presumably have been added, since there was no access of air from below to sustain combustion.

Our own century has seen a decrease in the number of campers who light, or attempt to light, camp-fires. Portable stoves are more convenient and reliable. The smallest may boil a kettle on a single pellet of solid 'meta fuel'. Bottled propane gas is available in rucksack size for gas-ring boilers, or in larger sizes for caravans. Primus-type oil stoves are also used for caravans, although they are potentially more hazardous. The stove is lit by pumping a fine spray of paraffin in air over an annular trough containing burning methylated spirit. Once the spray of air–paraffin mixture has ignited, the heat generated by the combustion is sufficient to maintain the supply of pre-mixed vaporized fuel.

7

Fire for destruction

Many English people will know one thing only about King Alfred, who ruled Wessex from AD 871 to 899: that he burned some cakes. Sheltering in a humble cottage, he agreed to keep an eye on the good wife's baking, for the use of fire in cooking requires judgement and skill. But the king was so preoccupied with the well-being of his realm that he allowed her cakes to burn. The legend, probably apocryphal, does not specify whether they were slightly blackened, charred right through, or totally consumed by flames. The heat of the fire can 'destroy' a material in different ways. At high temperatures in a generous supply of air, it may catch fire and burn, to give mainly gaseous products and airborne soot. At lower temperatures, or if oxygen access is limited, a solid may merely char. Other solids may melt and liquids boil before they oxidize, and some materials, such as glass, can be broken into smaller pieces by rapid heating and cooling. Over the ages, people have ingeniously exploited a variety of such changes to improve their lot.

Mankind's first use of fire for what we may call constructive destruction was probably for land clearance. Early nomads must have been grateful to find patches of fairly clear land in the wake of a forest fire, and they would have had ample opportunity to observe the destructive effect of a camp-fire which got out of hand. A natural step would be to initiate a fire in order to destroy undergrowth, a very much quicker and more effective method than that of hacking down scrub with a stone axe, or even with tools made of metal. The

T'ang poet Liu Yü-Hsi describes a Vietnamese tribe burning forest to produce arable land about one thousand years ago:

Wherever it may be, they like to burn off the fields,
Round and round, creeping over the mountain's belly.
When they bore the tortoise* and get the 'rain' trigram,
Up the mountain they go and set fire to the prostrate trees.
Startled muntjacs run, and then stare back;
Flocks of pheasants make *i-auk* sounds.
The red blaze forms sunset clouds far off,
Light coals fly into the city walls.
The wind draws it up to the high peaks,
It laps across the blue forest.
The blue forest, seen afar, dissolves in a flurry,
The red light sinks – then rises again.
A radiant tarn brings forth an old *kau*-dragon;
Exploding bamboos frighten the forest ghosts.
    E.H. Schafer, *The vermilion bird*, California University Press (1967)

Some primitive communities first cut down trees and then set fire to the forest. The reverse happened in Amazonia: the trees were killed by fire and then felled. In China, the trees were first killed by bark-ringing and then burned, and in Greek olive groves the stumps of felled trees are killed by fire. With careful management, fire can be used to clear the undergrowth of a forest without harming the more mature trees. It is also useful for the preservation of particular types of vegetation such as heathland in Scotland and Wales (see Plate 9) and pampas veld in Southern USA. It destroys both young saplings and low-growing plants; but the latter regenerate quickly, and the misty purple hillsides of Scotland would not have survived if the heather had not been protected in this way from encroachment by the forest (see Chapter 22). The same method has been used to regenerate turf roofs in Iceland, but care must be exercised not to set fire to the house as well. Fire is still used for land clearance. It has been claimed that 118 000 square kilometres of Amazonian rain forest are destroyed each year in 'slash and burn' agriculture. In England, stubble was often burned off after harvesting as late as the 1990s, despite complaints by motorists about the dangers of the heavy smoke and by environmentalists about the harm to animal life. Some gardeners prefer a flame gun to chemical herbicides for clearing weeds from paths.

* Refers to the use of a tortoise shell for divination.

Early peoples must have found the fire-cleared areas of forest much easier hunting territory than the dense undergrowth. Over the ages, fire has also been exploited by hunters in several other ways. Rabbits are an easy target when driven by a front of advancing flame in a forest, prairie, or stubble field. But not all animals are kept at bay by a fire. Some are attracted by its light, only to be blinded or mesmerized. Seals, elk, and wild geese were lured by lamps on land and fish by floating torches, now replaced by propane lamps.

Fire may be used as a repellent. Snakes and fierce beasts are often deterred by a camp-fire (and a circus lion will cringe at a red-hot poker). Insects, however, are often attracted to light, and the moth whose wings are singed by the candle is a common literary image. Mosquitoes, too, are lured by a flame. A simple but ingenious Chinese device for killing them is a candle burning inside a pitcher pierced with two holes, through which the insects are lured and sucked into the flame by the upward draught.

The destructive power of fire is also widely used for the disposal of all types of unwanted material. Cremation of human corpses is but one example; others are garden bonfires, demolition waste fires, hospital incinerators, and ignited urban tips. (The composite cloying

Fishing lights

and acrid smell of orange blossom and burning rubbish is particularly evocative of Southern Spain.) Burning not only destroys much of the discarded matter, but also kills the associated micro-organisms. Fire is sometimes used for simple sterilization, for example of dental instruments in the flame of a spirit lamp.

Fire is useful for separating something useful from a more flammable component, as in Bhutan where wheat is ignited to destroy the straw but to leave the grain. Careening involves partly burning marine growths off the undersides of ships before scraping them clean. Old paint can be part burned, part softened for scraping off wood by means of a blow-lamp (a hand-held paraffin lamp with a hot pre-mixed flame similar to that in a Primus stove). Destruction by burning is not, however, restricted to solids, but can be used to get rid of unwanted oil, from an ocean slick or broken oil-rig. Waste gases from an oil refinery can also be burned off (see Plate 10), often at the top of a tall chimney. A few centuries ago, 'firedamp' in mines was intentionally ignited in order to rid the galleries of it. (The methane was detected by a flint wheel, struck by a boy who went ahead of the miners; brightening of the sparks revealed its presence before it reached explosive concentrations.) Nowadays, methane is burned off decayed plant matter when rubbish tips are ignited. Methane is also formed in digestive tracts of animals, particularly of ruminants, but also of man, and so may be emitted by waste matter which has passed right through the human gut. Members of submarine

Ignition of firedamp in a mine during the 1860s. The fireman is wrapped in damp sacking

crews are taught to ignite such flatulence so as to convert the methane into its combustion products, carbon dioxide and water, and so to prevent the build-up of flammable gas in a confined space. Since the ignition, effected by holding a lighted match at a distance of 8–9 centimetres creates an impressive pop, the practice was also carried out in prisoner-of-war camps to relieve the boredom. The seat of the trousers protects the wearer from any pain, since the cloth acts analogously to the wire gauze in a Davy lamp, conducting the heat away from the burning gas.

Fire, often localized, can also be used to alter the properties of a material, rather than to destroy it. Wood was worked by converting a small area to charcoal, scraping this away and repeating the process. In this way, trees were felled, logs cut, and dugout canoes made. Fire was used for shipbuilding at least up to the seventeenth century to produce the required curvature in the oak planks for the hull. One side of the plank was flamed for as long as 2 hours. Hardwoods ignite only slowly but the heat causes dehydration and structural change, naturally most markedly near the surface and decreasing gradually into the wood, which therefore curves. Once the charred layer is scraped off, the mechanical strength of the wood is unimpaired. Charring on a smaller scale discourages fungal decay at the bases of fence posts; and a red-hot poker can be used to decorate a wooden surface.

Identification marks can be branded on to living flesh with a hot iron and, appear to have been used to identify Egyptian cattle as early as 2000 BC. Human flesh was similarly branded, to denote lowly status. Slaves in ancient Greece were marked with a Δ. More frequently, branding was used as a punishment for petty crime. In ancient Rome F denoted a thief (furs) or a deserter (fugitivus), while in eighteenth-century Britain those convicted of coinage crimes were branded R (rogue). The Chinese were more specific, using different characters to mark a 'stealer of corn', 'stealer of silver' etc. As recently as 1832, French gallery slaves could be branded TR (*travaux forcés*). In some cultures, fire is used by barbers instead of knife or scissors; and in the UK singeing of hair was carried out until fairly recently in order to counter 'split ends'.

Still smaller changes are those involved merely in melting or vaporizing another substance. A stone, hot from the fire, can melt a hole in ice for fishing, or can convert water into steam for a sauna bath. In both cases, some heat from the fire passes into the stone and is transferred to the ice, or the water, lowering the forces of attraction between the component molecules; the ice then melts to water and the water vaporizes into steam. An old-fashioned soldering iron, heated in the fire, similarly transfers heat to the working material, in this case to melt an alloy into a small gap between two pieces of solid metal. If surfaces of the metal attract, rather than repel, the molten solder, they remain joined after the solder has resolidified. The shaping of molten metals by casting is discussed in Chapter 8. Sometimes, the use of fire for working a material may involve burning a little of it, as when we use a lighted match to melt sealing wax or to cut (and seal the ends of) polypropylene rope.

Even metals may be cut with a flame provided that it is hot enough. The oxy-acetylene flame, at a temperature of over 3000 °C, can melt steel and is used both for cutting and for spot-welding. In spot-welding, small regions of adjacent pieces of metal are liquefied and fuse together. But metals can also be worked in the fire without becoming liquid, provided that oxides and other impurities are melted off the surface. Red hot iron, cleaned and softened in the fire, can be wrought into intricate shapes and can be welded together by hammering.

In one previous use of fire, the technological importance far exceeded the internal material changes which, on the molecular scale, are not very impressive. Fire was used to heat rock, the components of which vibrated rather more vigorously than before, causing the rock to expand a little. The rock was then doused in cold water and the sudden local contraction set up such strain that it cracked. This

Splitting rocks by fire-setting in the 1860s

method of 'fire-setting' was widely used for mining in ancient times; and up to the beginning of the nineteenth century, fires were left burning in the mine over the weekend in the Harz mountains in Germany. In China in the second century AD, fire-setting was also used for road making and for engineering new courses for rivers, in order to prevent flooding. The coolant was usually water but it was sometimes replaced by vinegar, both in Europe and the East, because of vinegar's supposedly 'cooler' nature. Although fire-setting has long been superseded, the civil engineer of today is as dependent as ever on fire for modifying the terrain; but his fire now comes packaged for instant use, as explosive charges (see Chapter 12).

Not surprisingly, we have also turned the destructive power of fire against our fellow human beings, often with the approval of society. Its symbolic associations make it an ideal instrument for the execution of people and the destruction of objects which are deemed to be 'unclean' (see Chapter 23). But the main destructive use of fire has been military. Incendiary warfare requires that combustible material be introduced into enemy territory, either after it has been ignited, or in a form which ignites spontaneously on arrival. It should burn with such vigour that it sets fire to nearby material before it burns out. However, the first recorded use of fire in warfare was for defence. An Assyrian relief from the ninth century BC shows the inhabitants of a besieged city routing attacking troops by hurling torches and firepots doubtless containing bitumen or pitch. Incendiary attack was sometimes carried out on the spot, by stealth. The outer walls of a city were often supported by wooden props which a saboteur could smear with a mixture of pitch and sulphur, and then ignite. An alternative idea put forward was that part of a city could be undermined by digging tunnels and supporting them with wooden props which could be ignited at salient points when the work was finished. The fire would spread throughout the tunnels and the buildings above would cave in.

More often, however, the fire is not started on the spot, but travels from the attacker's territory into the enemy's to destroy both matter and morale. Fire pots and incendiary javelins were thrown by hand, but muscle power could be used more effectively with the aid of the bow and the catapult. Incendiary arrows were used during the Peloponnesian War of 429 BC; and in an ancient Greek proverb fire lies between 'sea' and 'woman' as one of the three major evils. In India, cats, monkeys, and birds were used to take fire into besieged cities; presumably torches were lashed to the rear of the animal and then ignited, so that the terrified creature rushed for cover. Fireboats were used from antiquity until the nineteenth century; they played a major role in the Greek War of Independence (1821–33), giving the Greeks control of the sea. The space between the decks was packed with incendiary materials such as pitch, resin, and tallow, and, in recent centuries, with iron containers holding gunpowder. The crew brought the fireboat within close range of the target ship, then lit a fuse to the flammable materials and themselves escaped in a small craft which had been towed by the fireboat. Fire-vehicles, with bellows behind, were used in antiquity for military fire-setting to play flames on to the walls of besieged cities.

The ancient world had access to a number of incendiary materials from the oil-rich Middle East. Pitch was particularly useful against enemy ships, as it burns floating on water. Naphtha was obtained from Babylon (where the word means 'that which burns') and from the region between the Black and Caspian Seas. There has been much discussion about the nature of the viscous liquid known as 'Greek fire'. Its composition remains a secret, and this is not surprising, since it was a capital offence to reveal it. However, it was probably a mixture of crude oil, sulphur, and saltpetre. Common salt was often added to colour the flame yellow and so make it appear more fearsomely hot (see p. 50). Greek fire could be squirted from pipes for considerable distances, and must have been very slow to run off its target. Since it remained alight on the surface of water and may even have been self-igniting (see p. 28), it was particularly valuable for naval warfare. It was much feared and was used to defend Constantinople until as late as 1453. The use of Greek fire, or indeed of any incendiary material, against human targets, had been banned in 1139 by the Second Lateran Council.

Greek fire used in naval battle (from a tenth century Byzantine manuscript)

Over the centuries, incendiary weapons have been used in increasing variety. Hannibal sent oxen with lighted faggots on their horns to draw off the guards from a pass held by the Romans in 217 BC. In medieval times, incendiary grenades were widely used. Naphtha balls fired at elephant cavalry in India in AD 1008 caused great panic. In the thirteenth century, the Mongols had special corps of flame throwers, and the Arabs used to ride at the enemy with both riders and horses wearing protective clothing covered with burning Greek fire or fireworks.

Incendiary weapons were much used by both sides in the Second World War. The fear they produce has not diminished but there is now no ban on their use against fellow humans. Indeed napalm (see Chapter 3), the horrific descendent of Greek Fire, was developed for that very purpose. Aircraft and missiles rather than animals take the fire, now packaged, to enemy territory; and human muscle-power has been replaced by propellants (see Chapter 11) of surprising antiquity. The first incendiary-tipped Chinese bamboo rockets have evolved over the last millennium to target-seeking missiles such as 'Exocet', which on impact produce intense heat by allowing an oxygen-avid metal, such as magnesium or aluminium, to abstract the oxygen from another metal oxide in which it is less tightly bound. Since many of the targets are planes or warships, themselves constructed out of light alloys containing much magnesium or aluminium, these too will burn in air, provided that the missile generates enough heat to initiate the combustion.

Fire is used also by retreating armies, who often employ a 'scorched earth' policy to ensure that the advancing enemy will have little of value left to capture. Such tactics were employed by Moscow against Napoleon in 1812, and against the Germans in 1941. During the brief Gulf War of 1991, Iraq ignited over 600 oil wells in Kuwait to prevent them from being used, as well as using ditches of burning crude oil to hinder advancing tanks (see Plate 11). Especial care is of course taken to destroy, again by fire, any military equipment or documents. The incendiary materials used in document destroyers are similar to those used in incendiary missiles, since they produce much heat without generating the large volumes of gas which would cause an explosion.

Fire has, of course, its uses for the individual criminal. The Islandic saga of Njall tells how his enemies killed him by setting fire to the chickweed in his loft. (They did, however, allow the women, children, and menservants to escape while the fire was still small.) Today, pouring petrol over someone and igniting it is an infrequent but not unknown method of murder. In the 1980s the frequent forest fires in Greece were often started intentionally, with a view to harassing the government or to laying bare the land so that it could be used for building rather than forestry. But by far the most common crime involving fire is the illegal burning of buildings. Owners burn their own property in order to make fraudulent insurance claims; but more often the criminal burns the property of someone else. In the USA arson is on the increase, the known arsonists containing a higher percentage of juveniles than the population at large. In the UK in 1984 about one-quarter of large fires whose cause could be ascertained were started deliberately. Motives for arson vary from an intent to murder the occupants to doing it just 'for kicks', the thrill often being accompanied by sexual excitement. It must be difficult to draw a hard line between the desire to obtain this type of stimulation, and the pyromaniac's irresistible desire to set things on fire. Arson may alternatively be prompted by more personal aggression, such as a wish to mete out punishment or revenge, or to express racial or social hatred. Some commit arson to bolster their self-esteem. A burning building gives an impressive display of the arsonist's power, and moreover may give him an opportunity to indulge in heroics in fighting the blaze. Professional fire-fighters have been known to succumb to the temptation of arson. Some arsonists wish to draw attention to some disadvantage they suffer, such as unemployment. There are also more hardheaded motives. A fire is seen as an effective way to destroy evidence of some other crime such as theft or even murder.

We have so far restricted our discussion to those fires which burn in air at the familiar speeds of bonfires, burning buildings, and wildfire. The destructive power of fire in propellants and explosives has also been very widely harnessed, by no means entirely for aggression; but since these materials contain their own oxygen supply and burn extremely fast, we shall discuss them later (see Chapters 11 and 12). We have also used the terms 'constructive' and 'aggressive' from a purely human standpoint. However, as Zervos has pointed out, *Homo sapiens* is not the only victim of its own power over fire. The first small clearing burned in the forest marked the onset of mankind's adaptation of the environment to suit its own needs. The scale of this modification was soon to outstrip even the massive felling and dam-building of the beaver, whose impact on the landscape was probably greater than that of any other creature. Mankind's early ability to manipulate the environment was for most other species the beginning of a catastrophe which continues to this day.

8

Fire for craftsmen and chemists

The earliest fire-tamers must have noticed that raw meat is not the only material in which fire makes useful changes which stop short of destruction. The clay around a fire becomes dry and hard. Ashes from a wood fire built on the green rock malachite might yield a lump of reddish metal. From such observations grew the ceramic and metallurgical arts, without which our range of materials for buildings, tools, weapons, and daily life would have remained severely limited. Fires built against limestone or gypsum could have led to the chance production of quick lime or plaster of Paris; and simmering cooking pots could have paved the way for 'wet' chemistry. In this chapter we shall look at some of the ways in which fire has been harnessed to alter materials and to make new ones.

The firing of clay pots in Anatolia goes back at least six thousand years. Earlier pots, hardened only by the sun, were used for the storage of dry cereals, but would soon have collapsed in contact with water. The first ceramic vessels were fired in an open hearth, and heated gradually so that any water bound within the clay was expelled slowly, without causing bubbles or explosions. The final temperature was probably 600–700 °C, high enough to drive off all the water, but without causing any gross changes in the structure of the clay. The pots were rigid and water resistant, but remained porous and unglassy; and as they were not removed from the fire until after the ashes had cooled, they were marked by charcoal and smoke. Later vessels of improved appearance were taken hot from the open hearth and cooled in the air. Decoration, by painting a design on the pot with a different clay before firing, was practised as early as 3500 BC; each clay takes on a different colour during the firing process.

Kilns, built in brick from about 4000 BC in Mesopotamia, enabled the pots to be placed on a perforated floor directly above the fire, rather than in contact with it. The domed roof reradiated the heat back into the kiln and heat loss by escaping gases was reduced. At the higher temperatures achieved (750–800 °C), the clay undergoes some vitrification, so that the pots are stronger and less porous. Similar results can be achieved without a kiln, provided that the fire is large and is covered by a layer of earth or vegetable matter in order to prevent heat loss. This type of firing was carried out in Nigeria up to the twentieth century; the fire, like that of the charcoal-burner, was kept alight for several days. Firing at a high temperature for a prolonged period, either with or without a kiln, naturally required a lot of fuel and so the ability of a region to produce pottery depended

(a)   (b)

Reconstruction of ceramic kilns from: (a) Mesopotamia about 350 BC; (b) Egypt about 3500 BC. (This material originally appeared in *Technology in the ancient world* by Henry Hodges (1970), and is reprinted by permission of John Johnson Ltd., London.)

9 Burning off heather in Scotland

10 Burning off at oilrig

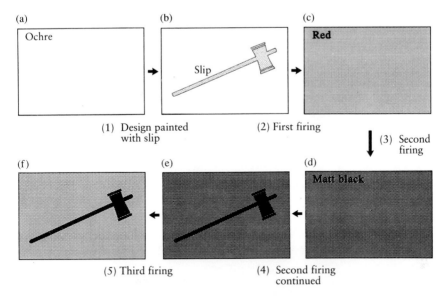

(1) Design painted with slip
(2) First firing
(3) Second firing
(5) Third firing
(4) Second firing continued

The firing of red and black Attic vases: (a) Polished air-dried ochre clay partially painted (1) with slip of fine clay. (b) Ochre clay, fired (2) at 850 °C in excess air. (c) Red (Fe_2O_3) surface, fired (3) at 850 °C in presence of damp leaves. (d) Dull black (FeO and Fe_3O_4) surface, heated (4) under same conditions for 5–10 minutes. (e) Surface of painted area sinters to protective glaze. Heated (5) at 900 °C in excess air (f) Unglazed surface re-oxidized to unglazed red Fe_2O_3. Protected glazed design remains glossy black.

not only on deposits of suitable clay, but also on the supply of fuel. Most pottery was, and still is, fired only once.

The famous black and red Attic ware, produced in Greece about 500 BC, was, however, fired in three stages. A kiln, unlike an open fire, allows the potter to control both the temperature of firing and the composition of the gases surrounding the pots. The red and the black parts of the Attic designs were produced from the same clay, which was separated by sedimentation in water into fractions containing either fine or medium sized particles. The pot was fashioned out of the medium particles and, after air-drying and smoothing, the design was painted on using a suspension of the fine ones, mixed with wood ash. The first stage of firing was carried out at 850 °C using an atmosphere of air; the clay particles, whatever their size, lose water, and the Attic clay, which contains iron, turns the rusty terracotta red of the oxide Fe_2O_3. The furnace is filled with wet leaves and air is

Attic black-on-red vase, showing forge (sixth century BC)

Attic red-on-black vase, showing vase-painter at work (about 430 BC)
(Ashmolean Museum, Oxford)

excluded; a reducing atmosphere of carbon monoxide and hydrogen is formed and these gases change the red oxide into one of the black iron oxides FeO or Fe_3O_4. The temperature of the furnace stays the same. At this temperature, the very fine clay particles vitrify in the presence of wood ash, although the coarser particles of the bulk of the pot do not. The pot becomes black all over: the painted parts a shiny, glassy black and the unpainted ones matt and porous. On the third firing, the temperature is raised to 900 °C and air is reintroduced. The unprotected matt black oxides are changed back into red Fe_2O_3 (still unglazed), while the painted areas, now vitreous, are inaccessible to air and remain black. The process is a masterpiece of technological control, happily coupled with the consummate sensitivity and skill of the draughtsmen (see Plate 12).

Greek kilns, like their Egyptian and Mesopotamian predecessors, were vertical, with a chimney hole at the top; and until fairly recently most, but not all, European kilns were of similar design. But Chinese pottery, much of which is of great beauty and antiquity, was often fired in a horizontal kiln, which retains the hot gases longer, and so keeps a more even temperature. Much of the impetus for development of Western pottery sprang from Europe's admiration of Chinese work and its unsuccessful attempts to imitate it. Higher temperatures were slowly achieved; the famous Dresden ware which was being fired in 1710 required a temperature of 1300–1400°C, an increase of only about 100°C on that used for the Stoneware produced in the reign of Charlemagne.

The art of the potter was not of course restricted to the making of pots, but included beads, and figurines of people and animals; and the baking of clay was exploited also for building. Bricks, at first only sun-dried, were fired as early as the third millennium BC for use in the walls of Babylon, and they have been used as a cheaper alternative to stone ever since, previously for roads as well as for buildings. Fired in large, long kilns for several days per brick, a variety of fuel has been used, dried turf being popular in Northern Europe in the Middle Ages. Modern kilns can hold several million bricks. In Clamper kilns, the bricks are arranged in piles, with the fire in the channels between them. Firing may last from 3 to 6 days. The Hoffman kilns are constructed so that the fire moves from one heating chamber to another; the incoming air is passed over the fired bricks and so acquires heat from them. Alternatively, the bricks may be moved through a fixed fire.

Fired clay has also been widely used for tiles of various types: flat and overlapping roofs in Northern Europe, curved and overlapping for Mediterranean roofs, totally flat for walls and floors. In modern times, ceramics are also extensively used for basins, lavatories, and underground pipes. Fired clay is, however, more or less porous, unless sealed by a layer of vitreous 'glaze'. Most glazes contain a small amount of lime, which must itself be produced by fire: calcium carbonate, in the form of chalk limestone or marble, has been heated in kilns since 2500 BC in order to expel carbon dioxide and produce calcium oxide (or 'lime'). Mixed with water and suitable sand, ground stone or ground brick, it was used in a wide range of mortars and cements. Plaster for covering internal walls of buildings was produced in a similar way by heating hydrated gypsum (calcium sulphate) in order to drive off the water, and has an equally long history.

Although lime is not a necessary component of glass, it is present in most modern glasses (except for lenses and lead glass) and in almost all ancient manufactured glass. Glass can however be prepared simply by fusing sand with soda or potash, but unless lime is added the temperatures needed are higher than those that were accessible to the early glassworkers. It is speculated that the nuggets of glass which have been found may have been formed when mixtures of sand and wood ash were later fused by lightning: hence the name 'lightning stones'. A glassy material was used to produce a green glaze over stone beads as early as 12 000 BC, while the first known object made solely of glass is a deep-blue amulet from about 7000 BC. Although these artifacts, and many later innovations of elaborately worked glass, were found in Egypt, they may have originated in Asia Minor.

Glassy materials have two great advantages over fired clay: they are non-porous, and both their colour and their opacity can be changed by the presence of very small quantities of additives. A glaze not only renders a vase, tile, or basin non-porous, but it also provides infinite scope for decoration. The same is true for objects made solely of glass, and for enamels, which are made by fusing a glass layer on to a metal base. The temperatures needed depend on the composition, but for ancient glass are often in the region of 1000 °C, which

Glassmaking in Italy, early
eleventh century

was then the upper limit of the potter's range. Nowadays sheet glass for such purposes as window panes is manufactured by a continuous process carried out at temperatures of 1500 °C or 1600 °C. A tank may have a capacity for over 1000 tons of glass and may operate for up to 3 years before it has to be cooled for repairs. Raw materials are fed into one end of the tank at exactly the same rate as the sheet glass is drawn off the surface of the molten glass at the other end.

Perhaps the most technologically significant gift bestowed by fire is the power it gave to extract and to work metals (cf. p. 85). Although an alloy of silver and gold ('electrum') could be found in river beds, and veins of elemental copper were occasionally found in rocks, the supply and the variety of native metals was very limited. Even if a lump of meteoritic iron should arrive from the gods, it was of no use to mankind without a very hot fire and the skill of a practised blacksmith. The first extraction of metals may well have occurred accidentally; but although the mineral malachite yields its copper at the very modest temperatures of an open fire, other metal ores are more demanding. The skill of the Middle Eastern bronze-smiths in the second millennium BC would not have developed without the prior knowledge of ceramics. Brick furnaces were needed to provide an adequate temperature for smelting, whether a mixture of tin and copper ores, or ores of tin alone, so that the metal might later be added to copper. Bronze-smiths also relied on the potter for ceramic moulds for casting, since bronze, unlike copper, cannot be shaped by alternate cold-working and annealing. Many of the moulds were made of two or more parts which fitted together and were therefore reusable. The most impressive collaboration between the arts of the potter and the smith must however be the casting of unique metal pieces by the lost wax ('cire perdue') process, in use to this day. The required object is first sculpted in wax. The wax model is next encased in clay, in which a few small channels are left. The clay is then fired and the molten wax escapes through the exit holes, leaving a space into which the molten metal is poured. Since the clay mould must then be broken in order to release the casting, this technique produces a unique artefact.

Iron posed further problems. At the temperatures (of about 500 °C) accessible to the first iron-smiths, iron could be freed from its ores without even being melted. The resulting metal contained little carbon and was soft enough to be hammered into shape (and to be easily mis-shapen by hard use). The higher temperatures made

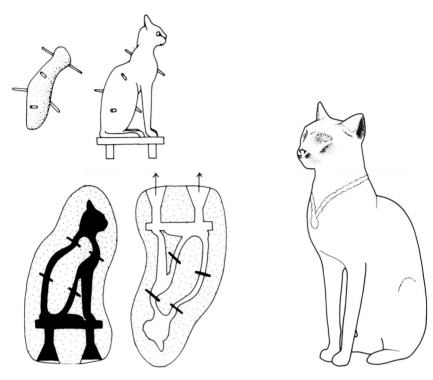

The lost-wax process, using a clay core. (This material originally appeared in *Technology in the ancient world* by Henry Hodges (1970), and is reprinted by permission of John Johnson Ltd., London.)

accessible by aerating the fire with bellows gave liquid iron, which contained up to 5 per cent carbon. This could be cast, but the solid was too brittle to be wrought. In order to produce iron containing exactly the right amount of carbon for a particular purpose, some of the carbon in the molten iron must be oxidized, so that it can escape as gas, leaving a steel which contains roughly 1 per cent carbon. Sword makers have for centuries been making fine Damascus and Samuria blades, but their steel-making recipe was kept secret; only in the nineteenth century was iron converted to steel on a large scale, in either open-hearth or Bessemer converters.

Today's continuously running furnaces are direct descendants of those of the early metal workers. Copper is smelted in a 'reverberatory' furnace at around 1000 °C; the red sides and arched roof promote efficient internal reflection of the heat from the flames. In

The 'Gloucester' candlestick, cast in gilt-bronze by the 'lost-wax' process, early twelfth century.

the 'blast furnace' iron ore and coke (together with a flux) are blasted with pre-heated oxygen-enriched air which reacts with the carbon in the coke to form carbon dioxide which combines with more coke to give carbon monoxide. The first reaction liberates heat and the second absorbs some of it. But the hot carbon monoxide gives out heat as it removes oxygen from the iron ore, and the temperature is thus kept high enough for the resulting iron to escape as a liquid.

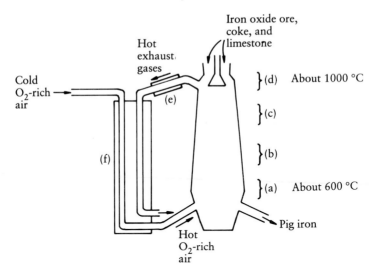

The blast furnace. (a) Coke reacts with hot oxygen to give carbon dioxide. Heat evolved. (b) Coke reacts with carbon dioxide to give carbon monoxide. Heat absorbed. (c) Silica (from the ore) and lime (from the limestone) form slag. (d) Carbon monoxide and iron oxide ore form carbon dioxide and molten iron. (e) Ash removed from exhaust gases. (f) Heat transferred from exhaust gases to incoming air

This solidifies as brittle carbon-rich pig iron. Conversion to steel involves remelting the pig iron and injecting it with liquid oxygen, which both burns off unwanted carbon and maintains the temperature of the melt.

During the Christian era, fire has been widely used to make new substances as well as to craft new artifacts. It was the chief experimental tool of the alchemists in their search for the Elixir of Life and the Philosophers' Stone, believed to turn base metal to gold. These quests, part mystical and part scientific, involved liquids and gases as well as solids and despite their frequent disreputability, laid the basis of much of what we now call Chemistry. To this day fire is used as a major promoter of chemical change, whether in a school laboratory or an industrial plant. The alchemists did not require the high temperatures needed by potters, iron smelters, and glass makers, but they did depend on the skill of these craftsmen to provide them with apparatus. The new technique of distillation was certainly practised in Alexandria at the beginning of the Christian era by alchemists who had at their disposal sophisticated vessels of glass or pottery. About

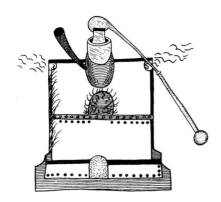

Distillation apparatus as used by medieval alchemists and their predecessors

the same time, Spanish alchemists were able to distil mercury from its sulphide ores and to make use of the 'bain-marie' or water-bath which allowed a vessel to be heated at the constant temperature of boiling water, a device traditionally attributed to, and named after, the female alchemist, Mary the Jewess.

It was probably about another thousand years before distillation of wine produced a satisfactorily drinkable form of concentrated alcohol. The monasteries with their vineyards and herb gardens led the way with the production of liqueurs, some of which have monastic names to this day. By the end of the thirteenth century, distillation was sufficiently widespread for there to be rules govern-

Woman using bellows to tend furnace for distillation of brandy, 1512

The manufacture of sulphuric acid in the eighteenth century

ing the excessive consumption of strong liquor, which was, however, widely prescribed by physicians during the Black Death in 1348, but whether this was for physical or for purely psychological reasons is not known. Gin and brandy originated during this era, which also saw a marked increase in the manufacture of 'aqua vitae' by distilling malt-fermented barley.

Distillation was used for the small scale preparation, and later for the bulk manufacture, of new substances which were later to become key industrial chemicals. Sulphuric acid was first made in the sixteenth century by destructive distillation of blue or green 'vitriols' (sulphates of copper or iron). In the nineteenth century, methyl alcohol was prepared from wood in a similar way, while products as diverse as carbolic acid and synthetic dyestuffs were obtained from coal tar. Distillation of the crude oil which had just started to be drilled both in Texas and in Romania yielded paraffin and lubricants. There was as yet no use for the lightest 'petroleum' batch of the distillation.

Fire is now put to a further use in the treatment of crude oil: that of making more petrol by 'cracking', in which the molecules of vaporized oil are broken down and then reassembled, by means of appropriate catalysts, to give custom-built molecules. The process is carried out at the moderate temperature of about 500°C, often produced by a coke fire. The products provide not only fuels for specific purposes but the building blocks for making most of the materials produced by today's industrial organic chemists: the synthetic polymers which provide us with man-made fibres, plastic containers and wrapping, foams and laminates, paints, varnishes, and adhesives.

The use of fire for such constructive destruction is not new. Wood has been slowly pyrolysed for many centuries in order to obtain charcoal, itself a fuel, which can be burned more cleanly and with more control than wood, and which is still in demand by barbecue cooks and artists. Slow heating of coal similarly yields coke, another valuable solid fuel. A more recent development combines rubbish disposal with fuel production: the pyrolysis of discarded tyres gives gaseous and liquid fuels which can be used to heat the furnace, while steel and carbon can be reclaimed from the solid residues.

9

Fire for movement: (1) External fires

Smoke rises upwards from a fire, and mobiles near a heater move merrily in the draught. When food is boiled in a covered pot, the lid rattles up and down as the steam escapes. The heat from a fire increases the speed of movement of the minute particles within all nearby matter, but the effect is most noticeable in gases, in which the molecules are free to move. Any increase in temperature of a gas is therefore accompanied by an increase in pressure (if the gas is enclosed in a container) or an increase in volume (if the gas is able to expand). Around a fire, the hot gaseous products of combustion rise freely and are replaced by the cooler denser air from the surroundings. When this flow of gas is channelled inside a chimney, the draught can produce quite a strong upwards pull. Burning paper is readily sucked up a domestic chimney and a multitude of children's requests to Father Christmas were despatched in this way before open fires declined in popularity and awareness of safety increased. In some rural fireplaces, the convective force of the updraught was sufficient to pull a large log slowly from the room into the hearth as the burning end was gradually consumed. Among Leonardo da Vinci's many intricate designs was one for harnessing this force to turn a spit. The updraught was intercepted by a vaned wheel, which rotated, windmill-fashion, and via a series of cogs turned the shaft on which the meat was impaled. The rate of rotation of the spit was

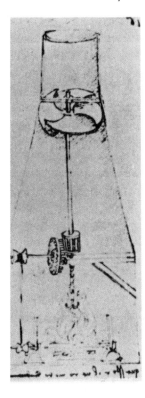

da Vinci's smokejack

Angel chimes

regulated automatically; the hotter the fire, the stronger the up-draught, and the faster it turned. 'Smoke-jacks' of this type were incorporated into the kitchen ranges of eighteenth century England (see Chapter 6); and the popular Christmas decoration 'angel chimes' works on the same principle. Hot gases from candle flames rise and turn a vaned wheel carrying angels who hold rods, attached by rings. As the wheel rotates, the centrifugal force makes the rods swing outwards and strike a bell.

Some successful machines driven by fire were in fact constructed some 1400 years before da Vinci's time. Hero of Alexandria, who probably wrote his *Pneumatics* around the first century of the Christian era, described a number of ingenious devices driven by the higher pressure produced when air is heated in a container. In one machine, a fire was lit on a metal altar, and the increased air pressure

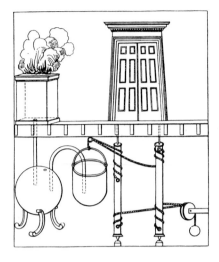

Hero's door-opening machine. Hot air from the altar drives water into the bucket which descends, turning the door spindles by means of a rope.

inside a metal box below the altar opened a pair of temple doors. The same principle was used in an automaton featuring two figures standing by the fire. The figures held cups, from which concealed tubes led down below the altar to the bottom of a reservoir, partially filled with wine. When the fire was lit, the increased air pressure in the reservoir forced some wine up the tubes and out of the cups; the figures appeared to be pouring libations on the fire. A later model included a hollow metal snake with a narrow slit of a mouth; as hot air streamed out of this tube, the snake hissed. Today's whistling kettle works on the same principle.

Some of Hero's other devices involve jets of steam. In one of the simplest, a pith ball appears to float in air above a small bowl, at the base of which escapes an upward jet of steam. His famous 'steam engine' was a hollow sphere which rotated about a horizontal axis when two jets of steam escaped in opposite directions tangentially from its equator; its meagre power was not, however, harnessed. Another toy which was based on rotary jet-propulsion was a revolving disc bearing a number of dancing figures. Hero specified that the disc should have a transparent (glass or horn) cover, since he thought that the reaction of the jets on the inside of the cover caused the disc to turn. It seems surprising that he did not recognize the similarity of the disc to the sphere which he had described earlier. Like the jet engine and the rocket (see Chapters 10 and 11), the device moved by reaction. When matter (such as steam) is ejected fast in one direction

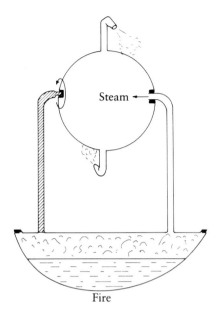

Steam ◄

Fire   Hero's steam turbine

the container moves in the opposite direction, initially with the same product of mass and speed. So when a rifle fires forward, the butt kicks backwards; when a rocket emits hot gases downwards from its base, the rocket moves upwards; and when a disc, or a Catherine wheel, emits gas tangentially to its rim, it rotates.

Most of the rest of this chapter will deal with machines in which the outer casing is stationary, and some inner mechanism is moved by the expansion of a gas into a region of lower pressure. The driving force is usually provided by steam, which may be produced by a fire at some distance from the moving parts. It was seventeenth century Europe which saw steam power start to develop into the major technological force which did so much to shape the history of the following two centuries. But the first 'steam-engines' were different, even in principle, from their eighteenth and nineteenth century descendants. They did, indeed, use steam to create the required difference in pressure; but the role of the steam in these early European models was to produce a *low* pressure (that is, a partial vacuum) rather than to provide the increased pressures which both Hero and the post-1800 engineers used to harness the heat of the fire in order to perform mechanical work.

During the seventeenth century, mining engineers were much concerned with the need for more efficient drainage of mines: the flooding became ever more serious the deeper they dug. The suction-pumps then available functioned by partially removing air from a cylinder by a hand-operated piston. The pressure of atmospheric air forced the water in the mine up into the partial vacuum. The maximum height of about 10 metres through which water can be raised by this type of pump is fixed by the pressure of the atmosphere. This limitation was not understood at the time and in an attempt to extend this height, Papin devised a prototype machine which created a much better vacuum than that achieved with the hand-operated suction pump. A little water was enclosed in the cylinder containing the piston and, when the water was heated, the steam pushed the piston to the top of its container, where it was held by a catch. The tube was then cooled to condense the steam back to water, which takes up less than one-thousandth of the space, so that, when the catch was released, the pressure of the atmosphere pushed the piston down again. Papin's device was for demonstration only; the cylinder was only 7.5 centimetres in diameter and no attempt was made to harness the power.

The first steam engine to be put to industrial use was the huge drainage machine made by the Englishman Thomas Savery, who named it 'the Miner's Friend'. Described as an 'engine to raise water by fire' or, more simply, a 'fire engine', it used steam to produce pressures that were both higher and lower than that of the atmosphere. Unlike Papin's device, the Miner's Friend contained no piston; its only movements were those of valve action. A tube led from a large, egg-shaped pot into the flooded mine-shaft. The pot was filled with steam, which was then cooled to produce a partial vacuum into which water was sucked from the mine. The shaft tube was then closed, and steam was admitted to the pot at a high pressure, which forced the water out through an exit tube, sometimes to a reservoir to be drained by a second such machine, working higher up. The alternate heating and cooling of the pot was, of course, very wasteful of energy, and the technology of the period was inadequate for the safe use of high pressure steam; nor did the machine raise water sufficiently to be of much use in mine drainage. It was, however, used in the early eighteenth century for pumping water to large buildings, for driving water wheels, and for filling a tank in an ornamental garden; and, despite its many shortcomings, the 'Miner's Friend' is of great historical significance.

Improved steam engines followed as fast as patent restrictions,

11 Burning oil-wells in Kuwait (© Scurr/Cedri/Impact Photos, London)

12 Attic cup: red-on-black, c. 500 BC. Ashmolean Museum, Oxford

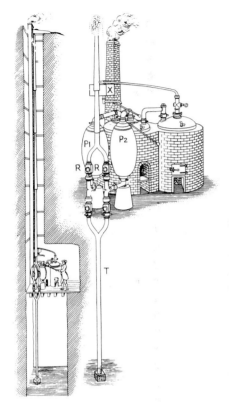

Savery's 'Miner's Friend, or an Engine to Raise Water by Fire'. Steam is admitted to the oval vessel P1 and displaces the water upwards through a check-valve R. When P1 is emptied of water the supply of steam is stopped and cold water from a cistern X is poured on P1 to condense the steam there. This creates a vacuum and water is sucked through T and Valve R. P2 is filled with steam while P1 is being cooled.

limited financial resources, and the engineering skills of the period allowed. Newcomen used two cylinders and pistons, connected by a beam. Steam was introduced at only atmospheric pressure, and cooled to create a partial vacuum. Engines of this type were more powerful than Savery's (5.5 as compared to 1 horsepower*), although they were only 1 per cent efficient in terms of the useful work obtained from the coal burned. For mine-drainage this was not important, as the fuel did not have to be transported and the steam boilers were fed with low-grade, unsaleable coal. The Newcomen engine was widely used in Britain for drainage, and for supplying water which could itself be used to work machinery needing uniform rotary, rather than intermittent vertical, motion. Its use spread rapidly to continental Europe and, by the mid-eighteenth century, to the New World. A large version was sent to Russia in the later part of the century to empty the naval docks of Catherine the Great. One used

* 1 horsepower = 746 watts.

for colliery work in Derbyshire was in operation from 1791–1918 and the last survivor was dismantled in 1934 after over a century of almost trouble-free service.

The last quarter of the eighteenth century saw another great step forward. James Watt realized that engine efficiency would be greatly increased if the cylinder were kept hot throughout the working cycle and not cooled at the end of each stroke. He therefore introduced a separate condenser, at some distance from the cylinder. In his first models, a piston was driven down the cylinder by the pressure of steam on its upper surface, expelling air through an exit valve. A valve in the piston now opened to equalize the steam pressure above and below the piston, which could then be raised by a weight and pulley system. Watt employed a canon-maker to bore his cylinders with the necessary precision (and one of his first two steam engines was used to supply air to the borer's blast furnace). Watt's later models were 'double-acting', with steam being introduced into the cylinder alternately above and below the piston. The supply of steam was cut off early in each stroke, the rest of the stroke being driven by the *expansion* of the steam.

Many improvements followed the expiry of Watt's patent in 1800. Engineering practice could now cope with high-pressure steam, which was used in Philadelphia to drive small moderate-pressure engines for grinding and sawing. Higher pressure steam engines were

Mobile steam-engine driving a threshing machine, about 1840

Paddlesteamers racing on the Mississippi

made in the early nineteenth century, many by the Cornish mining engineer Richard Trevithick. Their use was not restricted to mining, but also included rolling iron, grinding corn, and milling flour.

During the last quarter of the eighteenth century, whilst fire was being gradually harnessed to manufacturing technology, more dramatic innovations were being attempted in France. In 1783 came the first successful steam-driven locomotion: a paddlewheel steamer sailed up the river Saône near Lyons. Successful paddle-steamers were soon made in America and also in Scotland, but did not rapidly become commercially widespread. The American inventor, John Fitch, was hamstrung by financial difficulties; and the Scots, mindful even then of the need to care for the environment, declined to develop steam traffic on their rivers, lest the wash erode the banks. Paddle-steamers were, however, developed enthusiastically for river transport in America, as many beautiful nineteenth century prints bear witness. However, by the time that the paddle-steamer had been adequately adapted for ocean voyages, it was already being seriously challenged by steamers with screw propulsion in the mid-third of the nineteenth century. In 1842 the US Navy introduced (in the 'Princeton') a screw-engine designed so that all the machinery should have the protection of being below the waterline. The first trans-Atlantic screw-steamer crossing was achieved in the following year. The early steam-driven pumping engines were huge stationary machines, fed by low grade coal. Much ingenuity was needed to design steam-driven engines which would fit into the confines of a nineteenth century ship. Ocean-going mercantile vessels had to carry a sizeable supply of coal, often sufficient for the whole voyage; and naval ships were often limited in their sphere of active service by their inability to come ashore to a friendly refuelling station.

The use of steam power for land transport was developing over the same period, but it faced different problems. The engines had to be used in an even more confined space, but refuelling could be carried out *en route*. French and English experiments on steam powered road carriages date from the last third of the eighteenth century, and in 1800 Trevithick demonstrated a vehicle which was able to carry several people. He later designed a locomotive which could pull heavy loads along a cast-iron tramway at 8 kilometres per hour. During the Napoleonic Wars, the rising cost of horse-fodder provided stimulus for experiments on steam locomotion, which in 1820 culminated in the famous railway engine 'The Rocket', designed by George and Robert Stephenson. The subsequent development of a

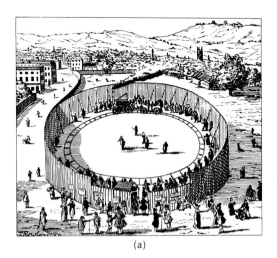

(a)   (b)

The world's first passenger railway: (a) the track; (b) Trevithick's engine, the 'Catch-me-who-can' (1808)

railway network throughout Britain, and very soon also throughout America and continental Europe, transformed land transport and was a major historical force throughout the century. Engines became larger, more powerful, and more efficient. Speeds, loads, and non-stop range increased accordingly. A major development was the introduction of the 'compound engine' where the steam can be made to yield more useful work by allowing it to expand in successive stages in different cylinders working at decreasing pressures. More energy was obtained from the fuel by improved fire-boxes, designed to achieve complete combustion. In the 1860s British locomotives, which were legally required to 'effectively consume their own smoke', became able to burn coal, instead of the more expensive but less smoky coke which previously had to be used. In many countries, wood was the main fuel, while Russia was already experimenting with oil.

Toward the end of the nineteenth century, steam power was used to drive prototype road vehicles such as cars and tricycles, but for most purposes was soon ousted by the internal combustion engine (see Chapter 10). However, the heavy steam-driven rollers used in road mending and construction were a familiar sight until the Second World War. Steam also powered the first successful airship, which transported its pilot for 17 miles around Paris as early as 1852, but the 3 horsepower engine was not powerful enough for serious use.

The development of steam-power was not confined to locomotion. Effective stationary steam engines were required not only for blast furnaces and general industrial duties, but also to drive the generators

Steam tricycle, made by Léon Serpollet in 1887

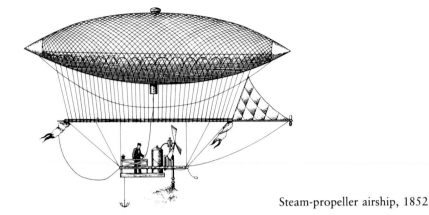

Steam-propeller airship, 1852

for the new electricity industry. Compound engines were naturally used, and by 1900 these could deliver up to 2900 horsepower (over 21 600 watts). By then, however, the power of expanding steam was being differently harnessed. In the steam turbine the force of expansion of high-pressure steam is used for direct production of rotary motion without the intervention of the linear motion of a piston in a cylinder. The principles employed are both simple and ancient. The energy with which a stream of gas strikes a vaned wheel has long been harnessed by the familiar North European windmill; and the rotation of a sphere in reaction to the angular escape of a jet of steam was described not only by Hero of Alexandria but also by Watt and Trevithick, whose experimental 'steam wheels' and 'whirling engines', similarly based on jet-propulsion, met with only limited success, because such devices are efficient only when they are rotating at rates very much higher than were then attainable.

In 1884, however, the British engineer Charles Parsons patented a turbine in which steam was passed through a static tube containing a moveable shaft. The shaft and the inner surface of the tube were fitted with alternating layers of vaned ribs. As high pressure steam passed from one set to the next, its energy of expansion was transferred gradually and efficiently to the shaft. Moreover, the vanes of the inner surface of the tube were set at such an angle to the shaft vanes that the steam issued in jets from the edge of the shaft, accelerating its rotation and so the engine achieved a speed of 18 000 r.p.m. By the end of the century, the first turbine-driven ship, the 'Turbina', had been launched, demonstrating a speed of 34.5 knots (about

The *Turbinia* (1897)

63 kilometres per hour); and by 1910 turbines generating up to 70 000 h.p. (over 52 000 kilowatts) were in use in liners and in British naval vessels. For many purposes, the harnessing of fire power via steam has now been replaced by the more direct use of fire in internal combustion engines (see Chapter 10). In one field, however, the steam turbine is still supreme. Much of the world's electricity is generated in this way, using inlet steam at about 600 °C and 300 atmospheres. This expands in twenty or more stages to generate 75 000 h.p. (nearly 56 000 kilowatts).

All steam engines require some container in which water can he converted to steam, often at considerable pressures. Although industrial boilers have developed a long way from the domestic kettle, they work on the same principles. A vessel containing water is placed near a source of heat. For rapid boiling, the fire should be hot, the kettle should be in intimate contact with it, and the base of the kettle should allow heat to pass readily through it. The temperature of the flame depends not only on the fuel but also on the pre-combustion temperature of the fuel and air, and on how much of the generated heat is used in heating up non-useful substances such as nitrogen and unburned excess oxygen. For this reason, the hottest atmospheric flames are achieved when the ratio of fuel to air is exactly that needed for complete combustion; and still higher temperatures are reached if the air is replaced by pure oxygen, so that no heat is wasted in raising the temperature of the unreactive nitrogen which comprises about 80 per cent of the air.

The incoming fuel mixture can be pre-heated by heat exchange with the hot flue gases, and the heat of the flame should be readily transferred to the water. The most economical boilers are compact (giving low heat loss to the surroundings), with a large area of contact between the water and the fire (or its flue gases) achieved by a convoluted system of piping. The hot flue gases may be piped through the water reservoir, as in 'fire-tube' boilers, which are not very compact and generate steam rather slowly; but 'water-tube' boilers, in which tubes carry water through the fire-box are much more widely used. The combustion gases should be as turbulent as possible in order to prevent the formation of a stagnant layer of insulating gas around the water tubes. A coal-fired boiler is usually stoked mechanically, often with a chain grate which supplies the coal to one side of the fire and removes the ashes at the other. The water may be pumped around the tubes, being either circulated several times, or forced through once only. Since heat is transferred by radiation as well as by conduction, the sooty luminous flames from the burning coal and oil are preferable to the non-luminous flames of natural gas, since they emit radiation over a wide range of energy. For the same reason, radiative transfer is facilitated by a covering of soot on the tube; the layer of soot should be thin, however, or else its insulating properties will decrease the transfer of heat by conduction. The fire-box must, of course, be designed to facilitate reradiation of energy; and it must be built of materials which are themselves both good radiators and sufficiently refractive to withstand the high temperatures produced.

Not all externally-fired machines need enclosed boilers, however. In the early nineteenth century a Scots teenager, Robert Stirling, was experimenting with an engine in which the working gas was not steam, but air. He heated an enclosed quantity of air and allowed it to expand, thereby moving a piston. The gas was then cooled and compressed at this lower temperature. Clearly it needs work to compress a gas, but since less work is needed to effect the compression at a lower temperature than can be obtained by expansion of the same gas at a higher temperature, the cycle provides a route for converting the heat of the fire into mechanical work. Although Stirling, and later the American, John Ericsson, had modest success with air-engines about 1830, they met many practical problems and their ideas lay fallow for over a century. Attempts were then made to revive the Stirling engine, working either on air or on some light gas such as hydrogen or helium. It has been claimed that the twentieth century models can generate enough power to drive ships and vehicles and are moreover smooth-running, low on pollution, and quiet enough to be used for blowing an organ. Small Stirling engines have been used to drive electricity generators in remote places and have the advantage that they are not fussy about their fuel. The heat they need can be obtained by burning almost anything from garden waste to salad oil. But until the designers have overcome the considerable problems involved in transferring heat from the fire to the cooled gas, and from the hot gas to the coolant, such engines are unlikely to be widely used.

Fire for movement: (2) Internal combustion

Leonardo da Vinci's smoke jack (see Chapter 6) was to be powered by flue gases rather than by steam. Since combustion normally generates more, and hotter, gas than it consumes, its products have potential as working gases, probably of greater efficiency than the external ones discussed in the previous chapter. Much energy is lost from the smoke jack, however, both by heating the excess air which is sucked into the fire and by escape of hot gases between the vanes and the chimney. Efficiency would be enhanced if the combustion took place inside a cylinder fitted with, say, a piston or turbine.

The first internal combustion engines were not a success. Towards the end of the seventeenth century, Papin, Huygens, and others experimented with a piston fitted into a cylinder in which gunpowder was exploded. The piston was indeed driven upwards, but both the removal of the exhaust gases, and the recharging of the hot cylinder with gunpowder, posed intractable problems. Understandably, gunpowder engines were not developed further.

About a century later, a British patent was taken out for an internal combustion engine which burned town gas, but only in the mid-nineteenth century was a satisfactory machine of this type produced, probably by Lenoir. The gas–air mixture was ignited by an electric spark, but at atmospheric pressure without compression, giving an efficiency lower than that of contemporary steam engines.

Moreover, since town gas was then available only near gas works, these internal combustion engines were not only stationary, but could be used in only a very limited range of locations.

A French scheme of 1862 sought greater efficiency by compressing the gas–air mixture before igniting it, but the design was never used. The same principle was, however, the basis of a horizontal gas engine

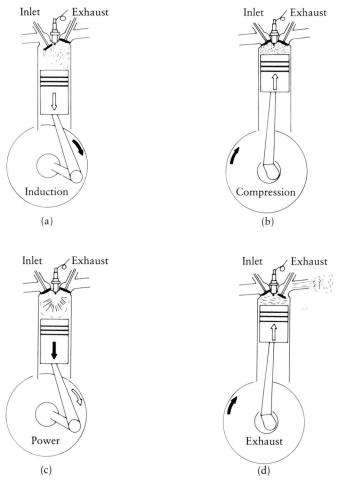

The four-stroke Otto cycle: (a) Induction. Inlet open, exhaust shut. Rotating flywheel lowers piston. Fuel gases sucked in. (b) Compression. Both valves shut. Rotating flywheel raises piston. (c) Ignition. Both valves shut. Ignition forces piston down and powers flywheel. (d) Exhaust. Inlet shut, exhaust open. Rotating flywheel raises piston. Products expelled.

constructed (probably independently) in Germany by Otto, in 1876. The piston in Otto's engine went through a four-stroke cycle which formed the basis of the vast majority of subsequent internal-combustion piston movements. On the first stroke, downward movement of the piston and opening of air and fuel intake valves in the cylinder head sucks a mixture of fuel and air into the cylinder. On the second stroke the piston is moved upwards and the fuel–air mixture is compressed at the top of the cylinder. An electric spark from a plug in the cylinder head then ignites the compressed fuel mixture, a flame front passes rapidly downwards, and the hot combustion gases expand and force the piston down again. This third stroke therefore uses the energy of combustion to provide the power which moves the piston. On the fourth and last stroke of the cycle, the piston moves upwards again and expels the combustion gases through an exit valve. Like earlier gas-engines, Otto's engine was condemned to a sedentary existence near to a gas works; but as the first sessile sea squirts may have formed the basis for the evolution of the vertebrates, so Otto's engine was not only a major stride in the development of land transport as we know it today, but also the parent of powered aviation. Present-day engines can perform fifty Otto cycles in a second.

The breakthrough came with the experimental use of fuels derived from petroleum. The heavier fractions were widely needed for paraffin lamps (see Chapter 5), but at that time there was no use for the lighter fractions, which were highly flammable, and so difficult to store safely. As a possible fuel for locomotive engines, it was more transportable than gas and was preferable to coal in that it flowed readily and burned to give more heat for its weight.

Primitive petrol engines, built by the Austrian Siegfried Markus around 1870, precede the Otto cycle, but the acknowledged pioneer of the petrol engine is the German, Gottlieb Daimler. Already experienced with town-gas engines, he patented his first petrol engine in 1885. The fuel–air mixture was prepared by sucking air through petrol on its way to the cylinder, and was ignited by an externally heated tube in the cylinder head. A bicycle driven by petrol was produced in 1886, followed by a carriage, and similar engines were soon used in small boats and stationary machinery. Also in 1885, Karl Benz patented a petrol-driven car which used electric spark ignition. The early years of the twentieth century saw the petrol engine harnessed to driving propellers in prototype aircraft designed by the Wright brothers and others. Dramatic success was achieved in 1909 with Bleriot's crossing of the English Channel.

Experiments were also being carried out with fuels from heavier petroleum fractions, which might sound unpromising, since they both vaporize less readily than the lighter ones, and also ignite less readily if sparked. However, in 1892 Rudolph Diesel patented an engine in which a mixture of air and heavy oil vapour could be

Benz motor-car, 1888

Petrol horse: a tractor
patented in France in 1897

The Wright brothers' flying
machine, 1903

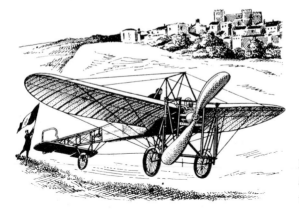

Bleriot landing at Dover
after the first crossing of
the English Channel, 1909

ignited by compression alone (see Chapter 3). Since his first engines
were difficult to start cold, he tried ignition based on an external
compressed-air turn-over, and external pre-heating of the engine.
Diesel himself never lived to see the success which his engine was to
achieve; he disappeared during a Channel crossing in 1913, assumed
to have jumped overboard as a result of the apparently insoluble
financial problems into which his inventions had landed him. But
even before he died, the small island of Guernsey, UK, was using
diesel power to generate all its electricity supply.

In the century following the appearance of the first satisfactory
internal combustion engines there have been many improvements in
design, fuels, and materials; and the adoption of any particular
model is, of course, a compromise between a number of conflicting
factors. In the petrol-driven, spark-ignition system, for example,
there are theoretical reasons for favouring a 'lean' fuel mixture which
has a higher proportion of air than that needed for complete combustion. But when these weak mixtures are burned, some energy is
dissipated in 'cracking' some of the unburned fuel. Less dissociation
occurs if the mixture is richer in fuel, so rich mixtures give a larger
quantity of useful energy, and hence better performance, even though
slightly lower temperatures are produced. Moreover, the combustion
products of fuel-rich mixtures are less harmful to the engine. So
slightly fuel-rich mixtures are often to be preferred, even though
criteria based on fuel economy favour weaker mixtures. The design
of a carburettor which produces exactly the right amount of fuel
admixed with the in-going air is a considerable challenge, as the
'right' amount varies with the load on the engine. Any imbalance

which leaves unburned fuel leads to inefficient and uneconomical performance and, of course, to worse atmospheric pollution (see Chapter 17). Introduction of the fuel into the cylinder by direct injection of the correct amount is much more satisfactory; but it is also much more expensive.

Theory also shows that efficiency is favoured by a high compression ratio (that is the ratio of the highest to lowest volumes within the cylinder during the cycle), by a high initial pressure, and by a low initial temperature. Obviously the first two factors are related: the initial pressure can be increased by prior compression. Such 'supercharging' is essential in aircraft engines which may fly at high altitudes with low external pressure, but it has also been applied to other types of engine. The initial temperature cannot be lowered much, since it has to be high enough to vaporize the fuel. Nor is it possible to increase the compression ratio above a value of about 10:1 for those spark-ignition engines and fuels which are generally available. Too high a compression produces an effect similar to that exploited to ignite a diesel engine. The hot-compressed fuel mixture ignites spontaneously before the flame front reaches it. The engine 'knocks' and its efficiency decreases.

The preparation of suitable fuel in spark ignition engines is yet another factor which has to satisfy a variety of criteria. Branched hydrocarbon fuels burn more slowly and steadily than those with straight-chain carbon backbones, as they are slightly more resistant to pyrolysis into radicals. Such fuels (usually pre-fixed by iso-, as in iso-octane) contribute to the smoothness of engine performance. Low boiling components are easier to vaporize and so give fewer problems with cold-starting; they also produce less soot and other undesirable products of incomplete combustion. The most important characteristic of a fuel is, however, often considered to be its knock-resistance, which is greatest for fuels with the shortest chains and, for a given chain length, for chains with the most branching. The knock-resistance of a fuel is normally expressed as its octane number, which is defined as that percentage by volume of the highly branched substance iso-octane in a mixture with the unbranched n-heptane which has the same resistance to knock under certain defined conditions. As some fuels are now more resistant to knock than pure iso-octane, these have octane numbers slightly greater than 100. The octane number of a substance can often be increased by additives known as antiknocks which facilitate smooth combustion. Until recently, these were usually compounds of lead, but now that the dangers of lead pollution are so widely recognized, other less toxic additives are being used as antiknocks.

Attempts to decrease pollution of the air by exhaust gases from petrol engines are not limited to the avoidance of lead additives. Oxides of nitrogen, and soot, have rightly received much attention (see Chapter 17). In some engines, water is injected to act as a coolant, which improves the performance and economy in high compression ratio engines (with both spark and compression ignition). Pollution is markedly decreased but at the expense of more complex, and hence more costly, equipment. A lean mixture allows the use of a higher compression ratio before knocking occurs, and so gives more complete combustion, increased efficiency, and less pollution. A disadvantage is that lean mixtures burn more slowly and may misfire unless the design of the piston can be adapted to increase the turbulence of the flame and so speed up the combustion. In some engines, a small quantity of fuel-rich mixture is ignited in a partially separated chamber from which the flame spreads to the leaner mixture in the main body of the cylinder. In other models, specially shaped pistons and combustion chambers produce turbulent swirl in the combustion gases and allow the use of fuel mixtures up to 33 per cent leaner than normal, thereby decreasing pollution and improving fuel economy.

Spark ignition engines, particularly those specially designed to have a high compression ratio, run well on fuels such as ethanol, LPG (liquefied petroleum gas), and CNG (compressed natural gas), which are lighter than petrol. As these fuels contain only small molecules, seldom with more than four carbon atoms apiece, they do not readily generate the free radicals which are thought to cause knocking. The engine runs coolly and smoothly. Moreover, since they burn relatively completely, they cause little pollution. Compared with petrol, however, they generate less energy per kilogram of fuel carried. In some countries, such as the Netherlands, which already have an extensive LPG network, cars are adapted to run on either petrol or LPG and have one tank for each fuel. But the cost and upheaval needed to extend or change any country's fuel distribution system would be enormous.

The many improvements which have been outlined above are all modifications of the Otto engine composed of cylindrical combustion chambers containing close fitting pistons which move up and down on a four-stroke cycle. But more radical changes have also been

13 Launch of Space shuttle *Atlantis*, July 1992

14 Hot air balloon with blow lamp

made. In 1956, Wankel designed an engine in which a piston of roughly triangular cross-section rotated inside the (slightly flattened) cylinder, carrying out the operations of fuel induction, compression, spark ignition, and exhaust in the spaces between the faces of the piston and the walls of the cylinder. Since the rotary motion in a Wankel engine is simpler than the conventional reciprocal movement, smoother operation would be expected. However, the strong, light alloys required to overcome the mechanical strain added greatly to the price, and the design has not been widely used.

An alternative approach to the four-stroke engine, which in prototype antedates Otto's patent, is to employ a shorter, simpler cycle. A two-stroke engine has the apparent advantage that it produces power on alternate strokes, whereas the Otto engine does useful work only on every fourth stroke, which has to power the three subsequent ones by means of energy transferred to a heavy fly wheel. In the usual single-cylinder two-stroke engine, the fuel-mixture inlets and exhaust outlets are so placed that the piston alternately blocks or exposes them. Induction, followed by compression, takes place as the piston rises. Ignition causes the piston to fall, providing the power stroke and expelling exhaust as it does so. The design has changed little from that developed by Day in 1891, and the problems which he encountered have not yet been fully resolved. There is still lack of total precision in the amounts and composition of the fuel mixture sucked into the cylinder, and the exhaust is not completely expelled; the running is low-powered, rough, and noisy. Two-stroke engines are therefore used only for small, extremely basic cars and for machines such as lawn-mowers, marine outboard motors, and mopeds, where weight must be kept to a minimum and little power is needed.

The development of the spark-ignition petrol engine was accompanied by similar evolution of the compression–ignition diesel engine, which runs on the same four-stroke cycle. The induction and compression stages, however, deal only with air. The fuel is injected at high pressure as a fine spray into the compressed air, which is swirled to effect turbulent mixing. This injection continues for a substantial part of the power stroke. The compression ratios, which are usually in the range 14:1 to 20:1, are appreciably higher than those in conventional petrol engines. As with spark ignition, efficiency is greater the higher the compression ratio, the leaner the fuel, and the lower the temperature. With a given fuel, however, compression ignition always has lower efficiency than spark ignition. Moreover, higher temperatures are required in order to achieve ignition. Diesel engines use fuel mixtures leaner than the theoretical value in order to try to achieve complete combustion, even if mixing is incomplete, and thus to avoid excessive 'diesel fume' pollution and deposits of soot and tarry residues inside the engine. Ignition of lean mixtures may be facilitated by 'indirect injection' of fuel into a precombustion chamber containing about half the total air at a compression ratio of about 20:1. As the piston moves down, the combustion spreads to the leaner mixture.

Diesel engines are much simpler than spark ignition ones, since they contain no carburettor and no ancillary electrics for ignition. They are therefore much more rugged and reliable and are particularly suitable for heavy duty commercial vehicles and for railway engines and ships, where they are in almost universal use. Although atmospheric pollution is an increasing problem (see Chapter 17), diesel engines are also used in some private cars.

As diesel engines are not subject to knock, many will run on cruder fuel that is needed for spark ignition; and no lead compounds, or other antiknocks, need be added. Indeed, since compression ignition is required, pro-knocking agents are added as ignition promoters. An explosively rapid burn is needed, and so the fuel contains a high proportion of straight-chain hydrocarbons which are readily pyrolysed. Present-day diesel fuel, which contains heavier oils than those in petrol, typically with sixteen to eighteen carbon atoms per molecule, has now largely overcome the early starting problems. In those parts of the world where petroleum products are not readily available, diesel engines could be run off fuels of similar molecular weight such as oils from coconut, soya, and sunflower.

As we saw in Chapter 9, the energy of expansion of a hot, high pressure gas can be harnessed to produce motion by means of turbines and jets, as well as by piston and cylinder. Hot combustion gases, produced by burning vaporized fuel in highly compressed air, can be used, as can steam, for either or both of these functions. The production of hot exhaust gases by combustion which does not involve atmospheric oxygen is discussed in Chapter 11. In a pure gas turbine engine, the expansion of the gases is used only to drive the turbine; in the aeronautical turbo-jet, some energy is taken from the exhaust gases to drive the air-compressor, while the rest supplies jet thrust;

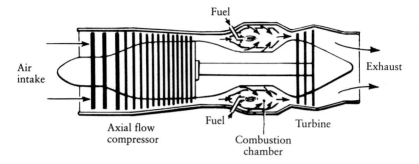

Jet engine.

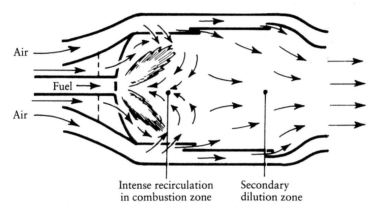

Combustion chamber of jet engine

and in ram-jet aircraft engines, compression is produced entirely by the forward movement of the plane, which is powered by the undiverted energy of the burned gas.

The design of turbines and jets is complicated, partly because the range of operating conditions is very wide, and must be adjusted to power output. The problems encountered are, however, by now familiar. The working temperature must be low enough not to damage the engine. This can be achieved by use of a very fuel-lean mixture. Such mixtures do not, however, ignite readily nor do they give a strong stable flame (particularly within the steam of very high velocity gas). These problems are overcome by injecting a fine spray of the fuel into only 30 per cent of the air, at high temperature and pressure. Most of the burnt gases are then directed backwards through the flame to maintain its stability, and to create vortex turbulence. The rest of the air cools the outside and inside of the combustion chamber, becomes extremely hot, and mixes with the escaping jet of combustion gases. Such recoil devices are the basis of much world travel and most manned aerial warfare.

11

Fire for movement: (3) Pre-packed oxygen

Whether toy or turbo-jet, all the machines described in the last two chapters convert chemically stored energy, first to molecular motion, and then into mechanical action. The fuel is burned, externally or internally, in air. But the oxygen which is needed for its combustion can also be obtained from richer sources such as pure gaseous or liquid oxygen, or salts such as saltpetre which liberate oxygen when they are heated. A more generous supply of oxygen accelerates the combustion, sometimes to the point where it is instantaneous and explosive (see Chapter 12). Here we shall discuss the use of pre-packed oxygen to produce motion by fast, but non-explosive, combustion.

Naturally occurring saltpetre has long been used to impregnate tinder, which can then be ignited by a spark. A mixture of charcoal and saltpetre burns rapidly even in the absence of air, and faster still if sulphur is also added. Both carbon and sulphur form only gaseous combustion products and so generate a large volume of hot gas. If the so-called 'black powder' is ignited in an enclosed space, it may explode, but if the gases are allowed to escape in a jet from one part of the container, this will move by reaction (see p. 101) in the opposite direction. Mixtures of this sort must have been available over one thousand years ago in China where fire crackers were used for family celebrations during the T'ang dynasty (which spanned the seventh to tenth centuries of the Christian era). Over the intervening millennium, black powder changed its name to gunpowder, and the various solid mixtures descended from it have been developed into increasingly vicious explosive weapons and coaxed into ever more beautiful fireworks (see Chapters 12 and 13).

The recorded use of black powder for military jet propulsion dates from the mid-thirteenth century when the Chinese used incendiary rockets against the Mongols, who in their turn used them to capture Baghdad in 1258. The Arabs thus acquired a knowledge of rocketry which they introduced into Europe. Military rockets were used in the siege of Orleans in 1429. In 1806 the British fired 200 rockets with the intention of destroying the French fleet, then anchored off Boulogne; but the rockets were deflected by wind and fell on the town instead. In the late eighteenth century rockets were used to fire a rescue line between a distressed ship and the land. (At first, the rescue rocket was fired from the shore; but it was soon realized that it was easier to hit the shore from the ship than vice versa.) More than a century earlier, Cyrano de Bergerac had made some science-fantasy suggestions about space travel, including the idea that a rocket could take a man to the moon. But this was the musing of a mere man of letters; space travel had to wait until the end of the nineteenth century for serious technological consideration.

The rocket was, of course, the obvious space locomotive, since its movement requires neither the resistance, nor the oxygen, of the earth's atmosphere. But even the most powerful military rockets available in the nineteenth century had minuscule thrust compared with that needed to escape from the earth's gravitational field. The development of larger and more powerful rockets naturally stimulated the search for the best possible propellant, the most important requirement being that its demise should result in the liberation of a great deal of heat, and a great many molecules of gas, preferably of very low mass.

Until the twentieth century, rocket propellants were always solid, but in 1903 the space-travel pioneer Tsiolkovsky (1857–1935) suggested the use of liquid hydrogen and liquid oxygen, which combine to evolve jets of very hot water vapour. The idea was publicized in the German science fiction film *Frau im Mond*, made in 1929 and featuring just such a rocket landing a girl on the moon. The first successful liquid-fuel rocket was launched, also in Germany, in 1935 and laid the basis for the military rockets, including the famous 'V-

II', used by the Germans in the Second World War (as a reprisal weapon, or Vergeltungswaffen). The period 1920–39 also saw a surge of interest in the application of smaller, solid-fuel rockets to all types of locomotion. There were many attempts, serious and otherwise, to fit them to cars, boats, gliders, trains, cycles, and even skates.

Of the new liquid-fuelled rockets, most employed the bipropellant system consisting of two liquids which are stored separately and meet only in the combustion chamber. One of the most popular bipropellant systems is indeed liquid hydrogen and liquid oxygen. The hydrogen can be replaced by other light fuels such as diborane (B_2H_6), acetylene or 'ethyne' (C_2H_2), or hydrazine (N_2H_4) or even by paraffin; and, as the very reactive light element fluorine combines avidly with all these fuels, liquid oxygen can be replaced by liquid fluorine. (Plate 3d shows a stream of hydrogen burning in an atmosphere of bromine, a heavier and less reactive analogue of fluorine.) With hydrogen as fuel, oxygen can also be replaced by a range of other so-called oxidants, but many of these (for example ozone, O_3, and light compounds of fluorine, such as F_2O, NF_3, and F_2O_2) are so unstable that handling and storage are extremely hazardous. A more convenient oxidant for liquid hydrogen is chlorotrifluoromethane, $CClF_3$, which liberates far less heat than liquid oxygen. On the other hand, it is denser and so a lower volume is needed, which in turn implies smaller and less weighty fuel tanks.

The choice of fuel involves a large number of factors in addition to the chemistry and thermochemistry of the combustion process, and considerations of health and safety; so there is a fine balance between the advantages and disadvantages of any particular bipropellant system. The combustion of paraffin in liquid oxygen produces the relatively massive oxides of carbon in the exhaust gases and hence gives a lower thrust than do many other bipropellants. On the other hand, paraffin is cheap, non-corrosive, and easy to store. It needs no heavy refrigeration units, nor the robust tanks needed for the storage of compressed gases. Liquid fuels are often used also to cool the combustion chamber, and for heat exchange purposes they should be thermally stable, flow easily, conduct heat well, and absorb a lot of heat for a given change in temperature. If intermittent ignition is needed, as for the smaller, off-centre, jets used for steering, it is best to use a 'hypergolic' bipropellant, that is two separate liquids which ignite spontaneously when mixed. Occasionally, homogeneous liquid propellants are used. Such monopropellants may be premixed mixtures of fuel and oxidant (such as methanol, CH_3OH, and nitromethane, CH_3NO_2) or single very unstable substances, such as hydrogen peroxide, H_2O_2. However, only few liquids which decompose so energetically on ignition remain intact under storage.

Problems of storage may be minimized by using a single solid propellant charge. Solid propellants cannot, however, be used also as coolants; and they cannot compete with the best liquid propellants in terms of thrust. Two main types of solid propellant have none the less been used. 'Double base' solid propellants contain two oxygen rich substances which are mixed to give the required combustion characteristics and mechanical properties. For example the explosive plasticizer nitroglycerine can be mixed with nitrocellulose, which acts as a binder to give a rigid, almost homogeneous, charge. 'Composite' solid propellants, on the other hand, contain particles of oxidant (usually ammonium or potassium salts of the oxygen-rich perchlorate or nitrate ions) dispersed in a flammable matrix (e.g. of an organic polymer such as polyethylene). Powdered carbon, or metals such as aluminium or beryllium, may be added as fillers, since they combine avidly with oxygen to form very stable oxides, liberating much heat in the process.

As we saw in Chapter 2, the combustion of solid fuel is much more complicated than that of a premixed gas. When a solid rocket-fuel charge is ignited, the surface ejects a stream of oxygen and pyrolysed matrix, together with solid particles, which radiate heat back to the burning surface. The rate of mixing of oxygen with combustible materials depends in a very complex way on particle size and on pressure, which of course varies with the environment of the rocket. If the external pressure drops, the burning may cease. However, the temperature may well be so high that the charge continues to decompose just below the burning surface. The gases generated will increase the pressure in this region, and ignition will start again spontaneously, only to stop again when the accumulated gas has been consumed. This sporadic combustion is the cause of 'chuffing'. Pierced charges of many different shapes have been used in order to achieve the most effective rate of combustion.

Multi-stage rockets do not necessarily use the same propellant for each stage. In the space shuttle, for example, the three main engines run off a liquid bipropellant, the 549 000 litres of oxygen and 1 476 000 litres of hydrogen being carried in a reusable external tank. The two 500 000 kilogram boosters use a solid propellant of powdered

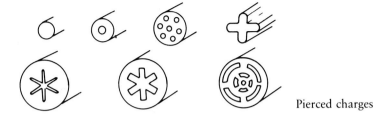

Pierced charges

aluminium, ammonium perchlorate, and a binder, while the small rockets used for manoeuvres and reaction control again use a liquid bipropellant, in this case hydrazine (N_2H_4) and dinitrogen tetroxide. The power of a modern space-rocket can be enormous, see Plate 13. As early as 1969 the Saturn C-25 engines generated, in 2.5 minutes, almost 1 000 000 000 kilojoules of energy.

From that first lunar landing of Apollo-II, less than two centuries had elapsed since mankind's first successful attempt to rise above the Earth's surface. This achievement, too, was dependent on fire, which enabled the Montgolfier brothers to heat the air inside their balloon and so to lower its density. The hot-air balloon then rose through the denser surrounding air. Unlike aeronauts, who contend with gravity, and astronauts who escape from it, balloonists exploit the gravitational

Explosion of the hydrogen-filled airship *Hindenburg*, 1937

force; and, in the eighteenth century, hot air was the only gas lighter than atmospheric air. The first hot-air balloons were filled by being held in place over an open bonfire. Since the air cooled (and the balloons therefore descended) after about ten minutes, the balloonists braved the fire-hazard and carried up a bowl of embers. This was soon replaced by a blow-lamp. Hot-air balloons were superseded by hydrogen balloons as soon as the technical difficulties of making gas-tight balloons and filling them with large quantities of the dangerously flammable hydrogen were thought to have been mastered. However, as late as 1937, the hydrogen-filled airship Hindenburg caught fire at the end of a transatlantic flight, killing thirty-six people, probably because a spark ignited a small hydrogen leak. Hydrogen was then gradually replaced by helium which is totally unreactive, although expensive and twice as dense. Hot air remains, however, the cheapest 'working fluid' for balloonists, and the Montgolfier hot-air balloon, complete with blow-lamp, still finds favour with present-day enthusiasts (see Plate 14).

12

Fire for movement: (4) Explosives

How does the 'almost instantaneous' combustion of an explosion differ from the 'exceedingly fast' burning of, say, a rocket propellant? Let us look first at the much simpler case of a column of stationary gas. In normal burning, or 'deflagration', the flame front travels through the gas at a speed of between 10 centimetres and 10 metres per second; and the pressure and density of the combustion gases decrease as distance from the flame increases. If, however, the flame travels much more rapidly (say 2 to 3 kilometres per second) and the combustion generates a lot of gas, the pressure and density of the products build up very suddenly to produce a supersonic shock wave, which compresses the reaction zone, raises its temperature, and increases the speed of reaction still further. The reaction accelerates violently, and explodes, or 'detonates'.

The simplest explosions are those which take place in mixtures of gases. Some of these occur because heat is generated by the reaction more quickly than it is lost by escaping molecules. The temperature increases and the reaction accelerates, generating yet higher temperatures. In other gas reactions, explosion may be caused by 'chain-branching': one highly reactive fragment (or 'radical') may give rise to several others. Some of these active species may be deactivated by collision with the walls of the vessel, or with each other, and some will react to form products. However, if radicals are produced more quickly than they are consumed, their total concentration will increase and these reactions too will accelerate. Many gaseous explosions involve both thermal and chain-branching acceleration. Moreover, since both heat loss and radical deactivation depend not only on the temperature and pressure of the gas, but also on the shape of the vessel and on the material of which it is made, it is very difficult to predict the exact conditions which produce an explosion. At any particular temperature, there is always a minimum pressure below which no explosion occurs. Above this pressure, there will be an explosive range, until a second limit is reached, when the fragments are so close together that they recombine. At still higher pressures, the rate may be so great that there is a third explosive range. Much research has been done on the explosive properties of mixtures of oxygen with simple gases; and for hydrogen (see Plate 6c) and carbon monoxide, the many component steps in the overall reactions

$$2H_2 + O_2 \rightarrow 2H_2O$$
$$2CO + O_2 \rightarrow 2CO_2$$

have now been largely unravelled.

In some gaseous mixtures, such as propane and air, there may be a region of pressure before the first explosion limit, in which transient 'cool flames' occur. The oxygen and propane first form a number of highly reactive radicals, together with energy-rich molecules of formaldehyde. These may emit energy as light, accompanied by only a little heat. The luminous zone which passes through the gas does not even char paper; the rise in temperature never exceeds 150 °C, and in some reactions is almost zero. The concentrations of the light-emitting species build up and decrease in an oscillatory way, so that a number of these cool flames may be seen before the explosion occurs.

A quite different type of explosive mixture is a suspension of very fine solid particles in air. Almost any solid in contact with air contains more energy than the oxides which would be formed by combustion. Many solids, however, do not normally burn, since the heat generated by any combustion at the surface would be conducted into the bulk of the material, thus lowering the surface temperature below that needed to sustain the reaction. In practice, the heat generated by surface combustion increases with surface area, while the removal of heat into the bulk of the material decreases with decreasing mass. So a small burning particle becomes hotter than a larger piece of the same substance and reradiates more heat to its neighbours. Thus, the smaller the particles, the faster they burn, and if they are so small as to constitute a fine dust, the combustion may occur explosively fast. Although an iron nail is not flammable, iron filings burn vigorously in air (see Plate 6b). Mists which contain very small droplets of flammable liquids may also explode.

Explosions in dust-suspensions and mists, like those in gases, are of interest mainly from the view-point of accident prevention (see Chapter 19) and of pure research. The great majority of intentional explosions make use of solids, which may be roughly divided into three classes. *Primary high explosives* can be detonated by any method of ignition, such as heat, flame, electrical spark or mechanical impact. *Secondary high explosives* will detonate under the influence of an external shockwave, but if ignited by a flame merely burn without explosion, or 'deflagrate'. Detonation of a high explosive can be considered instantaneous and generates pressures of several hundred thousand atmospheres. *Low* or *deflagrating explosives* burn extremely rapidly, although not instantaneously, and generate lower, but still very high, pressures, of several thousand atmospheres. The distinctions between these classes are not rigorous, since high explosives may burn momentarily before they explode, whilst low explosives may, on occasion, be persuaded to detonate. The total power released may be similar for all types of explosive, but de-flagrating explosives generate their power more slowly. They can therefore be used as rocket propellants, which must produce a rapid, but steadily sustained supply of power, in order to overcome the force of gravity without destroying the rocket casing (see Chapter 11).

It is not surprising that the large scale development of high ex-plosives had to wait until the latter half of the nineteenth century. All explosives, other than black powder, require the skill of the preparative chemist, based on knowledge and techniques previously unknown. Black powder, on the other hand, was made by adding together naturally occurring substances, without chemical reaction (although not by simple mixing). Before the saltpetre was added, the sulphur was forced into the interstices of the carbon structure by milling it with the charcoal, which had been prepared with great care. Although black powder deflagrates rather than detonates, the combustion of some of its forms in a confined space can generate explosive pressure and it has been used over the centuries for many tasks which are today performed by high explosives.

Charcoal-burning in the early eighteenth century. A, woodstack; B, preparing
the heap of wood; C, covering it; D, a freshly-lit, and E, a nearly burnt-out
heap; F, uncovering a carbonized heap.

The earliest use of black powder was probably for fireworks (see
Chapter 13). Military applications are known from mid-eleventh
century China and anticipated its use in civil engineering by several
hundred years. The first weapons containing black powder, which
were presumably fired with an ignited fuse, were dropped, thrown or
catapulted both by land forces and by warships; but it is not certain
whether these bombs were explosive or merely incendiary. In 1232,
black powder was first used as a military propellant, or 'gunpowder',
for blowing solids out of a bamboo tube. The earliest description of
the powder in the West was in Roger Bacon's *Opus majus* of 1267–8.
Guns appeared in Europe during the fourteenth century, at first firing
stones. By the end of the century, stones had been replaced either by
small lead balls, or large iron ones for cannons. Although small guns
were used at the battle of Crecy in 1346, the early heavy artillery was
extremely cumbersome. By 1445, a big gun could be fired twice an

Cannon, fourteenth century

hour (whereas the archers could fire amour-piercing arrows at the rate of one every five seconds), and the saltpetre for the charge often cost more than the gun. The fifteenth century also saw the military use of the rocket (see Chapter 11) and the development of the shell, which started as a hollow iron ball, pierced with a hole and filled with gunpowder. The shell was set off by igniting a flammable outer layer which burned until the flame reached the hole and the powder exploded.

Until the end of the fifteenth century, guns were usually fired by putting a piece of burning twine impregnated with saltpetre (a 'slow match') into contact with the gunpowder, at first through a touch-hole in the barrel. In later hand-held guns, a lighted slow match was pushed down on to the firing powder (without extinguishing it!) after the trigger had been pulled. Such match-lock guns were difficult to handle on horseback and were replaced by those fired by a wheel-lock in which the release of a keg-wound spring allowed a rough wheel to rotate and spark against a piece of pyrites. Although used in the Franco-Italian wars of 1494–1559, it was slow to rewind and was succeeded by the much more satisfactory flintlock, in which a flint was cocked against a spring. When the trigger was pulled, the flint was released and sparked on a roughened metal plate. The gun was first developed by the French for the new sport of shooting birds on the wing, but was later used by Louis XIV to re-equip his army during the 1660s. Although the great majority of firearms are aimed against fellow humans, the gun is still widely used for hunting and for culling over-populous species such as rabbits and deer.

Spring and steel firing mechanisms were also used to set off 'infernal machines', triggered either by a clock, or by touch. Some machines shot the person who touched them, while others merely set fire to the surroundings. From the late sixteenth century come descriptions of such devices concealed in purses, chests, stools, and letters; and from the first part of the seventeenth century in a basket of eggs and a wine cask. A macabre subject for social enquiry might be the type of disguises used for such booby traps in different historical periods. In 1881, there was a plot to kill Czar Alexander III by bombs hidden in peasants' caps, to be thrown in apparent jubilation during his coronation procession. In the austerity of the Second World War, explosive devices were contained in such irresistible objects as cigarette packets and bars of soap, while in 1985 an Irish boy was killed by a booby trap dog. When a particular person is the target for terrorism, a bomb is often taped under the victim's car, to be activated by the ignition system.

The eighteenth century saw a widening of the range of the military use of gunpowder. The Russians buried it under lumps of ice and lit the fuse just before the enemy passed by. A similar device, using rocks as ammunition, was used in Gibraltar in 1771. The first torpedo was launched only five years later.

The civil use of gunpowder was restricted to pyrotechnics for about five centuries. Explosives seem to have first been used for mining in Hungary in the early seventeenth century. Germany followed, and by the end of the century blasting was being carried out in Cornish mines in the UK using the 'miners' squib', a paper tube, half filled with gunpowder. The empty end, which was twisted and dipped in molten sulphur, burned steadily when ignited. Similar squibs, which were used as bird-scarers, had fuses of different length, so that the explosions were staggered. Guns were fired up chimneys so that the pressure waves would dislodge the soot. In our own time, the sound waves produced mainly by blank ammunition are used for warfare simulation (in military training and in drama), for crowd control, for starting races, for informal celebration, and for formal salutes such as state birthdays and funerals. Those receiving doctorates from the University of Stockholm are honoured by a salvo fired from a warship in the harbour.

15 Fireworks

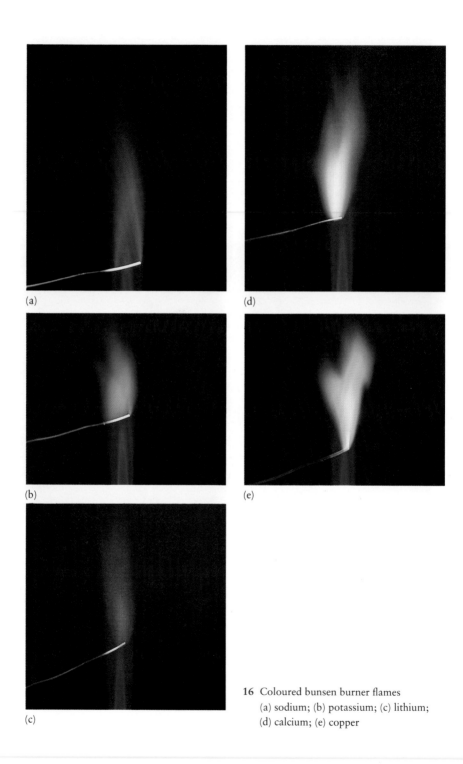

(a)

(d)

(b)

(e)

(c)

16 Coloured bunsen burner flames
(a) sodium; (b) potassium; (c) lithium;
(d) calcium; (e) copper

Vast development occurred during the nineteenth century. At its outset all explosives were a form of black powder; but by the end of the century, there was a considerable range both of secondary high explosives and of primary ones with which to detonate them. The first primary explosive, probably mercury fulminate, $Hg(ONC)_2$, was patented as 'percussion powder' in 1809 by the Scottish Presbyterian minister Alexander Forsyth, whose interest in firearms was sporting rather than military. Unstable to both heat and mechanical shock, it decomposes extremely readily to give only gaseous products and to generate a detonating shock wave. The use of similar powders (which often contained also the oxygen-rich potassium chlorate) led to the invention of the percussion cap, ignited by a hammer blow when the trigger was pulled. Unlike the flint-lock, this system was weather-proof and when it had, tardily, been adopted it transformed the design of armaments. More recent detonating explosives include azide (N_3^-) salts of heavy metals, such as lead, and organic compounds such as lead styphnate and hexanitromannitol, which also decompose instantly on impact, generating a large volume of gas. Since the last compound contains no heavy metals, it is less toxic than the others, and also cheaper. But the choice of primary explosive depends primarily on its use. Lead azide explodes on impact, but it is not sensitive to flame and so cannot be detonated by an electrically heated wire. It is also susceptible to damp. Lead styphnate is very sensitive to electrical discharge, and mercury fulminate is so unstable that both manufacture and storage is extremely hazardous (see Chapter 19).

The explosive which have now largely replaced black powder were mostly developed in the second half of the nineteenth century. Unlike gunpowder, they are detonated not by flame, but by prior detonation of the primary explosive. Most are organic compounds and many contain the unstable oxygen-rich nitro-group $—NO_2$. But many other compounds are also explosive, particularly those containing the oxygen-rich groups $—O—O—$, $—O—O—O—$, $—OClO_2$, and $—OClO_3$, or the groups $—N{=}N—$, and $—N{\cdots}N{\cdots}N—$, which break down readily to form nitrogen gas. Other groups which may make a substance explosively unstable are $—N{=}C{=}$ and $—C{\equiv}C—$, and some combinations of metal atoms with organic compounds.

The first nitro-explosives were based on molecules which had linear backbones of carbon atoms. Glycerine was nitrated to give nitroglycerine, the 'blasting oil' which blew up the Nobel factory in

H$_2$C — ONO$_2$
|
HC — ONO$_2$
|
H$_2$C — ONO$_2$

Nitroglycerine,
NG

O$_2$NOH$_2$C   CH$_2$ONO$_2$
\ /
C
/ \
O$_2$NOH$_2$C   CH$_2$ONO$_2$

PETN
(pentaerythritol
tetranitrate)

TNT
(trinitrotoluene)

[C$_6$H$_7$O$_2$(ONO$_2$)$_3$]$_n$

Nitrocellulose,
NC

RDX (cyclotrimethylene,
trinitramine)

Picric acid

NH$_4$NO$_3$

Ammonium
nitrate, AN

HMX (tetramethylene
tetranitramine)

Lead styphnate

Formulae of some explosives

1864. Carbohydrates were nitrated to nitrostarch ('gun cotton') and nitrocellulose. Nitroglycerine was found to be safer to handle when absorbed on the mineral kieselguhr to give 'dynamite'; but the kieselguhr absorbs heat from the combustion and contributes nothing to it. More active absorbants are preferable: combustible substances such as wood pulp, flour or collodion add to the heat generated, while sodium nitrate increases the supply of oxygen. Mixed with a fairly low percentage of nitrocellulose and some of these additives, nitroglycerine forms the useful gels 'gelignite' and 'blasting gelatine'.

Nitrocellulose itself may also be treated to form a gel which can be rolled into sheets and dried, to give 'cordite' or 'smokeless powder'. Another class of nitro-compounds is based on the hexagonal skeleton of the benzene ring, often containing three symmetrically placed nitro-groups and one other group. Examples are TNT, picric acid, ammonium picrate, and TETRYL, in which the additional group is $-CH_3$, $-OH$, $-ONH_4^+$, and $-N(NO_2)CH_3$ respectively. TNT is used, often in combination with other substances, for both civil and military work. On its own, it can pierce armour 30 centimetres thick and explode on the other side. Other highly nitrated military explosives are based on skeletons containing a five-membered cruciform structure (to give PETN), and six-membered and eight-membered rings containing alternate carbon and nitrogen atoms. The nitrogroups are attached to the nitrogen atoms to give substances called RDX and HMX respectively. These last three explosives all have detonation velocities greater than 8 kilometres per second. The most powerful, HMX, detonates at 9124 metres per second and is also of high stability.

In addition to these explosive solids, and to absorbed nitroglycerine, various liquids have been used. Sprengel explosives, which were used in 1885 to remove Flood Rock from the navigation channel in New York harbour, consisted of bags of potassium chlorate which were lowered first into tanks of nitrobenzene and then into the boreholes. The ANFO class of explosives, widely used in modern mining, also contain solid pellets of oxygen-rich ammonium nitrate soaked in fuel oil. In LOX blasting explosives, the solid component (active charcoal) acts as the fuel which is dunked in liquid oxygen and detonated before the oxygen can evaporate. Despite the cheapness of LOX explosives, they are now little used, as they are lethally temperamental. Combustible liquids such as paraffin oils can be mixed with one or more nitrated explosives of the type PETN or RDX to form a marzipan-like paste, mouldable by hand. Generally known as SEMTEX, the plasticity of these explosives enables them to be readily concealed by terrorists. A liquid component can also be used merely as an inert base, as in the water gel explosives: a saturated aqueous solution of ammonium and other nitrates is treated with solid ammonium nitrate, pellets of TNT, a gum, and maybe another gelling agent. The resulting slurry can be fortified with other fuels and aerated to a predetermined extent so that it sets to a gel of the required density.

There is now considerable scope for designing explosive materials to meet a wide variety of specifications. Military explosives, for example, should not be too sensitive, since they must not be set off by rough transport or handling, nor by nearby fires or gunfire. They must be powerful, not too bulky, not too heavy, and unaffected by moisture. Grenades and other weapons directed mainly against people must shatter their outer casing and project the fragments, since it is these that cause the injuries. Bombs and shells do their work over a much larger area, causing destruction by the shock waves they generate. Their explosives sometimes contain added fuels, such as powdered aluminium, which evolve a great deal of heat when they combine with oxygen. Some bombs are based on fuel–air explosives, which consist of fine powders or droplets of substance such as ethylene oxide $(CH_2)_2O$, which burn readily in air. The military analogue of custard powder (p. 188), they detonate on ignition, producing a strong, sustained pulse of high pressure, which pushes on the target rather than shattering it. Since such weapons rely on air for combustion, they are lighter than those which are self-sufficient in pre-packed oxygen.

Armour-piercing weapons must be particularly insensitive to shock, since the detonation must occur inside the target and so be initiated by a time fuse and not by the original impact. Armour-piercing is greatly improved by making a conical depression in the front of the charge, and lining this with metal. As detonation occurs, part of the cone becomes a jet which travels forwards at armour-penetrating speeds of up to 6 kilometres per second. The rest of the cone is shaped by the detonation into a slug which passes through the hole made by the jet. The well-known bazooka is a shaped-charge weapon of this type. An alternative tank-piercing weapon, the squash-head, contains an explosive which spreads over a large area

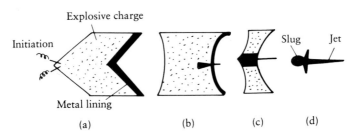

The formation of a shaped charge jet

inside the pierced vehicle before it detonates. When it does explode, it removes a large scab of metal from the inner surface of the armour and projects it into the interior of the tank. Military high-explosive weapons have now reached a high level of unpleasant sophistication, and it is only because of the even grosser inhumanities which can be perpetrated by nuclear and biological warfare that 'conventional' weapons are sometimes spoken of as if they were almost benign.

Happily, much skill has also been applied to more constructive uses of high explosives. Here one of the major considerations is that the charge should supply exactly the right power for the job. In blasting, which accounts for a large quantity of commercial explosives, the explosion must break down the rock without projecting the fragments far, or violently, into the surroundings; and in civil demolition work, the unwanted building should collapse where it stood without bombarding the surroundings with debris. The type, size, and distribution of the charges must therefore be meticulously matched to the damage needed. The explosives widely used in coal-mines are designed to minimize the hazards of accidental explosions from accumulations of methane or from a suspension of coal dust in air. Since methane–air mixtures ignite only at high temperatures and after an appreciable delay, the explosion should occur extremely quickly without producing too high a temperature. Salt acts as a coolant and may be added; or it may be formed during the detonation by use of mixtures such as sodium nitrate and ammonium chloride. Danger from dust explosives can be reduced if limestone is added to the charge (to generate carbon dioxide) and water introduced into the borehole.

Perhaps surprisingly, explosives are also needed in firefighting (see Chapter 22) and safety work. The application of very high pressure at a safe distance can be a valuable tool in situations which are too hazardous to be handled at close range. Explosive foam containing bubbles of an air/acetylene mixture can be gently pumped over a minefield and then detonated, in order that the resultant vibrations set off the mines. It can get into awkward places, such as under rocks and can be detonated at leisure (or even not at all, should there be a change of policy). Explosives are also used to extinguish oil spout fires; if a charge is set off at the mouth of the burning oil jet, the hot gases are dispersed so rapidly that the explosion 'blows out' the flame. Other uses for human safety are the activation of ejector seats in aircraft and the diversion of lava flow after volcanic eruptions.

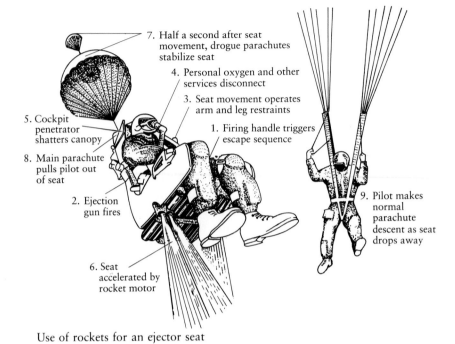

7. Half a second after seat movement, drogue parachutes stabilize seat

4. Personal oxygen and other services disconnect

3. Seat movement operates arm and leg restraints

5. Cockpit penetrator shatters canopy

1. Firing handle triggers escape sequence

8. Main parachute pulls pilot out of seat

2. Ejection gun fires

9. Pilot makes normal parachute descent as seat drops away

6. Seat accelerated by rocket motor

Use of rockets for an ejector seat

There is, however, the danger that interaction of a small charge with a stream of hot lava could itself cause a devastating explosion. Plans to blast the lava stream from Heimaey in Iceland, to prevent it from blocking the harbour, were abandoned for this reason.

High explosives have also been used for underground and submarine geological mapping. The sound of an explosion is monitored at various distances from the point of detonation, having travelled to the sensors both directly and after reflection from underlying boundaries between strata. Such 'seismic' research enables geologists to obtain a three-dimensional map of the substrata, and has helped to locate oil-beds in the North Sea.

Many much smaller jobs also use explosives to produce high pressure by remote control. The techniques of demolition and quarrying have been scaled down to allow burglars to blow open locks and farmers to excavate ditches, remove tree stumps, and break up the top soil. The sinister shaped-charge weapons have been tamed to pierce the clay plugs which seal blast furnaces, allowing them to be tapped quickly and safely. Small, carefully controlled explosive charges are now widely used in metal-working. The pressure of an explosion can harden the surface of steel to a predetermined depth or can coat it with a cladding of an incompatible metal such as aluminium by forcing the two layers into intimate contact. Small pieces of metals can be shaped into complex dies, inaccessible rivets expanded, and graphite converted into tiny diamonds for industrial use.

Lower powered, deflagrating explosives are employed mainly in rocket propulsion (see Chapter 11), firearms, and fireworks (see Chapter 13); but they are also used to scatter various substances into the atmosphere. Since many organic compounds decompose when strongly heated, pesticides, fungicides, crowd-control irritants, and other organic toxins should be dispersed at low temperatures, and flameless propellants have now been developed for this purpose. Various metals can also be distributed into the atmosphere to act as meteorological markers. The yellow trail left by sodium, for example, is used for studying ionospheric winds at altitudes of 150 kilometres. Barium is similarly used for research on magnetic fields. The reaction between propellant-dispersed aluminium powder and oxygen to give AlO produces a blue glow which is used to map atmospheric temperatures.

As well as helping us to obtain information about the weather, propellants can be used in attempts to modify it. Clouds may be dispersed, producing rain; and rockets are fired over vineyards to ensure that any precipitation falls as rain rather than hail. Propellants have been used over airfields to blow holes in fog of sufficient size to allow aircraft to take off and land, and it has been claimed that they can break up the destructive power of a hurricane. It would be good if explosive power could be harnessed to oppose the destructive forces of nature, as well as to augment them. But however distasteful may be our aggressive use of explosive combustion, it would be hard to overestimate the benefits that explosives have conferred on mankind through civil engineering.

13

Fire for special effects: (1) Pyrotechnics

The two previous chapters have traced the development of black powder into propellants and explosives which deliver ever-increasing loads to yet more distant destinations or create more-and-more powerful shock waves. But since we do not put men on the moon, nor even expand rivet-heads, by force alone, we have simultaneously been learning to harness this vast power with ever-increasing control. The pyrotechnics discussed in this chapter have also evolved far from their T'ang firecracker forbears but, as their loads are very light, only little power is needed. Progress has been in the variety and control of the combustion, with the result that some of today's fireworks are of such breathtaking beauty that the whole assembly of onlookers gasps as one (see Plate 15).

Knowledge of fireworks, like that of military rockets, (see Chapter 11) came to Europe from the Far East via the Arab World, and the basic oriental techniques were little changed before the end of the eighteenth century. Until then, only saltpetre was used as the source of oxygen, and the main fuels were the charcoal and sulphur of traditional 'black powder'. Sparks of different types could be produced by adding iron or steel filings, or lamp black. For the bright flames of 'white fire' salts of antimony or arsenic were added. Combustible binders such as shellac, starch, and dextrin were often added to increase the time of burning.

The Chinese produced coloured displays by igniting fireworks inside coloured lanterns but the first interestingly coloured flame appears to date from 1630, when a greenish tinge was obtained using a mixture of sal ammoniac and verdigris, from corroded copper. A similar reddish tinge, possibly from some salt of strontium, was claimed in the early eighteenth century. We know that sodium salts (such as common salt) colour flames deep yellow (see p. 50). Salts of other metals can be used to produce different colours, provided that the flame is hot enough both to volatize the salt and to provide enough energy to excite the metallic component of the vapour. The excess energy is reradiated, emitting a colour which is characteristic of the metal (see Plate 16). The early fireworks might seem unimpressive today, since it was not then possible to produce flames hot enough to give strong colours; but they were very popular at the time. Their social use in China goes back at least one thousand years and they have been used in European religious festivals and public displays for almost half of that period (see Chapter 23).

Considerable variety was available even to the early pyrotechnists. Stationary fireworks could project sparks and flames to give effects of cascading water or burgeoning vegetation. Alternatively, a large number of cigarette-sized fireworks, each giving a single lance of fire, could be mounted on a frame to outline a pictorial design or depict lettering. Mobile fireworks, propelled by jet action of the combustion gases, included sky rockets and squibs. Jet action also turns wheel fireworks, which are formed from a flat coiled tube. At the centre of the coil is a space, through which the coil is loosely pinned to a stand, in either a horizontal or a vertical plane.

The manufacture of fireworks in the seventeenth century was led by pyrotechnic schools in Nurenberg and in Italy, but public displays had long been popular in many European countries for national celebrations of victory, peace or royal occasions, for local festivals, and for public spectacles in parks and gardens. Queen Elizabeth I of England was said to have been very enthusiastic about them until, during such an occasion, a nearby house burned down, killing all its occupants. For national occasions, the artillerymen, being familiar with the handling of gunpowder, were responsible also for peacetime pyrotechnics; in Britain such displays were in the charge of the Master Gunner until as late as 1856. The fireworks were often supplemented by simpler forms of fire, such as flares and torches; the river display for the Lord Mayor's procession in London in the early seventeenth century was preceded by 'Green Men' who carried fire-emitting clubs.

Despite the relative simplicity of the fireworks, the pyrotechnic events became increasingly elaborate. The treaty of Aix la Chapelle in 1748 stimulated massive displays over much of Europe. The fireworks were mounted in enormous temporary 'temples'. In London, the total cost of the event was £14 500, of which rather over half was used on the actual fireworks;* and Handel was commissioned to write his famous 'Music for the Royal Fireworks'. In Paris there was a dispute between the French and Italian pyrotechnists as to who should be the first to light their display. In the event, both compositions were ignited simultaneously and both blew up, killing forty people and injuring 300 others. Not content with mounting displays from elaborate stands and temporary buildings, the English barbarously ignited fireworks on live animals such as bulls. The French produced aerial displays from balloons in which the fireworks descended slowly by parachute. Since many of the balloons were filled with hydrogen, this was a hazardous undertaking. In 1819 a Mme Blandchard, widow of a balloonist, was killed while giving such a display.

Pyrotechnics took a great step forward at the end of the eighteenth century when potassium chlorate ($KClO_3$) became available. A more ready source of oxygen than saltpetre, it produced higher temperatures and therefore could volatize more metal salts; so a wider variety of more brightly coloured flames was possible. A good red was obtained from some strontium salts, and apple green from barium ones. The familiar yellow sodium flame is easily produced by table salt. Blue flames were more difficult to obtain because many of the parent copper compounds were unstable to friction.

The first half of the nineteenth century also saw the introduction of the recently isolated metals, magnesium and aluminium, which, when finely divided, burn with an intense white flame in the presence of potassium chlorate. The particles of metal are hammered before use, because the tips of jagged fragments are more reactive than the smoother surfaces of powders which have been ground in a pebble mill (in the same way that the tip of an iron nail rusts in damp air more rapidly than the shank and that a dented piece of metal cor-

* These were not a success. Despite the rain, the main display caught fire and the Italian director drew his sword on the Controller of Ordinance, whose inefficiencies had characterized the preparations.

rodes more easily than a smooth one). The familiar 'sparklers' contain particles of iron (see Plate 6b) or aluminium, together with an oxidant, held together by a generous amount of binder. 'Snow-cones' derive their name from the white fall-out of oxide from burning magnesium (see Plate 6a). Aluminium gives a similar oxide, and such products can provide an effective smoke background for reflection of subsequent flames, whether white or coloured.

An indoor pyrotechnic diversion is 'Pharaoh's Serpent' or 'Snake in the Grass': a small pellet, which when ignited, expands grossly to give a coil of ash in the form of a worm cast. This 'snake's egg' was formerly mercury thiocyanate, but more recently nitrated pitch has been used, because this, too, gives a high volume ash, but is cheaper and less toxic. The 'grass', if present, is the green oxide of chromium, Cr_2O_3, which is the combustion residue of the oxygen-rich ammonium dichromate $(NH_4)_2Cr_2O_7$.

The art of the pyrotechnist is obviously critically dependent on the rates of combustion of the various parts of the firework. Although some fireworks are cast as pellets, many are packed into rolled paper cases. For rockets, fountains, and similar force and spark compositions, the case stays largely intact while the the firework burns. But those cases that contain flame-producing compositions are usually consumed and at exactly the same rate as the firework itself. It has been claimed that the rarity of certain Maltese postage stamps is due to the fact that the paper of which they are made burns at the same rate as the contents of a Roman candle. As the Maltese firework makers are exceptionally skilful, and as every village celebrates its saint's day with a pyrotechnic display which include Roman candles, surviving postage stamps are hard to come by.

Great care must also be taken when packing the 'composition' into the case. Any cavity may cause uneven burning which will certainly detract from the appearance and may well cause an explosion. The filling of firework cases is an extremely skilled job which is still normally done by hand. The meticulously symmetrical fireworks produced in Japan (often reminiscent of highly formalized chrysanthemum heads) demonstrate the peak of technique which can be achieved by precision filling. It is interesting to note how Japan's ancient aesthetic tradition of ordered composition was transplanted to the new pyrotechnic art which was imported into the country, not from China as one might have guessed, but from Holland. The Japanese also developed daylight displays in which weighted paper animals and figures were released from rockets and inflated as they fell.

The popularity of public firework displays continued throughout the nineteenth century and into the early years of the twentieth. With the many new developments in the art of pyrotechnics, the events became even more lavish than before. Delineation by lance fireworks resulted in recognizable portraits and detailed inscriptions, mounted on frames up to 60 feet high. Actors, depicting characters in stories such as Jack and the Beanstalk, wore asbestos suits covered with fireworks, as did matadors in combat with mechanical bulls. Highly complex set pieces involving movement or change were devised to represent sea battles, the changing seasons, and, more recently, cars and aeroplanes.

Some of the public displays were on a huge scale. Twenty thousand people came to the fête at the Crystal Palace, London, in 1865, and the display mounted to welcome the visit of the French Fleet to Britain in 1905 involved fifty-eight ships and 6 000 men. Firework competitions were also held under rigid categories and rules as to, for example, the number of permitted assistants. For elaborate set pieces in particular, the timing of the ignition is of paramount importance. Simultaneous (or effectively simultaneous) ignition of several components may be carried out by firing a rocket along a line in contact with the fuse papers of the individual units. Delayed ignition is achieved by cotton wicks impregnated with combustible material such as saltpetre. These 'slow matches' or 'fast matches', which can be prepared so as to give a wide variety of rates of burning, can connect various sets of fireworks with each other within a complex network of cardboard tubes.

The visual impact of fireworks is, for some onlookers, much enhanced by their noise. Indeed, 'bangers' have no other *raison d'être*. In addition to the bang generated by the very rapid production of a lot of very hot gas, some rockets containing picrates also emit an impressive whistling sound. The production of noise is also the sole object of caps for toy guns which, like more serious percussion caps, contain mercury fulminate (see Chapter 12) and detonate on impact. Cracker snaps, which also contain mercury fulminate, are detonated by friction with sand paper. Caps and snaps are the only pyrotechnic devices so far to be made entirely by machine. Larger versions of the snap have been used in less playful situations. In India, for example, 'throw-downs', consisting of fulminate and grit wrapped in paper, explode menacingly when dropped on a hard surface. Even more unpleasant missiles were used by terrorists at a prayer meeting led by Gandhi in 1948. Prepared by filling coconut shells with a mixture of potassium chlorate and yellow arsenic sulphide, they detonated dangerously on impact.

Pyrotechnics also have their utilitarian uses, but apart from the practice of adding salt to fuels to brighten the flame (see Chapters 5 and 7), they were little exploited before the nineteenth century. Only then did the richer sources of oxygen and the oxygen-avid metals become available for such devices as the photoflash (see Chapter 5). Flares for illumination often also consist of magnesium, together with an oxygen-rich salt in a metal binder. Aerial flares of this type, launched by rocket and kept aloft by parachute, were used by the Danish army as early as 1820 to illuminate a target. Before the introduction of infra-red sensitive film, night-time aerial photography relied on illumination by aerial flares which are the direct descendants of the photoflash. Flares placed on the ground can act as markers for a target or for an aircraft runway, or indeed as spoof markers, to mislead the enemy. One has even been thrown into a goal-mouth to disrupt an international football match. They can also be used to provide information about movement. Dummy bombs used in training do not explode, but instead produce a flash, so that the point of impact can be recorded photographically. One impressive application is in missile tracking. Flare cartridges weighing only 85 grams but producing 23 million candela, (formerly candle power) are ejected at regular intervals. The path of a missile travelling at a height of 25 000 metres is visible from a distance of 1600 kilometres. A large part of modern pyrotechnics is concerned with simulating weapons, both for military training and for depicting the many battle scenes, whether historical or contemporary, shown on film or television. The effects produced range from the humble booby trap to the atomic bomb, slowly producing its characteristic mushroom cloud.

Even in our era of radio and radar, pyrotechnic compositions are still used for signals from small boats in distress. Some flares which contain phosphorus compounds are self-igniting on contact with water, and the heat generated ignites a rocket. Red distress signals are often fitted with a parachute, and can burn for up to 1 minute. White flares warn other vessels that they are on a collision course. Before the days of radio, Colston lights were used to identify ships of different lines, each of which had its own pyrotechnic 'signature'. At first separate fireworks were ignited in the appropriate sequence, but later a company would often have its own combination prepacked. A somewhat similar use of coded pyrotechnics was the Very pistol, patented in 1878, which fired coloured flares, each combination representing a prearranged message.

We have seen that smoke plays an important role in pyrotechnics, both as a reflector and for the simulation of explosive weapons. It also has a range of other uses which are discussed in the next chapter.

14

Fire for special effects: (2) Smokes

Mankind has harnessed fire mainly in order to tap the energy it releases, often in the form of heat, but also as light, pressure change, and even sound. The smoke is normally considered to be a noxious by-product, to be minimized and expelled at a distance, whether it be a toxic hazard or merely an aesthetic nuisance. But we have seen that we can sometimes put even the smoke to our use.

Smoke from a fire contains finely divided solid particles, dispersed in a hot gaseous mixture of air, unburned fuel, and its pyrolysed, oxidized, and partially oxidized products. If the fuel is an organic material such as coal, wood or candlewax, the solid is usually soot, arising from incomplete oxidation of the fuel (see Chapter 2). On the other hand, the smokes of combustible metal, such as magnesium ribbon or powdered aluminium, contain fine fully oxidized particles of the metal oxides. The particles in smokes interact with any light which falls on them, and if their diameters are roughly similar to the wavelength of light, they will scatter it. The smallest such particles scatter only the light with the lowest visible wavelengths, and so look blue. Somewhat larger particles scatter light of all visible wavelengths and appear white. If the particles are appreciably larger than the wavelengths of visible light, they absorb some of it and scatter some of it, and so have the same appearance as the bulk material. Soot, for example, looks black, while smokes containing iron oxide (Fe_2O_3) look rusty orange.

The smoking of salt red herring over smouldering sawdust, a method which
had been used for several centuries before this print was made in 1772

The use of smoke as a food preservative appears to date from
prehistoric times, and depends on its power both to dry the food and
partially to decompose the fats. Many smoked fish, meats, and
cheeses are still popular with the gourmet, even though industrialized
societies no longer need to preserve food in this way.

Since smokes are often formed by incomplete combustion of
organic fuels, they may also be used as carriers to disperse some
efficacious (or deleterious) material which is not decomposed in the
flame. The active substance may itself form a smoke of small solid
particles, or it may volatilize and add its fumes to the combustion
gases. Naturally, an early use of dispersant smoke was in warfare,
always a powerful stimulant to technological advance. From the
third century BC or even earlier, toxic plants, such as henbane and
aconite, and minerals containing arsenic were burned in order to

17 Buildings on fire

18 Smoke and vapour trails: Red Arrows display team

stupefy and so to overcome the enemy. It was found advisable to add some pleasant fragrance, so that the victims would not get wind of the poison. It seems that Greek village boys during the Second World War would plunge burning plants into streams in order to dope the eels.

Fumes and smokes of various types have long been used to rid mankind of undesirable fellow organisms. Until recently, rooms were fumigated against infection, and greenhouses against fungi and insect pests, by the burning of sulphur candles to produce the toxic and acrid gas, sulphur dioxide. Smoke has been used against rats and burrow-dwelling animals. The insect-repellent smoke from burning incense, used in Chinese temples and (against bookworms) in libraries, is familiar to the Western tourist as the mosquito coil, often essential for a comfortable night. A smoke machine, used at an open air concert at Salisbury in 1991 to protect the orchestra from mosquitoes, much detracted from the visual images projected on to the cathedral wall. The flambeaux now used to light alfresco suppers also generate a smoke which keeps insects at bay. The medieval alchemists supposed that smoke was also efficacious against the devils who must be exorcized before the Elixir of Life could be prepared. Smoke can also be a valuable aid to the hunter. Animals such as bears can be smoked out of an underground nest by igniting it. Woodchucks were hunted by sending a turtle into their holes, with a burning oil-soaked wick tied to its tail. When the turtle turned round to come out again, the woodchuck was smoked out. Sometimes the smoke kills the prey, as in the Congolese method for collecting termites, which were suffocated before they were eaten.

Low concentrations of smoke, of suitable composition, can be extremely pleasing to many people, particularly if the smoke contains nicotine. Tobacco smoking, despite the seriousness of the many health warnings, has been widely practised in both primitive and technological societies, including our own, and has many pleasant social associations. The use of smokes as carriers of deeply narcotic substances probably accounts for their use in magic, and hallucinant smokes may have given rise to the animal faces seen by some alchemists. Since the age of the Egyptian pyramids, mixtures of conifer resins and herbs have been burned as incense, producing a smell which was 'pleasing to the nose-trills' not only of the gods (see Chapter 23) but also of their worshippers. Although many of us retain a childhood nostalgia for the smell of burned fireworks, we would probably not assert that the smell positively promoted good health. Such a claim was, however, made by the people of the Chinese town of Canton where the Governor had banned the use of fire crackers as 'wanton'. Happily, he relented; but whether or not he was persuaded by the argument is uncertain. It has also been optimistically claimed that smoke can remedy baldness.

Many other uses of smoke depend on its visibility and opacity rather than on the particular types of substances it carries. Smoke has a long history both as a cover for hostile activities and as a signal. In classical times, mustard was burned as a smoke screen for those undermining an enemy city. More recently, the smoke from guns has provided a useful, if accidental, cover for movement of troops. Smoke signals, originally from burning grass, may now be coloured, often by the rusty iron oxide Fe_2O_3, which, being cheap and non-toxic, is used for daytime distress flares at sea. Iodine (violet) and cinnabar (red mercury sulphide HgS) have also been used, but are costly and poisonous. Organic dyes are also expensive and are decomposed by too hot a flame, often into carcinogenic fragments. A recent use of coloured smoke is in aeronautical displays. Like the tail of a stunt kite, it acts both as an accentuator and as a short-term memory of the intricate figures performed (see Plate 18). The 200th anniversary of the French Revolution was celebrated with an aeronautical display using red, white, and blue smokes which diffused to form a tricoleur trail. The best opacity however, is obtained, both for screening and signalling, if the smoke is white. Pellets of white phosphorus, coated in rubber to slow down combustion were once widely used, but have now been replaced by a smoke of aluminium oxide, generated by a mixture of aluminium, zinc oxide, and hexachloroethane.

Just as smoke can act as a barrier to the passage of visible light, so it can prevent the passage of other types of radiation. A layer of smoke over an orchard prevents heat loss, acting as an artificial reinforcement of the greenhouse effect. On the other hand, smoke acts as a shield which prevents access of radiation from outside. A large Canadian forest fire, which was initiated in 1985, partly to kill off diseased trees, was used to predict the possible effects of a heavy layer of smoke from a nuclear explosion on the screening of sunlight from the trees below. If the product of the smoke is accompanied by emission of light, as in the burning of magnesium or aluminium, to form dispersions of the metal oxide, reflection from the white particles can greatly enhance the brilliance of the flame, an effect which is exploited in the photographic flash bulb and in firework displays.

As smoke is so opaque, even quite small amounts of it are visible, and so its movement can easily be seen. The way in which smoke leaves a chimney tells the landsman much about the speed and direction of the wind. Smoke can be used as a simple monitor for blocked drains and leaking pipes. As early as the fourteenth century, smoke has been used as a detector of disturbed ground under which gunpowder may have been concealed. Resin was burned under an upturned pot, which became full of smoke. When the pot was lifted, the smoke spread out evenly over the surrounding area except above those places which had recently been dug, from which it rose rapidly.

Very small quantities of smoke can also be detected by smell (while it is understandable that King Alfred forgot the cakes, he should surely have *smelled* them burning). Smoke is a most useful indicator (see Chapter 20) of the early stages of accidental fire; and if the fire is allowed past its early stage, then the smoke has to be taken very seriously indeed (see Chapter 18).

15

Fire as timekeeper

Awareness of the likely lifetime of a fire is essential for planning an adequate fuel supply. The wise virgins of Christ's parable must have had a fairly easy task in predicting whether theirs would last out, as they were dealing with liquid fuel and with lamps they could adjust (and presumably also shelter from draughts). Solid fuel fires probably require more experience; but in a particular hearth, logs of the same material and size, if laid in the same way and protected from the wind, would burn for a similar period. Once mankind could gauge the time a particular fire would burn, it would be natural to use the lifetime of a similar fire to mark the passage of that period. Often only rough timing is needed; the death of a fire can function like a school bell which heralds to all concerned that the lesson period has ended, rather than announcing that exactly 40.00 minutes have passed since it last rang. Up to the twentieth century some North American tribes used fire in this way to determine the duration of their council meetings. Discussion stopped when the fire went out, a procedure which seems more conducive to rational decisions than the all-night sittings of some present-day parliaments.

Burning which proceeds at a regular, predictable speed can be used not only to mark the end of a period, but also to achieve delayed-action ignition. A simple example is the paper fuse, labelled 'Light Here and Stand Back' which protrudes from a firework. The combustion zone moves relatively slowly from the point at which it was lit, allowing the igniter time to withdraw to safety before the hot region reaches and ignites some more violently flammable material.

Similar fuses were widely used both for blasting and for blowing up bridges and other military objectives. Often made from hemp string impregnated with saltpetre, they burned at the rate of about 2.5 centimetres every 5 minutes. The precise timing was not important, provided that the fuse did not burn faster than intended. Delayed-action ignition has also been carried out using mixtures of finely divided metallic, or metalloid, elements with oxygen-rich salts, such as tellurium with barium peroxide or manganese with lead dichromate. Less sophisticated 'slow matches', based on diffusion of oxygen from the air, have also been used. Many a saboteur found that a lighted cigarette served very well, the rate of travel of the smouldering zone depending on the brand and the air flow.

Delayed action ignition may require much more precise timing. In free-fall parachuting, for example, slow matches have been used both to set off a small charge which activates the mechanism to open the parachute, and to ignite flares. A complex series of slow-burning devices can be used as 'delay trains' to set off successive blasting explosions, or to ensure the very precise sequential ignition of fireworks in the sophisticated pyrotechnic set-pieces described in Chapter 13. Such delay trains have been made for a wide variety of timings; any period from 1/250 second to 16 seconds may be required for the combustion zone to travel 1 centimetre. Nowadays, however, such ignition, be it for military or civil purposes, is often carried out electrically.

We need not, of course, focus only on that moment when a fire burns itself out, or when the flame reaches the charge at the end of the slow match. If we know the time needed to consume all the combustible material, we need only to assess the amount which has been burned (or that which remains) to estimate how much time has passed. So, provided that the fuel burns at a constant rate, we can use fire as a clock.

One of the most primitive methods of using combustion to measure time was observed in Hawaii. A number of candle-nuts, which are rich in oil, are threaded on a string. A child, traditionally the youngest in the family, holds the string vertically, and ignites the top nut; and as flames rise upwards, the nut below it is unaffected. When the child judges that the oil in the top nut is nearly exhausted as its flames are subsiding, he inverts the string, and holds it in this position just long enough to ignite the second nut before returning it to its original orientation. The passage of time is assessed by the number of nuts burned. Although the precision depends on the constancy of nut size, the absence of draught, and the skill of the operator, this labour intensive and quantized method of time-telling doubtless fulfilled the basic criterion of all scientific observation: that the precision of the measurements should match the needs of the observer.

In Europe, the use of a candle to measure time was attributed to King Alfred the Great but graduated candles, well protected from strong air currents, were probably in use much earlier than the ninth century. Arabian precision engineering transformed the humble candle into a striking clock, equipped with a pointer for denoting the time. In the late twelfth century, al-Jazari described such a device in which the weights of the wax and the wick, and the cross-section of the candle, are carefully specified. As the candle burns, it is forced upwards by a weight. A series of sheaths, rods, and pulleys couples its movement to the pointer, shaped like a scribe's pen, which indicates the time on a scale. Once an hour the mechanism frees a metal ball which rolls into the head of a bird, and drops from its hinged beak into a sonorous metal trough. It is no surprise that, in so intricate a design, care was taken to ensure that no moving part was ever clogged by resolidified wax. A much cruder device, used at auctions in the West of England well into the twentieth century, was a pin stuck into an ordinary candle. The sale went to him who had made the last bid before the pin fell from the molten wax. In France, even today, some rural auctions are concluded at that moment at which a candle burns out.

It was, however, in the Far East, that fire-clocks were most widely used, with considerable variety in both design and application. The Chinese used to observe the fall in the level of oil in a lamp in much the same way as Europeans used a graduated candle. A cord similar to an impregnated hemp 'slow match' was widely used in China. Divisions of the day were indicated by knots in the cord. A returning missionary related that such cords were used as a poor man's alarm clock. Cut to a suitable length, one end was placed between the toes and the other ignited before sleep descended. Most Far Eastern fire-clocks, however, involve the burning of some type of incense, be it in fairly soft upright joss-sticks, in harder horizontal sticks or helical coils, or in trails of powder. The joss-sticks were marked off vertically in hours. They are used, not only as timekeeping incense-sticks in temples, but also at sea and in coalmines, to time the ship's watches and miners' 3-hour shifts. In Geisha houses, they were set into holes in a box, labelled with each girl's name. As each stick burned to box level, another was lit and when the man left, a quick count of the stubs showed how much he owed. Joss-sticks were also used to mark the end of the permitted period for groups of elderly scholars engaged in composing poetry to time. A string, with a bell attached, was tied round the stick, and when the stick had burned down to that level, the bell dropped off and rang. A similar device involved a harder incense-stick, laid horizontally along the length of a boat-shaped dragon. Pieces of string, with a metal weight on each end, are laid under the incense-stick at regular intervals. When the smouldering zone reaches a string, this burns through and releases the weights into a gong dish below the dragon.

The length of a hard incense stick can be greatly increased by casting the incense into a spiral. Such coils are familiar in the West as mosquito repellents, centrally pivoted on a small metal stand. These green spirals of roughly 15 centimetres in diameter burn out in about 6 hours. Their Eastern predecessors were very much larger and were apically suspended from the ceiling in both temples and houses. They were used for timekeeping as well as for religious ritual and the discouragement of insects; some, equipped with string, weights, and gong-bowl, also acted as striking devices. A seventeenth century Jesuit traveller commented on the cheapness of this type of time-keeper, which put clocks within reach of a much wider range of households than was the case in Europe where clocks were mechanical, and therefore so expensive as to be restricted to the wealthy.

The most highly evolved form of fire-clock is surely the intriguing 'incense seal', so called only on account of its appearance, which

Shen-Li's 'Hundred Graduation Incense Seal' (AD 1073)

resembles a seal with an intricate, incised design. We are lucky to
have a full description of one designed in China in AD 1073, a year
when there was a drought so great that no water was available for
the water-clocks then in common use. We are told the names of the
designer, the publisher, and the craftsman and also of the owner,
who caused the design to be recorded in stone for posterity. The
device was a hardwood disc, about 3 centimetres high and of 33
centimetres diameter, within which was an incised folded loop nearly
7 metres long. The indented path was filled with powdered incense,
for which the recipe is given, and the trail ignited at the appropriate
point. The seal had 100 graduations, one per day, so it must have
been more like a calendar than a clock. Of the similar incense seals
used in Japanese temples, some had bamboo sticks to mark the
hours, while others had plates of different types of incense which
allowed each passing hour to be recognized by its distinctive smell.
From the beginning of the Ming period (which started in the fourteenth century of the Christian era) many beautiful examples were
made. Some are still used as incense burners, but have lost their timekeeping function, except for marking different phases in religious
ritual.

16

Fire as sleuth

Not all substances are combustible, but many of those which are not themselves ignited by a flame are in some way altered by it. We have seen in Chapter 8 how cooks, craftsmen, technologists, and chemists have used such changes to improve known materials and to create new ones. Since different substances react to increased temperature in different ways, we can learn much about a material by observing how it is affected by the heat of a flame. Fire has been a particularly valuable probe for the analytical chemist, but we shall see that its use is not restricted to sleuthing about the present; it can also give archaeologists and geophysicists information about the past.

The use of fire for analysis was first prompted by the quest for wealth. Ores were 'tried' in the fire for their precious metal content in Biblical times, and a description of gold assay was given by Theothrastus in the fourth century BC. But before we discuss the various changes involved, we shall look at some of the ways in which heat can affect a sample.

Heat produces many apparently diverse changes in matter, most of which involve a weakening of forces of attraction and an increase in disorder. Examples of changes from cold, sluggish order to hot, frenzied chaos include the melting of solids, the boiling of liquids, the colour of flames, and many chemical decompositions (including pyrolysis), especially those in which gases are given off.

The simple processes of melting and boiling have been widely used by chemists to characterize substances. If a solid sample consists of a single pure substance, it will melt sharply at one particular temperature; and a pure liquid will similarly boil at a single temperature (but as vapours, unlike liquids and solids, can easily be compressed, the boiling point of a liquid is very sensitive to the external pressure). The melting point of a solid and the boiling point of a liquid under a specified pressure form part of the substance's chemical fingerprint; and if a solid melts, or a liquid boils, over a range of temperatures, we know that the sample must contain more than one substance.

Substances often decompose on heating into simpler ones, so producing an overall increase in disorder. Many of us have heated the blue crystals of hydrated copper sulphate and seen them turn first pale blue and finally white, as the water in the crystals is driven off to give the anhydrous solid and highly disordered water vapour, which then condenses in the colder neck of the test tube. Simple laboratory investigations to identify unknown substances often start with the basic test of heating it in a bunsen flame, to see if, for example, there is a change in colour or evolution of a gas. Thus carbonates often give off carbon dioxide, some nitrates give oxygen, and others give brown fumes of oxides of nitrogen. On heating, the green copper ore, malachite (which contains hydrated basic copper carbonate), loses both water vapour and carbon dioxide, and turns into black copper oxide. This reaction was probably familiar to the early copper smiths, for when the copper oxide comes into contact with red-hot charcoal, it yields metallic copper and gaseous carbon monoxide, yet another example of the use of high temperatures to yield a more disordered state.

Naturally, when a substance breaks down into simpler components, the decomposition occurs at a particular temperature and the liberation of a gaseous product produces a definite percentage loss of weight. Measurement of how the weight decreases as the temperature is raised can therefore tell us exactly how the decomposition takes place. If we already know how two single substances, say the carbonates of magnesium and calcium, decompose when heated, measurement of the weight loss which occurs when a mixture of the two is heated can tell us how much of each component is present. This 'thermogravimetric' method of chemical analysis, although based on reactions which were first investigated in the heat of a bunsen flame, is now carried out electrically.

One modern method of chemical analysis, flame photometry, still uses fire itself to produce the high temperatures required. The pyrotechnists (see Chapter 13) were the first to exploit the characteristic colours emitted by volatilized metal salts. Familiar flame colours include the yellow of sodium and the lilac of potassium seen at the base of wood fires. Barium gives an apple green and calcium a brick red, while lithium and strontium both give crimsons, which although very similar to the human eye, may be distinguished with a spectroscope, which analyses the emitted light into its constituent energies. The colour (and spectroscopic analysis) of the flame tells us which element is present in a solution, while the intensity is a measure of its concentration. The method is widely used for the clinical determination of, for example, potassium and lithium in the blood (cf. Plate 16).

The analytical chemist often makes use of fire to bring about some change in a mixture of the sample with some other material. If he wishes to determine the minor constituents of many organic materials such as biological samples, they are often first ignited, in order to expel the carbon and hydrogen atoms (as carbon dioxide and water vapour) and to convert compounds of trace metals such as molybdenum into non-volatile oxides. These remain in the ash which can be analysed more easily if major constituents are absent; spectroscopic methods are often used.

Pre-instrumental techniques for identifying an unknown solid salt included converting it to a metal oxide and then heating it with charcoal, which changes some but not all of the oxides into their free metals. Another classical procedure involved incorporating the salt into a transparent bead by heating it with borax in a bunsen flame. Many metals give characteristic colours, reminiscent of stained glass: the cobalt bead, for example, is a deep blue. In the hands of an experienced analyst, these simple visual tests yielded a wealth of information.

The oldest use of fire for analysis was probably the testing of ores for their content of precious metal. So far as we can tell, the ancient procedures were similar to some still used for assaying gold and silver. The crushed ore is treated with lead oxide and a flux which will combine with the unwanted mineral matrix. Heating with charcoal converts the oxide to molten lead, which dissolves small amounts of the precious metals present; and further heating melts the minerals into the flux. On cooling, there remains a metal button, surrounded by brittle slag which can be hammered off. The button is placed in a 'cupel' (a shallow cup of absorbent material such as bone

The assay of copper ores (C) in furnaces (A and D) using lever-operated bellows (E) or steam aeolipile (F). The flux is prepared in pots (G) and the metal collected in assay crucibles (H) (1574).

ash) and heated in an oxidizing furnace. The lead is reconverted to (molten) oxide, which is absorbed by the cupel, leaving a much smaller metal button consisting of precious metals. The silver can be dissolved out using boiling nitric acid, leaving a brown residue of metallic gold. Annealing converts this to the familiar golden metal, which can be weighed.

Not only is fire an invaluable tool for the analyst, but the effects of ancient fires also have much to offer the sleuth. Even its destructive power can yield significant information. The worldwide appearance of soot in iridium-rich rocks deposited about 144 million years ago has been interpreted by some (but by no means all) geologists as evidence of a global fire caused by impact with a huge meteorite.

Fires of a more recent vintage have left a wealth of information for the archaeologist. Traces of charcoal on fossilized wood and bone tell us about the earliest users of fire, both for lighting and cooking (see Chapters 5 and 6). Most wood does not, however, become fossilized, but eventually rots away after hosting a variety of fungi and other organisms. One obvious contribution of fire is its ability to convert wood into charcoal which contains no nutrients and so survives. An estimate of the time elapsed since, as living wood, it absorbed carbon dioxide from the atmosphere, can be obtained from carbon-14 dating. When iron has been smelted in a fire, some of the carbon from the fuel is taken up by the metal, and so this, too, can be dated by the carbon-14 method. Forgeries of icons have been detected by finding that the carbon contained by the nails in the frame had far too high a carbon-14 content for the alleged date; the iron had been smelted together with wood which had been alive demonstrably more recently.

The high temperatures needed to fire and glaze pottery interrupt some of the geophysical processes occurring in clay and in objects made from it. Natural radioactive decay, for example, can dislodge an electron from its regular position in a soil particle, leaving a vacant electron site or 'hole'. The longer the sample is exposed to radiation, the more such defects accumulate. When a pot is fired, the high temperature enables these trapped electrons to move back to their former sites and a solid with fewer defects is regenerated. In a pot which is later buried, however, defects continue to be produced, and remain trapped in increasing numbers as the millennia pass. If the pot is again heated, the defects are removed as before; and since the ceramic returns to a slightly more stable state, a little energy is given out. There is a weak 'thermoluminescent' glow, in addition to the expected red glow of the ceramic at high temperatures. (A repeat procedure produces only the red glow, as the first heating has removed the defects.) Thermoluminescence, therefore, forms the basis of a method for estimating the time which has elapsed since removal of defects by firing.

Most clay contains iron, and many iron minerals are sensitive to the Earth's magnetic field. They do not often behave as permanent magnets, because, although small regions ('domains') of the mineral may act individually in this way, the domains themselves are oriented at random, or nearly so, and their effects largely cancel out. At normal temperatures, there is little chance for domains to change orientation, but at the high temperatures used in firing, the domains become free and some of them take up the orientation of the Earth's magnetic field. As the Earth's field gradually changes, it might seem that this 'thermoremnant' magnetism could provide information about when a ceramic was fired. We should, of course, need to know how the Earth's magnetism has varied at a particular firing site throughout the pottery-firing era, together with the orientation of the furnace relative to the magnetic pole, and of the ceramic relative to the furnace. The situation is not, however, as hopeless as it might seem, as magnetic data can be combined with results from other dating techniques. Some sites of ancient furnaces do survive and although pots were often placed higgledy-piggledy in the kiln for firing, more regular objects, such as tiles and bricks were indeed often stacked in a particular orientation. Measurement of the thermo-remnant magnetism can therefore help the geophysicist to obtain a picture of how the terrestrial magnetism has varied throughout the ages at various places. Once this 'calibration' system has been established, magnetic measurements will help the archaeologist to date at least those ceramic objects which were fired in a known orientation.

So in both thermoluminescence and in thermoremnant magnetism, fire acts as an archaeological 'stopwatch' by temporarily 'loosening' the ceramic lattice. But while the luminescence of pottery increases with age, because of the changes which occur within it, the magnetism of an artifact is fixed by firing and the subsequent changes observed are those which have taken place externally in the Earth's field.

17

Fire as polluter

We have seen in Chapter 14 that we use smoke to repel, or even to kill, some of our more unwelcome fellow creatures. The ill-effects of combustion products are not however limited to those organisms which mankind deems undesirable; they also impinge not only on ourselves but also on the entire planet. Major problems can arise in our fire-oriented technology even before ignition has occurred. Unless sufficient care is taken when collecting and transporting the fuel, coal-miners will succumb to such respiratory problems as silicosis, and marine habitats will be laid waste by oil slicks. Here, however, we shall concentrate on the products of combustion and discuss how they afflict our environment with a condition which, although chronic, is not necessarily untreatable. The acutely destructive effects of unwanted fire form the subject of the next section of this book.

Many of the noxious substances emitted by combustion in the course of man's activities are emitted in quantities which are small compared with those generated by natural processes. Mankind produces only about one-tenth of the total quantity of carbon monoxide in the atmosphere, the bulk of which arises from the combination of naturally occurring methane with insufficient oxygen to produce carbon dioxide. Only for smoke and sulphur dioxide does man outstrip nature. If the products of combustion were immediately dispersed throughout the atmosphere, they would do little harm. Unfortunately, however, they are generated in centres of population and industrialization, in some of which geographical and meteorological factors conspire to minimize dispersion. Such regions may suffer severely from atmospheric pollution.

Even complete combustion of a pure fossil fuel such as octane to carbon dioxide and water is an ecological hazard, although neither of these gases is toxic. Nowadays, more carbon dioxide is generated than can be dissolved in the oceans or absorbed by green plants during photosynthesis, and the increased concentration in the atmosphere contributes to the so-called 'greenhouse' effect. Some of the heat energy emitted by the sun is taken up by plants on the earth's surface and then re-emitted. Carbon dioxide can absorb some of this released energy as it is of just the right wavelength to make its molecules vibrate. Since the carbon dioxide in the atmosphere prevents the escape of energy from the earth's surface, an increase in the emission of carbon dioxide is one of the factors which, it is feared, might lead to global warming. At present the carbon dioxide concentration is increasing only extremely slowly, but the possible long term effects are causing grave concern since a few degrees increase in temperature could result in the reduction of the polar icecap and marked climatic and ecological changes. But since the temperature of the atmosphere is determined by several factors in addition to the carbon dioxide content, it is difficult to predict it with confidence.

The pollution of the atmosphere by man's activities is no new phenomenon. The smoke which hangs over the countryside after the burning of stubble must be little different from that generated since prehistoric times by 'slash and burn' land clearance. But the scale is changing. Astronauts have reported thick clouds of smoke hovering over Amazonia, and, after the Gulf War, over Kuwait (see Chapter 7).

Much of the nuisance value of large-scale burning is due, not to carbon dioxide and water, but to the irritant soot particles formed by incomplete combustion. Domestic fires, the industrial revolution, and the internal combustion engine have exacerbated the problem by introducing small amounts of highly noxious impurities: sulphur is a natural ingredient of coal and the heavier petrochemical oils, while lead has often been added to motor fuel as an antiknock (see Chapter 10). King Edward I, who reigned from 1272 to 1307, prohibited the burning of coal in London while Parliament was in session, the penalty for an offender being the loss of his head. John Evelyn described the atmosphere of London in 1661 as 'an impure and thick

Fire action

Any person discovering a fire

1 Sound the alarm.
2 Call fire brigade.
3 Attack the fire if possible using the appliances provided.

On hearing the fire alarm

4 Leave by the nearest available route.
5 Close all doors behind you.
6 Report to your assembly point.

Do not take risks.
Do not return to the building for any reason until authorised to do so.

Do not use lifts.

KNOW YOUR FIRE EXTINGUISHER COLOUR CODE

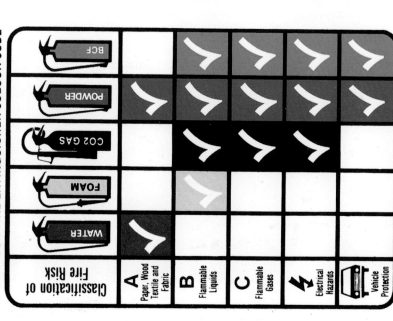

Classification of Fire Risk	WATER	FOAM	CO2 GAS	POWDER	BCF
A Paper, Wood Textile and Fabric	✓			✓	
B Flammable Liquids		✓	✓	✓	✓
C Flammable Gases			✓	✓	✓
⚡ Electrical Hazards			✓	✓	✓
🚗 Vehicle Protection				✓	✓

19 Fire action card

20 Capping a burning oil-well

Factory chimneys at St
Rollox soda works,
Glasgow, about 1800

Mist accompanied with a fuliginous and filthy vapour'. The burning
of coal, at first for domestic purposes, but later greatly reinforced by
industrial consumption, continued to poison the air of London until
the Clean Air Acts of 1956 and 1968, and was responsible for the
'pea-souper' smogs for which the city was notorious.

This type of thick khaki smog is most likely to form if sulphur-rich
smoke is emitted into a damp atmosphere at about 0 °C, and so
London, with its climate and its ready supply of bituminous, sulphur-
rich coal was particularly vulnerable. A smog-forming smoke contains not only sulphur dioxide, but also minute particles of solids,
such as soot, silica, alumina, and metal oxides. The smog is formed
'synergistically', that is, by the interaction of the components. The
cool water vapour condenses around the particles of solid, forming
tiny droplets of fog. The particles in the smoke have a high surface
area and can act as catalysts, speeding up the oxidation of sulphur
dioxide by atmospheric oxygen to give the trioxide. Both these
oxides dissolve in the water droplets: the dioxide gives the mildly
acidic sulphurous acid, while the trioxide forms the strongly acidic
sulphuric acid. However, sulphurous acid is more readily oxidized
than its parent oxide, so it, too, is liable to end up as the highly
corrosive sulphuric acid. Since droplets of a certain size are readily
trapped in the human respiratory system, such smogs are extremely
harmful, especially to young children, to old people, and to those
already suffering from respiratory disease. In 1952, over 4000 people
died in London from smog-related causes. The synergic nature of the
problem is emphasized by the fact that much less serious symptoms

were observed in workers who had been accidentally exposed to the same levels of sulphur, but in the form of the dioxide only. The presence of particulates and droplets naturally caused a decrease in visibility, often reducing it to only one or two yellowish metres. Stone, especially limestone, became eroded by attack from the acid, and the rate of corrosion of metals increased. The 'pea-souper' has been banished by removing only one of the factors responsible for its formation. The winter air of London is still cold, humid, and sulphur-laden, but the 'smokeless' fuels and more efficient combustion now required by legislation has reduced the particulates to a level below that needed to nucleate the smog.

Many other cities have also benefited from decreased emission of smoke. In the industrial north of England, for example, many buildings and trees were blackened by deposits of soot from factory chimneys. The predominant murk of such regions is reflected in the appearance of an urban variety of the Peppered Moth (*Biston betularia*). Before the Industrial Revolution, the moth had a pale, mottled appearance, well adapted to camouflage when settled on a lichen covered tree-trunk. As the air became more polluted, however, the lichen disappeared and was replaced by soot. A dark form of the moth became increasingly common in urban areas, although the paler variety persisted away from industrial regions. At present, the decline of the dark form is a happy confirmation of the decrease in the soot content of the atmosphere. Soot can also be an indoor problem, especially in churches where icons and statues have been blackened from centuries of candles and oil lamps. In many catholic churches, fire has now been replaced by coin-operated electric 'candles'.

However, reduction of soot by no means solves all the problems of pollution by industrial combustion. The sulphur dioxide in the atmosphere has increased thirtyfold since 1860, as a result of increased coal-burning to meet the ever-growing needs of industry and of electrical generators. Most of this increase has occurred since the Second World War. As we have seen, sulphur dioxide is readily converted to sulphuric acid in the presence of oxygen and water. It has long been known that unusually acidic rain falls in the industrial regions of the North East of the United States, neighbouring parts of Canada, and the industrial north of England. If the pollution is particularly acute, the rain can have a pH as low as 2, which is 1000-fold more acidic than the mild acidity of normal rain, caused by

Pepper moth, *Biston betularia* (a) on lichened oak, melanic form, f. *carbonaria*, above pale form, f. *typica*; (b) on polluted oak, f. *typica*, above f. *carbonaria*

dissolved carbon dioxide. A new problem associated with 'acid rain' results from the building of tall chimneys designed to remove the sulphur dioxide from the area in which it is generated. They are so successful that the corrosive rain may fall a considerable distance (as far as 1000 kilometres) away from its place of origin, often crossing national boundaries and causing grievous damage in countries which played no part in generating the pollution. Acid rain appears to cause more harm to crops and forests than it does directly to the animal kingdom, although the increased acidity of lakes and rivers has grave ecological implications. The effect is particularly serious on granite rocks, which, unlike many sedimentary ones, can do nothing to reduce the acidity. Acid rain also causes damage to buildings and statuary of marble and limestone, which are gradually dissolved by the acid.

As it is expensive to remove sulphur compounds from fuels before combustion, it is better to remove the sulphur dioxide either from the effluent gases or as it is being formed. Thus powdered limestone may be added to the fuel feed in fluidized bed combustion, and the resulting calcium sulphate removed as ash. The more radical solution of using coal which contains less sulphur needs serious consideration, despite the economic and social implications for countries whose coal is rich in sulphur.

A more recent form of pollution arises from the internal combustion engine, which generates various incompletely burned products, such as carbon monoxide, pyrolysed and partially oxidized fuel fragments (sometimes recombined), molecules and droplets of unburned fuel, and soot. At the high temperatures of the post-flame gases, nitric oxide, NO, is formed, probably both by direct reaction of free oxygen atoms with nitrogen gas and via a complex series of reactions initiated by reaction of oxygen gas with hydrogen atoms, and of nitrogen gas with fuel fragments. Some of these changes are activated by sunlight. As with the products of coal combustion, the components of the exhaust gases may themselves be harmful, and they may form further noxious substances by reaction with each other and with other species which are present in the atmosphere. Carbon monoxide, for example, causes behavioural disturbances in humans at those concentrations (85 parts per million (ppm)) reached in urban rush-hour traffic, and may contribute to accidents. In its normal concentrations (about 0.2 ppm) in industrial regions it has no direct influence on man, but any increase in this value leads to a decrease in the concentration of the hydroxyl group. This species (OH) consisting of one atom of oxygen and one of hydrogen, is unstable, and reacts with numerous other species, including many noxious ones generated by human activities. An increase in carbon monoxide output would therefore upset the balance of atmospheric reactions in which the OH group does an invaluable job as a scavenger for other pollutants.

The fate of the exhaust from internal combustion engines, like that of the emissions from coal-burning, is extremely sensitive to geographical factors. The conditions needed for smog-formation from traffic exhaust are, however, very different from those which gave rise to the synergic London pea-souper. They are exemplified by the city of Los Angeles, which has a warm, sunny climate and is situated by the sea, in a basin surrounded by hills; but many other traffic-ridden cities, such as Tokyo and Athens, have similar situations, and similar smogs. In Los Angeles itself, over 10 000 tonnes of exhaust gases are emitted daily. The geographical conditions cause the air temperature to increase with increased height above the city, instead of undergoing the normal decrease (as experienced by mountain walkers). This temperature inversion prevents the usual convective mixing by downward flow of cleaner, colder, more dense air to replace the warmer, lighter, and more polluted air at ground level. In effect, the layer of warm air across the top of the encircling hills acts as a lid which prevents the pollutants from escaping. The sunlight is necessary to trigger off the complex changes which give rise to the smog.

A fundamental step in the formation of a 'photochemical' or 'Los Angeles' smog involves the oxidation of nitric oxide NO to the brown nitrogen dioxide NO_2, and of atmospheric oxygen O_2 to ozone O_3. These reactions do not occur directly, but via atomic oxygen which is produced by the photodissociation of nitrogen dioxide. So the action of sunlight on air polluted by nitric oxide establishes an equilibrium between nitrogen dioxide and oxygen on the one hand, and nitric oxide and ozone on the other. Sunlight also breaks down some of the ozone to give excited oxygen atoms which attack the molecules of water and the traces of methane normally present in the atmosphere. The various fragments which are produced interact with each other and with the original pollutants, by a complex network of probably over 100 reaction steps, some of which are themselves also initiated by sunlight. The detailed pathways are not yet fully understood, but the pollutants which are present in low, but harmful, quantities include hydrocarbons (saturated, unsaturated, and aromatic), aldehydes, and peroxyacyl nitrates ('PAN').

As the formation of a photochemical smog depends both on the concentration of exhaust gases and on the intensity of sunlight, it is not surprising that the individual concentrations vary with the time of day. The harmful effects of the smog include decreased visibility, leading to more road and air accidents, respiratory diseases (from ozone and PAN), acute eye irritation (from PAN), increased vulnerability to cancer (from aromatics), and an unpleasant smell (from nitrogen dioxide, ozone, aldehydes, and aromatics). Many of the pollutants harm plants by suppressing photosynthesis. Ozone produced near ground level can cause damage also to some non-living matter, accelerating the rotting of fabrics, the bleaching of dyes, and the ageing of rubber. All exhaust fumes from fuels which contain lead antiknocks carry particles of lead oxide and lead salts which can affect the growing brain and are thought to cause hyperactivity and delinquency in young people. Clearly, it is desirable that these many noxious emissions be reduced as much as possible, even though some of the measures now available add to the cost of buying or running a vehicle. Social conscience must surely go some way to counterbalancing economic disincentive.

There are two main approaches to the cleaning-up of exhaust gases. The engine may be designed to produce fewer noxious substances and the products may be treated to make them less harmful before they are emitted. Unfortunately, the criteria for engine design are conflicting, and here again the details of the chemistry involved are not fully understood. Spark ignition engines normally run on fuel-rich mixtures in order to achieve good power and smooth running (see Chapter 10). Combustion is therefore incomplete and produces appreciable amounts of smoke, carbon monoxide, and hydrocarbon fragments. Use of a leaner mixture would decrease pollution from these sources, but would have other disadvantages. Not only would it reduce the performance of the engine, but it would increase the output of nitric oxide, which is favoured by a higher oxygen content of the fuel mix. Since nitric oxide is generated in appreciable amounts only at very high temperatures, its formation can be considerably reduced by injecting water into the combustion chamber as a coolant; but problems of economics and design have so far prevented commercial adoption of this ploy. One strategy is to improve engine design so that leaner mixtures can be used without loss of power. Formation of carbon monoxide and organic fragments is reduced, and the increased nitric oxide is partly removed after combustion. Modifications include the standardization of fuel mix between the cylinders, and stratified charge and pre-charge combustion chambers (see Chapter 10). A recycling procedure is needed to tackle the nitric oxide. The fuel mixture is diluted with up to 20 per cent of exhaust gas, which so lowers the temperature of combustion that the concentration of nitric oxide is reduced to less than half its former value; but this procedure may increase the concentrations of other pollutants.

Since it seems unlikely that improvements in engine design will succeed in producing combustion gases with an acceptable level of pollutants, it is probably best to convert these into a less noxious form before they leave the vehicle. The incompletely burned products, including carbon monoxide, may be fully oxidized to carbon dioxide after leaving the combustion chamber. The gases, mixed with air, flow through a platinum/rhodium mesh which catalyses their combustion with oxygen (see Chapter 3) so that they are converted to carbon dioxide. Some converters first decompose oxides of nitrogen to their elements. The engine is run on a fuel rich mixture, and the exhaust gases, which contain almost no oxygen, are passed through a platinum catalyst. Air is then admitted and the exhaust is passed through a normal catalytic converter to complete the combustion. Both types of catalyst are, however, inactivated by even a trace of any fuel containing a lead antiknock.

It seems that the problem of photochemical smog is not technologically insoluble; but it remains to be seen whether there is sufficient corporate will to overcome the social problems produced by increased cost and decreased convenience. The smog problem in such geographically sensitive cities as Los Angeles and Athens should be tackled both by reducing the emission of noxious substances from vehicles and by drastic reduction in the traffic flow. Social factors, such as legislation, economic incentives, and exhortation are clearly important, and a first-rate system of public transport is essential. Lead antiknocks are already banned in many countries and there are restrictions on the use of private cars and petrol-driven mowers in some smog-prone cities. Legislation to encourage the use of electric cars, as in Los Angeles, reduces the emissions leading to

Pollution near rocket launch pad

photochemical smog, but at the expense of higher consumption of current electricity and so of increased pollution from combustion of coal in the generating plant.

At the outset of the space shuttle programme, much concern was expressed about the possible pollution of the stratosphere. Although only small quantities of oxides of nitrogen are emitted, it was feared that ozone depletion might result from the use of ammonium perchlorate solid fuel boosters, which release hydrogen chloride gas during the launch. Recent estimates suggest that the effect is very small.

Pollution of upper atmosphere by solid fuel propellants of the rocket Ariane

Progress is also being made in the struggle against pollution by another type of combustion; that of tobacco. In addition to nicotine, the experiencing of which is one of the aims of tobacco smoking, the smoke also contains aromatic hydrocarbons, which are generally accepted to be carcinogenic, and enough carbon monoxide to worsen cardiac and respiratory diseases. It is believed that pollution caused by tobacco smoking is much more harmful than that which results from combustion of coal or motor fuel and can cause not only lung cancer but also heart disease and miscarriage. Moreover, it renders the smoker most vulnerable to the effects of these other pollutants, and has a deleterious effect on those members of the family or work-team who share the indoor environment, not least since the air oxidizes some of the components of tobacco smoke to give even more severely carcinogenic substances. Some 'passive smokers', such as the unborn, the old, and the unwell, may be more vulnerable than the smokers themselves. As with all forms of pollution, however, a balance must be struck between the good done by that form of combustion and the harm done by the side effects. The use of coal to generate electricity not only provides a service which is now considered essential to an industrialized community, but also minimizes the use of nuclear power, about which many responsible critics have expressed great concern. Tobacco smoking, despite its medical dangers, can also provide valuable relief from tension. All forms of combustion, whether for national economy or personal pleasure, should surely be undertaken with the good sense to use the least noxious material possible, to disperse the products as efficiently as possible, and to exercise consideration and restraint.

A pipe in the form of the tower of the Houses of Parliament; the 'Pipesmoker of the Year' award for 1992, presented to Mr Tony Benn, MP

IV

Fire as hazard

1838. January 27th. Early in the morning of Saturday, January 27th, a fire was discovered in the south wing of the University Press; happily, however, from the promptitude of those giving the alarm, and the admirable provisions made in that establishment, the fire was subdued in four hours, and the building has not sustained any material injury. The fire was confined to the large press room and the room over it, the loss consisting principally of type and paper. After a careful and minute investigation of the circumstances connected with the origin of the fire, it was the unanimous opinion of the Delegates that it was caused by the ignition of the timbers near the Western Store. The Board of Delegates have expressed both in words and liberal donations the sense they entertain of the important services rendered by all persons to the University on that occasion.

The Bible Committee were requested to consider the propriety of employing a watchman nightly upon the premises.

It was ordered that Messrs Arnett and Wright be requested every night to examine the rooms connected with the department immediately before retiring to rest. Extract from the Minutes of Delegates of the Oxford University Press,
27 January 1838.

18

Mankind versus fire: (1) The toll

On 28 January 1986, television viewers throughout the world were shocked and saddened to witness the deaths of seven trained astronauts during the tragic accident at the launch of the spacecraft Challenger. It seemed that, because of the cold weather, the shrinkage of a gasket allowed hot exhaust gases to leak slightly from the join between two sections of the solid booster. The heat eventually broke a strut and pierced the tank carrying liquid hydrogen. Ignition occurred in the wrong place at the wrong time; and fire took its toll of human life and of material resources. Happily the knowledge and skill of those engaged in space technology makes such accidents extremely rare.

However, fire takes its toll on human life in other ways. In the UK there are about 1000 fire deaths a year. Between 1961 and 1972 the number of people killed by fire in the USA was 143 550, over three times as many as those killed in action in Vietnam (45 925) over the same period. Of these, about two-thirds were in private houses and one-sixth in other residential buildings. Predictably, the majority of these fires occurred at night. For about 60 per cent of those killed in fires in both the UK and the USA, death is caused by inhalation of toxic gases or smoke rather than by burns or other injuries. And for every person killed by fire in industrial nations, there are about five hospital patients who need prolonged surgical or medical care, mainly for very severe burns. It is generally recognized that such injuries are difficult and distressing to treat, because of both the extreme pain which the patients suffer and the many serious secondary effects which often develop. Since the dangers of fire are all too familiar, it seems odd that a civilization with the technological skill to develop relatively safe space travel should allow fire to gain control and inflict such suffering.

It is of interest that domestic fires seem first to have been a problem in ancient Rome, although clumsy drunks who knock over lamps feature in the earlier literature of ancient Greece. The emphasis was, however, on the mess made by the spilled oil rather than on fires caused, probably because the Greek homes were so much more sparsely furnished than the Roman ones. The explanation of the high present-day toll of fire does not, however, rest entirely on the increasing affluence of a society which surrounds itself with combustibles, perhaps at a greater rate than it hedges itself with safety regulations. In the late 1970s the number of deaths per head of population in Canada and the USA was almost twice that in France, Japan, Sweden, and the UK, and almost three times that in Australia, Switzerland, and West Germany.

The toll of uncontrolled fire is not of course confined to human life and physical health; important though these are, we must also remember that undisciplined fires cause immense material and economic loss, and that this, too, is deleterious to human wellbeing. In the next two chapters, we shall discuss ways in which we can attempt both to prevent unwanted fires from starting, and to limit the harm they do if they should occur. But before we can discuss the tactics we should use in our fight against fire, we must consider how an accidental fire, once started, can develop. Since most fire deaths and casualties occur in buildings and vehicles, we shall first describe the spread of fire in confined spaces. Discussion of wildfire, which of course can also cause vast economic damage, will be deferred until Chapter 22.

Fire, as we have seen, requires a suitable mixture of fuel and oxidant at a temperature sufficient to break down the fuel into excited fragments which combine with the oxidant and so emit enough heat to keep the combustion going. If we exclude fires in factories which manufacture or make use of oxidizing substances, the oxidant is usually atmospheric oxygen, and the reactive gaseous fragments are provided by pyrolysis either of vaporized liquids or of solid fuels. Whether or not a flammable mixture of fuel and air is actually ignited by, say, a spark, or by fleeting contact with a hot object, depends not only on the nature of the mixture, but also on the heat source: on its temperature, its extent, and its duration. The ability of a fire, once ignited, to sustain and accelerate its growth depends partly on the flow of heat from the hot combustion products back to the potential fuel; and this feed-back depends on the surroundings. Laboratory experiments using a hood as a simulated ceiling have confirmed our experience that confined fires, in which heat is reradiated down on to the fuel, burn much faster than unconfined ones. If a reaction which generates a large volume of gas occurs in a confined space, such as a building, the pressure will increase rapidly and may cause an explosion, even though the same substance would burn normally, rather than detonate, in the open air.

In our present era, the main causes of accidental fires in buildings are cooking devices, cigarettes, and faulty electrical circuits, the last two factors being responsible for the majority of fatal fires. Let us follow the all too common series of events which occur when a lighted cigarette is inadvertently dropped down the side of an upholstered armchair. The smoker forgets it and leaves the room, closing the door behind him. The cigarette smoulders, as it is designed to do, without bursting into flame. It generates enough heat to pyrolyse and char the cloth upholstery, and some of the pyrolysis products will be oxidized by the air. However, the oxygen supply to the crevice between the cushion and the inner edge of the chair is limited, and the gaps in the weave of the cloth are increasingly occupied by volatile decomposition products. Oxidation occurs slowly, generating enough heat only to char neighbouring fibres, without producing a flame. The chair smoulders. The slow combustion may reach the filling of the cushion and the charred area becomes larger, moving into a region where air circulates more freely. Pyrolysis products, including toxic fumes and smoke, are emitted, and increased heat is generated. When the temperature and air supply are both adequate, the chair bursts into flame. A similar result is obtained if a lighted match is accidentally dropped on to many fabrics.

A smouldering fire may develop quite fast or moderately slowly, but once a flame has appeared, destruction progresses rapidly. The hot fumes and smoke from the, as yet localized, fire rise in a plume from the burning chair to the ceiling. Being less dense than the colder air in the room, the combustion products collect in the highest position possible, forming an increasingly hot layer which spreads rapidly under the ceiling, radiating heat back to the room, and pyrolysing the surface of any flammable object present. In a room 2.5 metres high, this happens when the ceiling temperature is about 600 °C. Within an alarmingly brief period, all combustible surfaces in the room have reached spontaneous ignition point and burst into flame simultaneously. Once this 'flash-over' has occurred, any attempt at escape or rescue from that room is out of the question. The fire will have taken its full toll.

What of the rest of the building? Unfortunately, the door of the fire room is not hermetically sealed, and hot pyrolysis products stream out round the top of the closed door, displacing the cooler air from the ceiling outside it. Cold air is sucked in from any available crack along the floor of the corridor; but it does not enter the fire room. Rather, when it meets the closed door, it is sucked up towards the hot pyrolysis products which are flowing away from the fire. Within the fire room, the oxygen supply is being used up, but the temperature is still very high and so large quantities of incompletely burned pyrolysis products stream out, together with flames, around the door, thereby enriching and heating the combustible gases below the ceiling. When these meet the incoming air, flash-over occurs in the corridor, too. The hot, buoyant, fuel-rich gases rise wherever they can, to the ceilings of passages and open rooms and up stairwells and lift-shafts. On contact with air, they ignite and the whole building becomes ablaze, almost literally in a flash. The difference in temperature between the burning region and the air outside can create large differences in pressure between the floors of a tall building, drawing smoke and hot gases through it with considerable speed. This 'stack effect' is held responsible for the rapid spread of fire in the MGM building in Las Vegas in 1981.

It is obvious that no living matter could survive the high temperatures generated at flash-over, or indeed the temperatures of the incompletely burned gases streaming from the fire room. The temperature of some burning polymers is 1200 °C (mild burns can be caused by exposure to a temperature as low as 65 °C for only 1 second). Even quite small increases in temperature cause dehydration and heat exhaustion, followed by collapse. The heat produced by the fire is not however the only factor which kills, nor even the main one. More than half of those who die in a fire are later found to have been killed by inhaling toxic gases and smoke before the body suffered severe burns. The main killer is carbon monoxide which owes its

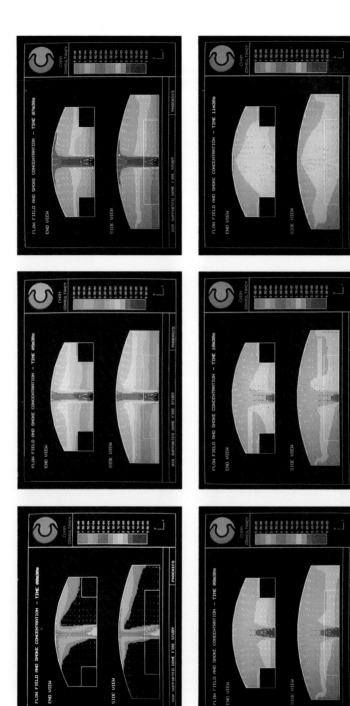

21 Fire modelling for a domed building

22 Forest fire

high toxicity to the fact that it combines with the oxygen-carrying haemoglobin in the blood 200 times faster than does oxygen itself. Even when uncontaminated air is again available, the carbon monoxide is slow to detach itself from haemoglobin and so it much reduces the amount of uncombined haemoglobin and hence the amount of oxygen which the blood can carry round the body. Moreover, even of those who survive carbon monoxide poisoning, one-third have lasting psychological and memory problems. Many fire victims are found to have inhaled more than the lethal amount of hydrogen cyanide, a highly toxic gas which is formed during the combustion of many of the synthetic acrylic polymers used for upholstery and decoration. (Almost all of these have, however, also inhaled carbon monoxide considerably in excess of the lethal amount.) Smoke exacerbates the danger of the combustion gases both because it irritates the lungs, making them more susceptible to toxins, and because the soot particles absorb various poisonous pyrolysis products, such as aldehydes, and so concentrates them in the lungs.

Discussion of the dangers of smoke-laden toxic gases cannot, however, be limited to mere numerical consideration of the period of exposure to particular concentrations of harmful products. Inhaled at well below the lethal level, these gases stupefy the victims, hindering them from making sensible decisions about what they should do. The reduction of the oxygen content of the air below the normal 21 per cent has a similar effect. At less than 15 per cent, judgement deteriorates, while reduction to 10 per cent leads to reversible collapse. Less than 6 per cent is lethal. More oxygen is needed for exertion, for those who are excited, for smokers, and for those who have heart–lung problems. Fear itself can kill, not only by causing a heart attack, but also by generating counter-productive panic instead of useful action.

Attempts to escape may be hazardous, or even fatal, if they involve jumping from an upper window, or becoming crushed and trampled at an exit. Those who remain in or near a burning building may be killed if part of it should collapse. And, as we have seen, many of those survivors who have suffered burn injuries do not survive the complications which may follow. Whilst taking full account of the gross physical damage which fire inflicts, we must not forget the psychological damage which fire does to those who have suffered injury, bereavement, fear and material loss, some of which may represent not only money but a lifetime of creative toil. Clearly, all reasonable attempts should be made to prevent fire from taking its horrific toll. The next two chapters are concerned with the scientific tactics which we use to minimize both the chances of accidental fire and the damage that such fire can do (see Plate 17)

19

Mankind versus fire: (2) Prevention

The best way of lowering the toll taken by uncontrolled fire is to prevent it from occurring. During the English Civil War (1642–6), a broadsheet was published, listing the causes of fire:

SEASONABLE ADVICE

For Preventing the Mischiefe of Fire, that may come by Negligence, Treason, or Otherwise

Ordered to be printed by the Lord Mayor of London.

And is Thought Very Necessary to Hang in Every Man's House, Especially in These Dangerous Times.

Invented by William Gosling, Engineer.

How many severall ways, Houses, Townes, and Cities, habe beene set a-fire.

Some hath been burnt by bad Harths, Chimnies, Ovens, or by pans of fire set upon boards: some by Cloaths hanged against the fire: some by leaving great fires in Chimnies, where the sparkes or sickles breaking fell and fired the boards, painted Cloaths, Wainscots, Rufhes, Matts, as houses were burnt in Shoreditch: some by Powder, or shooting off Pieces; some by Tinder or Matches: some by setting Candles under shelves: some by leaving Candles neere their beds: some by snuffes of Candles, Tobacco-snuffes, burnt papers: and some by drunkards; as many houses were burnt in

Southwarke: some by warming Beds: some by looking under beds with Candles: some by sleeping at worke, leaving their Candles by them, so many have been burnt of severall Trades: some by setting Candles neere the thatch of houses: some by snuffes or sparkes falne upon Gunpowder, or upon matts, rushes, chips, small coale, and in chinkes; so Wimbleton was burnt: some Townes were burnt by Maultkills: some by Candles in Stables: or by foule chimnies; some by Candles amongst hempe, flaxe, and ware-houses: some by Candles falling out of their Candlesticks: some by sticking their Candles upon posts: some by Lincks knockt at shops, stalls, sellers, windowes, ware-houses, dores, and dangerous places: some by carrying fire from place to place, where the winde hath blowne it about the streets, as it did burne St. Edmondsbury: some by warme Sea-coale sinders put in baskets, or woodden things, as did burne London-Bridge: And some have been burnt without either fire, or Candle, as by wet hay, corne, straw, or by mills, wheeles, or such like: all which hath been by carelesnesse. And some have been fired a purpose by villany or Treason.

Methods for preventing accidental ignition and (see Chapter 21) for combatting fires were also given.

Gamble, writing in London in 1925, attributed all unwanted fire to carelessness. If we exclude fires that are started intentionally by arsonists, rioters, and enemy forces, and those which result from earthquakes and volcanic eruptions, we must concede that most unwanted fires, like other accidents, do not 'just happen' but are 'caused', sometimes by a chain of human errors rather than a single act of carelessness. A survey in 1989 estimated that 43 per cent of domestic fires in the UK were caused by 'misuse' of equipment.

Fire safety may conveniently be discussed in terms of the familiar 'triangle' of oxidizer, heat, and fuel, since we can prevent ignition by adequate reduction of just one of these factors.

The most hazardous oxidizers are those manufactured for use as explosives and propellants; liquid oxygen for medical and technological use; and oxygen-rich salts for research and agricultural purposes. Such materials must be rigorously protected from contact with any potential fuel, and from hot spots which might cause decomposition. In the great majority of accidental fires, however, air acts as oxidant, streaming into the burning region to consume the fuel and spread the flames.

Most buildings contain much flammable material surrounded by freely circulating air, so it would seem that prevention of accidental fire would require absence of our third factor, i.e. any temperature high enough to produce ignition; but total elimination of hot-spots would preclude all conventional cooking, much space-heating, and any smoking. A more realistic target is to reduce the number (and temperature) of hot-spots, to minimize the supply (and flammability) of potential fuels, and to keep the two as far apart as possible. Unfortunately an accidental fire can be started by a very small amount of heat if the potential fuel is sufficiently sensitive. A mixture of a combustible gas with exactly the right amount of air can be ignited by an electrostatic spark carrying as little as one-thousandth of a joule of energy (i.e. about half that which would be given out if one-millionth of a gram of wood burned in air). Such a tiny spark can bring only a minute amount of the flammable gas-mixture to its ignition temperature, but once even a few molecules have acquired enough energy to react, the heat generated by combustion will augment and accelerate the process. A hot-spot which is harmless in one situation may well be lethal in another: the effect of throwing an unextinguished match into a scuttle full of coal is very different from that of throwing it into an open-work basket of waste paper. Since fuel gases are readily flammable when mixed with air (often over a wide range of composition), any region in which they could collect should be thoroughly ventilated.

There is much scope for human error to produce hot-spots in unintended places. Before the industrial revolution, they were almost always generated by the negligent use of pre-existing fire. Although candles were often fitted with perforated guards, many fires were said to have been started by candles which were used to search for objects which had rolled under the bed, or which were left too near the curtains of an open window. Oil lamps (and more recently also oil heaters) were often knocked over, spreading the burning liquid fuel. Open fires were a further hazard, since burning logs could roll out of them and glowing pieces could be ejected by the pressure generated by the burning of small pockets of gaseous pyrolysis products.

In present-day industrialized societies, naked flames are much less common and oil heaters are better designed to prevent fuel spillage. Open fires are enclosed by a fender and, if unattended, by a spark guard. Safety matches, unlike their strike-a-light predecessors, do not ignite accidentally; and hot discarded match-heads are less frequent in this era of cigarette lighters, and of battery, piezoelectric or catalytic lighters for gas burners. The naked gas flames of bunsen burners, which were a common cause of small fires in chemical laboratories, should never be used for heating flammable liquids. Electrically heated mantles can do the same job, not only more safely but also with finer temperature control. If naked flames must be used in regions which contain flammable vapours, the flame may be covered by a wire gauze flame-trap which conducts the heat away from the flame and so lowers the temperature below that needed for ignition (see Chapter 2). Some paraffin space heaters now incorporate a similar safety mesh. Despite all these precautions, many fires are still caused by misuse of flaming or smouldering materials, of which by far the most heinous is the lighted cigarette. It is not only for medical reasons that smoking is banned in libraries. Readers are not admitted to the Bodleian Library of Oxford University without swearing aloud that they will 'neither bring in nor kindle any naked flame'. The library was never lit by candles or lamps, but always closed at sundown until 1922 when electric lighting was introduced.

Severe hot-spots may also be produced by electrical phenomena. Lightning strikes high buildings as well as tall trees. An excess of electric charge builds up in a small region of material and its eventual discharge may release sufficient heat to cause ignition of, say, wood. Tall buildings are therefore fitted with protruding metal lightning conductors, through which the electric charge may safely pass into the earth.

Build-up of electrostatic charge or frictional heating can initiate explosive combustion of a mixture of air with either finely divided solids (see Chapter 12) or with flammable vapours. The hot-spot may be generated by a spark from moving machinery or even from the floor; a person walking on an unearthed woollen carpet in unsuitable footwear can generate a potential of 14 kilovolts. Explosions in flammable mists and in dusts of such varied materials as coal dust, custard powder, and metals may be self-initiating, since the charge may be built up by the movement of the particles in the air. The chance of electrostatic ignition from any source is much reduced by working in a humid, ion-rich atmosphere.

In domestic surroundings, current electricity is a much greater hazard. Red-hot wires, which form the elements of many electric heaters, are usually now adequately guarded against chance contact with clothing, paper, and suchlike, although the heater must obviously be kept away from flammable materials such as wood or upholstery. Most electrically generated fires are caused by a short circuit, often due to faulty insulation, either in the electric wiring system of a building or inside a piece of electrical equipment. Age is the usual cause, although rats and even hamsters enjoy gnawing rubber and plastic off exposed cables. Unfortunately, new electrical appliances can also be dangerous, through faults in design or installation. Some amateur repairs, such as cable-joining, may soon lead to disaster, although there are many skilled do-it-yourself enthusiasts who rightly pride themselves on working to a professional standard. An electric fuse should always be fitted according to the manufacturer's specification and never replaced by one carrying a larger current. Obviously, *in no circumstance* should a piece of ordinary wire be used instead of a fuse.

Since we shall never eliminate all hot-spots, we must also be vigilant in our handling and storage of any potential fuel. Although many of the materials within a building are combustible, they differ greatly in flammability. Fuels and flammable solvents should be stored away from buildings where people live and work. Gas pipes and connectors should be designed and fitted to prevent any possibility of leakage, and all users should be educated to act sensibly and promptly at the least sniff of escaping gas. (Even in the first quarter of the twentieth century many fires were caused by candles used to search for gas leaks.) Gas-fuel burners should always have the hot-spot available (often in the form of a pilot light) *before* the main fuel supply is turned on. Successful ignition should be checked by monitoring the heat or light generated or the increase in electrical conductivity (see Chapter 2).

In many accidental fires, the combustible material need never have been present. Flammable vapours or dusts can often be dispersed by adequate ventilation. Combustible waste adds greatly to fire hazard, be it a pile of empty cardboard boxes in a supermarket, used plastic cups under stadium seats, or even an accumulation of fluff under an escalator. The case for tidy housekeeping does not rest on hygiene and aesthetics alone.

In previous centuries, buildings were often of wood and thatch and were particularly flammable. Nowadays we use less combustible materials such as brick, stone, tiles, metal, and concrete, with relatively little wood. But even a well-ordered building is full of combustible materials, the most readily ignitable being paper and cloth, so present-day fire takes its main toll by the burning not of buildings but of their contents. We could of course make our homes much safer if we were prepared to alter our priorities: floors and walls could be of marble and tile, all furniture could be built of metal and glass, and curtains could be replaced by metal venetian blinds.

The ease with which a substance burns (its 'flammability') depends both on how readily it ignites and how quickly any flame spreads. The former factor is assessed by measuring the time taken for a substance to ignite when exposed to a given input of energy, and depends on: the amount of energy needed to heat up a particular volume; the ease with which heat flows away from the irradiated area; the ease of gasification; the pyrolysis temperature of the hot vapour; and the ease of heating the fragments to the temperature needed for oxidation.

The rate at which a fire spreads also depends on all the factors which initially determine ignition, and is further complicated by the fact that the heat source which irradiates the surface of the material is constantly increasing. This feed-back of energy depends on the area of the surface which is on fire, the amount of heat released by the burning pyrolysis products, and the proportion of this heat which is reradiated back from the flame to the surface. A sooty flame, which contains incompletely oxidized particles of carbon, will release less heat than if these had burned completely; but the glowing solids in a sooty flame radiate much more effectively than do the gaseous fragments in a clear, less luminous one. With so many variables, it is very difficult to predict the likely flammability of a particular material, or even to extrapolate the results of laboratory tests of flammability to assess how a substance might burn in a real fire. But we do know that, once any material has started to burn, it not only gets hotter, but the *rate* of heat production also increases; so the fire grows exponentially. However, as we have seen in Chapter 18 heat is not the most serious consequence of fire, since, if human escape is in question, the smoke and fumes are an even greater hazard.

Those who choose a material, either for building or for furnishing, must of course take into account many factors (technical, economic, and aesthetic) besides those relating to fire safety. Fortunately, it is often possible to treat the material in some way so as to reduce its flammability without spoiling its desirable properties. Of the several approaches which have been used to produce flame-retardant materials, the oldest is to coat the combustible substance with a non-combustible one. This acts as a barrier between the air outside and the flammable pyrolysis products inside, and may also act as a heat sink, retarding the rise in temperature of the potential fuel. The Chinese covered their straw roofs with a layer of mud, which was also used in classical times to protect the exposed parts of ships from incendiary attack. In colonial America, chimneys were made of reed or wood, but were rendered slightly less flammable by a lining of mortar. In our own time, some Christmas trees are sprayed with a fire-retardant. A more effective method for treating wood is to coat every fibre. This can be achieved by impregnating the wood with certain inorganic substances, such as borax and sodium silicate, which melt to form a glassy liquid. It is thought that alum was used in this way as early as 548 BC when the temple at Delphi was rebuilt. A similar method has been used to produce flame resistant cloth for over two centuries, but as the treatment forces the coating compound between the fibres, it causes some weakening, both of wood and of fabrics. Cloth can also be impregnated with a 'blowing out' agent such as ammonium carbonate or starch. When the substance is heated it produces a large volume of non-combustible gas which retards the spread of the flame by separating the hot upper fibres from the underlying fabric, and may even dilute the atmospheric oxygen so much as to prevent combustion. Some flame-retardants act primarily as a heat sink. At high temperatures, aluminium hydroxide $(Al(OH)_3)$ absorbs heat avidly and decomposes into the oxide Al_2O_3 and water vapour, which itself contributes to flame retardation by acting as a blow-out agent and a further heat sink.

The flame-retardants we have discussed so far work by limiting the supply of heat and oxygen to the combustible material. Others can interfere with the normal course of combustion to give a less harmful outcome. The retardant may either be applied to the surface of the fibre or, in the case of man-made materials, the combustion properties may be modified by chemical alterations during its synthesis. One strategy is to discourage pyrolysis fragments from reacting with oxygen by providing them with a preferred alternative, such as chlorine atoms which act as a 'radical scavenger'. Some synthetic polymers, such as PVC, which contain chlorine, burn only slowly for this reason, and those which also contain phosphorus or antimony may be even better retardants. Some phosphorus compounds discourage ignition of wood or cotton in a different way. At high temperatures, they form phosphorus oxyacids, which are so avid for water that they extract it from the cellulose fibres, leaving only carbon. The wood or cotton chars, but without emitting flammable gases.

Naturally, attempts to produce fabrics which are less dangerously susceptible to fire must be designed with a view to the eventual use of the fabric. Some synthetic materials, such as polyesters, melt before they ignite and are therefore well suited for furnishing but unsatisfactory for fire-protective clothing, for which the main criteria are low thermal conductivity (as in asbestos) and an ability to form a protective char (as in aramid, a high-melting relative of nylon, in which the short linear chains of carbon atoms in the backbone are replaced by 'aromatic' rings). Asbestos is now outlawed, as being a proven health hazard.

Blended fibres may require special treatment as the two components, or their pyrolysis products, may interact at flame temperatures; and it may be difficult to find either a retardant which works for both fibres or two retardants which are not incompatible. Blends of cotton with polyesters pose a particular problem, even though the components do not interact. At high temperatures the synthetic polymer melts, but does not drip away; it is held in the skeleton of the, probably charred, cotton and there provides fuel for combustion. Such blends burn more intensely than either fabric on its own. Since the high concentrations of retardant needed to inhibit combustion ruin the properties of the fabric, polyester cotton blends are little used for furnishing where high safety standards are required. The combustion behaviour of blends of wool with synthetic polymers is less well understood because of the complicated reactions which take place between the pyrolysis fragments of the two types of fibre. A further difficulty with flame retardants arises from the very fact that they inhibit combustion, often generating incompletely oxidized products. So, although they may retard the spread of flames, they may actually increase the amount of smoke and the toxicity of the fumes. Burning wood, for example, produces more hydrogen cyanide if it has been fire-retarded.

Even if a fire should occur, a building can be protected against its worst ravages by good architectural design. Since fire can spread rapidly from one room to another by the flow of pyrolysis products along corridors and up stairways and lift shafts, such fire-highways should be divided into compartments by fire-resistant doors. These greatly impede the flow of inflammable vapours, smoke, and toxic fumes, and so act both as barriers to the spread of fire and as relatively safe escape routes for the occupants. Stairwells may even be kept at a slightly higher pressure than the rest of the building, so as to discourage the seepage of flammable gases without making the escape doors difficult to open. The skeleton of a building should have regions of low thermal conductivity to slow down the spread of fire by the conduction of heat. Air is one of the best thermal insulators and empty pots were therefore incorporated into the plaster walls of eighteenth century buildings in France and later in England to prevent heat from reaching the wooden beams. Towards the end of the nineteenth century, machine-made hollow terracotta flooring blocks were manufactured in the USA to be followed by porous bricks, fired from a mixture of clay and sawdust, and by the present-day aerated breeze block and pierced air brick. Cavity walls provide a layer of air or insulating foam within a building. As many buildings collapse in a fire before they are consumed by it, iron and steel girders have been used since the nineteenth century, either as the main construction material or for reinforcement. The metals do not burn, but at temperatures of about 500 °C (well below those of about 900 °C reached in a typical building fire) they soften and buckle. The building then caves in, as happened to the 'fireproof' New York Crystal Palace in 1858. Happily a fairly thin covering of concrete provides sufficient insulation to prevent the metals from softening and also helps to support the load.

The use of thermal insulators has been developed on a smaller scale for the protection of valuables in fireproof containers. Several types of box and chest were made in the decade 1820–30. A simple French box from that period has double walls of metal, the cavity insulation being provided merely by air. In England, forerunners of the modern safe were made of double-walled sheet iron, separated by various thermal insulators such as marble dust, burned clay or damp cement (which on heating gave off a protective layer of steam). The insulator in a New England version was oak soaked in brine. Vault doors are manufactured similarly and can withstand fire for periods of 30 or 60 minutes (whereas most metal filing boxes survive only for 3 to 5 minutes). A vault door only 15 centimetres thick remained intact after the atomic explosion at Hiroshima although it was only 300 metres from the centre of destruction.

Similar measures can prevent the rapid spread of fire from one building to another. In twelfth century England, the law required that firewalls (16 feet high and 3 feet thick) be built between neighbouring buildings. Later, grain silos were protected by a moat. In the middle ages houses were built close together, and in colonial America they were often grouped around a central area where combustibles, including gunpowder, were stored and through which fire was transmitted extremely rapidly. Modern city planning allows more space between buildings, and if an industrial plant is particularly at risk from fire it is well separated from other structures. The space around buildings should be kept clear of weeds which become dry and flammable in summer and so allow fire to travel over open ground. Even large gaps do not, however, offer total protection. The Chicago fire of 1871 crossed the river. Buildings under threat from nearby fire, and ships under incendiary attack, were protected by being hung with wet hides in the same way that today a house in the path of a forest fire is protected by covering the walls with blankets and hosing them with water, which acts both as a heat sink and the source of a protective layer of steam.

Despite rapid increase in our knowledge of the way unwanted fires behave, it is still difficult to predict what will happen in an untried situation, e.g. in an underground train, a crashed airliner, or a blazing oil rig. For example, the rise in temperature in a small compartment may be much higher than expected, due to more efficient reradiation. Combustion will then occur not only faster, but also in unexpected ways, perhaps generating unexpectedly high concentrations of some toxic vapour. Progress is best made by carrying out tests under conditions which reproduce the real situation as closely as possible. When an accident does occur its causes should be analysed in great depth, and any definitive conclusions *should be used* by those responsible for subsequent modifications of structure or procedure, and for future planning.

Manufacturing plants which are at risk from explosions have special architectural requirements. The most sensitive part of the process may be carried out totally automatically to eliminate human error and to allow the plant to operate in an inert atmosphere (e.g. of nitrogen) or at least in an oxygen-reduced one. The amount of explosive or ignitable dust which is present can be reduced by using only a small plant, in which build-up of particles is minimized, and by adequate ventilation. As an explosion may totally destroy an unsuitable building, the plant should be housed in a steel-frame structure covered with cladding which is readily displaced at high pressure and so acts as a safety valve. (The cladding should, of course, also be restrained so that it is not projected off the building into the surroundings.) The same effect can be achieved by fitting the plant with explosion vents which open automatically if the pressure becomes too high.

So far, we have discussed mainly those fires which occur in buildings, vehicles, and ships. But fire is a hazard also in rural contexts. Wildfire, the one form of unwanted fire which is not necessarily due to human carelessness, is discussed in Chapter 22. Fires in large haystacks and grain stores must, however, be attributed to man's shortcomings. If they are improperly made of damp material, the resulting decay can generate enough heat both to dispel any water which was present and even to ignite the remaining vegetable material (see p. 29). Haystacks are therefore usually at some distance from dwellings. We are not, unfortunately, always successful in preventing serious urban or rural fires, even with the many means at our disposal. But we are often able to bring such fires under control using a wide range of methods which we shall discuss in the next chapter.

20

Mankind versus fire: (3) Weapons for combat

The first step in the control of any unwanted fire is, of course, detection. Here we shall be concerned mainly with fires in enclosed spaces; wildfire will be discussed in Chapter 22. It is essential that a fire in a building or vehicle should be detected, and the alarm raised, at the earliest possible stage so as to allow people to escape unharmed and to minimize damage to property. It is tempting to think that the best detector in a building which is being used by alert, able-bodied adults is the human sensory system. Surely a wisp of smoke from an unexpected source would be seen and smelt without delay? However, after the London underground fire at King's Cross Station in 1987, in which thirty-one people died as a result of one unextinguished match or cigarette end, it was learnt that smoke was seen issuing from the escalator one hour before it was reported. Moreover, since many fires occur in buildings which are unoccupied, or which are occupied only by people who are asleep, or drunk, or very old, it is much better to use technological sensing devices, provided that they are continuously in working order. Various types of detector have been developed. Some, which respond to any rise in temperature, are particularly suitable for large unoccupied industrial and commercial buildings where, since the primary interest is protection of property, heat is the main threat. The simplest such devices are activated when a particular temperature has been reached. They contain either a fuse or a bimetallic strip and are often coupled to automatic sprinklers (see p. 204). Unfortunately, they often give false alarms, since the temperature may rise gradually to the activating level for some harmless reason.

In an actual fire, however, the temperature rises rapidly once flaming combustion has started, and so a detector which is activated by a high *rate of increase* in temperature provides a more discerning sensor. It, too, can be quite simple and often consists of an air chamber with a small vent in it. When it is heated the air expands, and so increases in pressure. If the expansion is gradual, air leaks slowly out of the vent and the pressure inside the chamber stays much the same. But if the expansion is rapid, the air cannot escape fast enough to keep the pressure constant and the increased pressure inside the chamber then activates the alarm.

Many fires start slowly and may smoulder for some hours at a low temperature before any flame appears. Smouldering can be detected with an 'electronic eye' which senses the light scattered by the smoke particles. Some of these monitors are, unfortunately, also activated by heavy tobacco smoke, burning toast, steam rising from a hot bath, and even by swarms of small winged insects. Smoke and fumes may also be detected by the ion-chamber method, which consists of an air chamber which also contains americium-241. The particles emitted by the radioactive decay of the americium knock electrons off the species in the chamber, be they smoke particles, pyrolysis products or the normal components of air. These become positively charged ions, which can be made to move and so carry a current if a voltage is applied. The lighter the ions, the faster they move, and so the current is larger if the air is pure than if it contains smoke particles and pyrolysis fragments. Any drop in current activates the detector. The device is particularly useful for detecting 'clean' fires which burn with little visible smoke, but is unsuitable for use in kitchens, which are better served by the rate-of-heating type of sensor.

Once a fire has been detected, the alarm must be raised. If the fire has been discovered by an individual, raising the alarm may involve waking other people in the house, telephoning the appropriate person at work, activating an electrical alarm bell, and summoning the emergency services. All adults should ensure that they would be able to operate the fire alarm and to telephone the emergency services, even in pitch darkness, should the need arise. Automatic fire detectors usually sound an alarm both in the fire area and in the janitorial headquarters, and they may also be connected to the public emergency services. Naturally they must have an emergency supply of electric current from batteries or a generator, in case the mains supply fails. Unfortunately, automatic fire detectors are not infallible, not so much because they are intrinsically faulty, but because they are not always properly maintained. It is thought that the fire which destroyed a wing of London's historic Hampton Court Palace, killing the occupant, was undetected for so many hours because the sensors had not been properly reset after servicing, or after one of the many false alarms caused by maintenance work. Of course, there is no point in raising the alarm unless people heed it. The Great Fire of London (1666) was first noticed at 2 a.m. in a baker's where furze kindling was stored. At 3 a.m. the Mayor was roused and informed, but is reported to have said 'Pish! A woman might piss it out' and gone back to bed. The fire burned for several days, killing six people and destroying over 13 000 houses, nearly 100 churches, 52 livery company halls, 4 prisons, 4 stone bridges, 3 city gates, and many hospitals and public buildings.

Even today there is a tendency to overlook the potential seriousness of the small fire. Maybe people are afraid of being thought foolish if they seem to over-react by evacuating a building on account

The Great Fire of London consumes 'Paul's church and school'.
It made me weep to see it. The churches, houses and all on fire, and flaming at once, and a horrid noise the flames made, and the cracking of houses at their ruine.

Samuel Pepys

23 Aerial fire-fighting

24 'The Elements in Salvation: Fire. God appears in the burning bush. Column of cloud and fire leading God's people. God hidden in the fire and smoke on Sinai. Three young men in the burning fiery furnace. The new fire at Easter. The fire of the Holy Spirit at Pentecost.' Tapestry in St Albans Cathedral, Hertfordshire

of a little fire which could probably be controlled by one or two buckets of water. Many do not realize how quickly a small, but flaming, fire can accelerate to lethal flashover. But, however small the fire, it is clearly sensible to proceed as quickly as possible with the two tasks of controlling the fire and evacuating the occupants.

The principles of extinction of a fire are similar to those of retarding it by use of materials of reduced flammability (see Chapter 19); we must attempt to negate one or more of the three requisite conditions of temperature, fuel, and oxygen. Circumstance determines which factors to tackle. If a pan of hot cooking oil ignites, the cook will put the lid firmly on the pan, and will also remove the pan from the hot plate, thereby depriving the fuel vapour of oxygen and the fuel of further heat for vaporization and pyrolysis. (It has unfortunately been known for a panicky cook to take the flaming, uncovered pan to the door, so as to leave it outside to burn out. It is likely that, as the door is opened, the flames will be blown back on to his arms and face. Badly burned, he will drop the pan, and so spread burning oil over the floor, where it will set fire to any combustible material it meets. Pouring cold water into the pan would have similar results, as the water would vaporize and make the burning oil spit out of the pan on to the cook's hands or face.) Smothering a fire by cutting off its supply of oxygen is a valuable way of extinguishing small fires. A person whose clothing is on fire should be rapidly wrapped in a blanket, and rolls of fire retardant cloth are now a common feature of fire-protection in hotels and work-places. The sand bucket was a familiar sight in Britain during the Second World War for the immediate suffocation of fires started by incendiary bombs (and as a useful burial ground for unextinguished cigarettes).

The traditional fire extinguishant is, of course, water, or any largely aqueous liquid which is to hand, such as milk, urine or vinegar. (So familiar is water in fire-fighting that the modern reader perhaps needs to be reminded that it conducts electricity and so should *never* be used on fires caused by, or involving, electrical equipment.) The main role played by water is to cool the burning surface, and so to slow down the pyrolysis. Water needs to absorb an abnormally large amount of heat in order to raise its own temperature, and so can be a very effective coolant, provided that it can be kept in contact with the burning area. The steam which is formed dilutes both the oxygen and the pyrolysis products, and so slows the combustion yet further; and water has the further great advantage over all other extinguishants of being often (though, alas, not always) available in large quantities. The most serious problem is that of contact: water rapidly runs off the vertical surfaces up which flames so often travel and, being denser than many other liquids, immediately sinks below the burning surface of many liquid fuel fires. Water can be positioned over a burning surface more precisely and for a longer period if it is applied as a foam, which acts in several ways: as a coolant, as a barrier between the air and the pyrolysis products, and as an insulator which reduces the reradiated heat reaching the fuel.

Water is sometimes used as a fog of minute droplets dispersed in air, or as a foam of tiny air bubbles suspended in water, which is a useful extinguishant for fires involving either solids or liquids. The surfactant agent which is added as a foam-stabilizer is chosen to give exactly the right degree of miscibility between the froth and the fuel it is protecting. Repulsion between the fuel and the foam discourages combustible vapour from seeping upwards towards the air, but also discourages the foam from covering a wide area of the surface of the burning fuel. Greater compatibility between foam and fuel allows a wider area to be attacked, but increases the danger of flammable gases 'wicking' up to the atmosphere. A careful balance must therefore be struck. Aqueous foams for use on fuels such as alcohols which are miscible with water must contain 'rafting agents' which form a surface barrier between the foam and the fuel and so stop the foam from merely collapsing at the surface and mixing with the fuel. Previously, the foam concentrate contained a complex ion of ammonia and zinc. When the water was added for foam formation, this broke down to give zinc ions which reacted with the foaming agent to give a type of soap scum which supported the foam over the alcohol. Nowadays, starch-like 'rafts' are used to make foams which are viscous but stable, in much the same way as starch itself is used in the preparation of factory-made meringues.

Two useful extinguishants for liquid fuel fires are the gases carbon dioxide and nitrogen which act simply by diluting the oxygen to below the level needed for combustion. The former, despite its lack of chemical reactivity, can however cause explosions. Release of the gas into the air from a cylinder containing the high pressure liquid causes such cooling as to recondense the carbon dioxide, not to droplets, but to tiny particles of solid. These may carry enough electrostatic charge to initiate an explosion if released into a highly combustible atmosphere. Nowadays, carbon dioxide is applied from a metal horn, which, being a good conductor of both heat and electricity, prevents the formation of charged particles of carbon dioxide snow. Since the horn gets extremely cold, it should never be touched by hand. Occasionally nitrogen is released as a liquid, rather than as a gas. As it boils at $-196\,°C$, it acts as an effective coolant as well as a diluent.

Powder extinguishants are inorganic salts which fuse and cover the fuel with a protective layer. Bicarbonates, which are useful in liquid fuel fires, also generate carbon dioxide which acts as a gas diluent. Ammonium phosphate controls smouldering. Powder extinguishers do not, however, act also as coolants and so there is a danger of reignition (which may be reduced by applying a foam after the flames have subsided). Fires involving reactive metals such as magnesium may be combated by a mixture of salts, such as 'TEC' (which is the 'ternary eutectic mixture' of chlorides of sodium, potassium, and barium). 'Intumescent' graphite, in the form of an expanded powder, works on the same principle and is used to combat the combustion of the highly flammable alloy of sodium and potassium which is used in nuclear energy plants. It is thought that some of the powdered salts, in addition to forming a protective cover, may act as 'radical scavengers' and mop up activated pyrolysis fragments before they can react further.

The Halon extinguishants*, certainly react with pyrolysis fragments. Halon 1211 or BCF (of boiling point $-4\,°C$) is released as a spray of droplets which is more penetrating than just a stream of gas. Since it is toxic, the operator must take care not to inhale it. Halon 1301 (or BTM) is less toxic than BCF and so is to be preferred if people are present, even though it is gaseous. It is used to extinguish fires at computer terminals.

An addition to our armoury of extinguishants is one which has no counterpart among retardants: air. The fire-fighter can ventilate the fire. If a space is full of hot smoke and flammable gases, the breaking of a window, or the axing of a hole in the roof will allow the gases to escape, either spontaneously, or with the help of a powered fan. The cooler, cleaner atmosphere should slow down combustion by lowering both the temperature and the concentration of pyrolysis products. It will also reduce the smoke damage and allow the fire-fighters to breathe and see more easily. On the other hand, the

---

* Classified by their Halon number $wxyz$, derived from their formula $C_wF_xCl_yBr_z$.

increased oxygen concentration could accelerate combustion, even to
the point of explosion. The decision of whether or not to ventilate a
fire is clearly a matter of very fine judgement and the province only of
the expert.

Another question for the professional is whether to try to control a
fire at all. It may be better to evacuate the area around, say, a lorry
full of explosives and then let it burn out, rather than to risk the lives
of fire-fighters. In other fires, the major hazard may be escaped but
unburned material. It is usually safer to let a fire of liquefied natural
gas burn in a controlled way rather than to extinguish it completely,
thereby allowing the unburned fuel to form an explosive mixture
with the air.

Effective control of fire naturally requires an adequate and accessible supply of extinguishant and the means to apply it rapidly.
Bucket or spade technology for applying water or earth was used for
millennia and was still a familiar sight during the incendiary air raids
of the Second World War. The use of pumps is relatively recent, at
least in Europe; although a device to deliver a continuous stream of
water to a fire was described by Hero about two thousand years ago,
we do not know that it was ever used. The first pumps in general

Hand-pumped engine at the time of the Great Fire of London (1666)

use delivered discontinuous jets of water, and it was only in the eighteenth century that constant discharge ones were introduced. The foot-held, hand-operated stirrup-pump which delivered a stream of water from a bucket during the Second World War is a very close descendent of the 'Fire-Squirt' of 1750. 'Fire-engines' on wheels or runners were first manufactured in seventeenth century Nuremburg, at the rate of two per year. They were drawn by hand and consisted of a tank and a hand-operated pump. At that period, however, most streets were too narrow to allow them access. The tank was continually refilled by bucket from any available supply of water, which often had to be obtained by piercing the mains pipe and damming up the resulting flood. Later, suction pumps allowed water to be taken from stand pipes and from natural water supplies such as rivers; but the hoses were often so short that the engine itself was destroyed in the fire.

Modernization was stimulated by a number of city fires including the Edinburgh fire of 1824. The primitive hand-carts were replaced by horse-drawn engines, with the horses waiting ready harnessed. They could then be coupled rapidly to the engines, and they could also be uncoupled rapidly, so that any horse which fell could soon be put on its feet again. In the mid-nineteenth century, steam-power was introduced for pumping, and there was a brief period before the appearance of the internal combustion engine when steam engines were also used for traction. The last steam fire-engine to be used in New York was pulled by a tractor, and remained in service until 1932. The large fire services which now operate in most industrialized countries have trucks which can carry at least 760 litres of water, have 300 metres of hose, and can pump at rates of up to almost 6000 litres per minute. Trucks with turntables date from the 1930s and can now carry hydraulically operated telescopic ladders, reaching to 44 metres, or goose-neck cranes ('snorkels'), with two 12 metre arms leading to a basket, which can be used for both rescue and fire-fighting.

The nineteenth century also saw the development of the portable fire-extinguisher. The first, invented in 1816, contained compressed air and a solution of pearl ash in water. During the period 1884–1914, glass 'fire-grenades' were thrown on the fire and discharged carbon dioxide when they broke. The bottles themselves were of attractive appearance but were of little use in fire control. In 1902, a larger fire-extinguisher contained 150 litres of an aqueous solution of sodium bicarbonate and a separate bottle of sulphuric acid. When the acid was tipped into the bicarbonate, the carbon dioxide which was generated forced the aqueous solution through the nozzle, and itself also acted as an extinguishant. The chemical action was spent after about 5 minutes.

In many industrial and commercial buildings, and in some houses, water is applied automatically by a sprinkler activated by the alarm system. The water must, of course, be released at an early stage in the fire, before the buoyancy of the flames prevents the droplets from reaching the burning region. In this way, it is likely that the fire can be controlled and extinguished before it has a chance to spread, and also that water damage is minimized, since only the small area served by one detector is wetted. The first automatic sprinklers were available in London as early as 1852.

Water is not the only extinguishant which can be dispensed automatically when a sensor is activated. Some explosion detectors can supply a Halon 'radical scavenger' to suppress further explosion. Fire detectors can open pourers which supply foam of low expansion (of only about eight times the volume of the surfactant solution from which it is formed). Others can generate foam of very high expansion (up to a 1000-fold increase in volume) which is used in situations where the space is very limited or where water damage must be kept to a minimum. There may still be some truth in the old quip that the water used by fire-fighters does more damage than the flames. Should time and manpower allow, much water damage can be prevented if valuable articles on floors below the fire can be covered with water-proof sheeting.

The wide range of modern extinguishants available to the specialist fire-fighter can also be used from portable extinguishers by the individual operator (see Plate 19). The professional services, however, continue to rely heavily on water, which is now widely available from hydrants for urban fire-fighting (but see p. 213) and from natural waters for nautical work. When the Iceland volcano Heinaey erupted in 1979, the hot lava was sprayed with sea-water at a rate of 200 000 000 litres per hour. But water, like other extinguishants, is sometimes transported to the fire by lorry or tanker.

New applications of fire-combat principles have been needed in the attempts to extinguish the burning Kuwaiti oil-wells, of which there were over 600 at the end of the Gulf War. One approach is to prevent the crude oil and its flammable vapours from reaching the air at the surface. Side-shafts can be cut to divert the oil into underground reservoirs, or a quick-setting expanding resin can be pumped into the neck of a well so as to act as a tight-fitting plug. Alternatively, oil can be allowed to flow to the surface, but the supply of oxygen can be reduced, either by pumping liquid nitrogen down the shaft or by placing a huge upturned bucket-shaped snuffer over the mouth of the well, while simultaneously shovelling sand in through a valve. These newer methods supplement the traditional use of explosives for 'blowing-out' oil-rig fires (see Chapter 12 and Plate 20). Water, pumped in from the sea along former oil-pipes and stored in plastic-lined reservoirs, is widely used to discourage reignition.

To many, our first duty in the fight against uncontrolled fire is to prevent human death or injury. In the late eighteenth century, rescue equipment in Geneva included cloth chutes, baskets on ropes, and sectional ladders with wheels on the top section so that they could be pushed up walls. Ideally, though, rescue from a burning building should be unnecessary, as it should have been anticipated by prompt evacuation. The human factors required are discussed later in Chapter 21, but no amount of courage or good sense is likely to be effective without adequate, well-signposted, and well-lit exit routes which can be approached without suffocation or burning. Many older buildings still have external iron fire escape staircases. These may weaken in the heat and pull away from the building. But even if they are secure, they can themselves be hazardous in the dark and in bad weather, particularly for people who are very old, very young, sick, or disabled. Some of those trying to escape will have a fear of heights, and most will be afraid of the fire; at night, many may be only partly awake, others not totally sober. If the fire has taken hold, some may already be suffering the effects of toxic fumes. Other external means of evacuation, such as fire-retardant rope ladders, chutes, and counterpoised sling-belts are nowadays even more strongly out of favour for similar reasons.

Modern building design aims to contain the fire long enough to allow evacuation in an adequately smoke-free environment, protected by fire retardant doors to rooms, to abutting stairwells, and within corridors. It is also possible, given adequate initial expenditure, to increase the air pressure in the escape areas in the event of fire, in order to discourage entry of smoke. These areas of positive pressure may be complemented by application of negative pressure, or suction, in the fire area, in order to reduce the build-up of smoke.

If it should unfortunately be necessary to escape from a region which already has a heavily smoky atmosphere, it is best to keep the head as near to the ground as possible. In aircraft, emergency lighting is placed at floor level to facilitate such escape. The lowest 15 centimetres of air will be cooler than the atmosphere in the rest of the enclosure, and will contain less smoke and more oxygen. Evacuation of a building in which normal escape routes are cut off is a matter for the emergency services. The lucky may be rescued from a balcony or roof by extending ladder or even by helicopter, or they may be able to jump into a safety net; but in a bad fire, it is unlikely that all trapped victims will be fortunate enough to survive.

21

Mankind versus fire: (4) Collective strategies

The problem of uncontrolled fire is not restricted to the owner of the burning property; nor to those under his immediate roof. Flames spread from one building to another and throughout rural areas. It is in the best interests of the whole community that fire should be kept under firm control, and so it is reasonable that some collective responsibility should be taken both to prevent and to combat unwanted fire. The earliest organized fire-brigades appear to be the bands of slaves (Familia Publica) who fire-watched and fire-fought in ancient Rome, but in 300 BC were criticized for neglecting their rounds and being slow in arriving at the scene of a fire.

Much more efficient were the Vigiles set up by Caesar Augustus in AD 6–7. The corps, which existed for some 500 years, consisted of from 100 to 1000 men, with specialized jobs such as water carrier, pump supervisor, hooker (who pulled down burning roofs), and the inspector, who had to determine the cause of the fire. Heavy penalties could be imposed in the light of his findings. The Vigiles were nicknamed 'Sparteoli', since they used buckets made of tarred Esparto grass, as well as hooked poles, pick axes, felling axes, ladders, and wet blankets. They were entitled to enter a house that they suspected of being on fire, and there is a report of preparations for a feast being abruptly disturbed by their water and axes, on account of the large amount of smoke from the cooking: the problem of oversensitive sprinklers being set off by burnt toast is not new. Despite the presence of the Vigiles, however, Rome burned for eight days in AD 64 and much of the city was destroyed.

Roman efficiency was not practised by other European nations until over one thousand years later. In medieval England, fire was combatted by prayer and church bells rung in a reverse peal, both to raise the alarm and to summon help, a practice which persisted into the twentieth century. A bell was also tolled every evening in timber-built English towns to warn people that it was time to cover their fires with a metal lid and to extinguish their candles. Curfew (from the Old French 'cuevrefu') is said to have been introduced by King Alfred in 872, but the regulation was reintroduced, or at least more strictly enforced, by William the Conqueror.

The first English king to concern himself with building regulations to reduce fire hazards was Richard I (1189–99) who decreed that new houses in London should be built of stone, with roofs of tile or slate, and that thick and high party walls be erected between neighbouring buildings. He also legislated for the provision of labour, water, and equipment for fighting fire. Owners of big houses were to keep ladders, and a barrel of water if there was no fountain. In London each alderman was to be responsible for ten firemen, who should have a crook, chains, strong cords, and a loud horn.

There must have been many serious fires in the crowded wooden cities of the middle ages, but records are far from complete. We know, however, that London was largely destroyed three times (in 798, 982, and 1212) before the 'Great Fire'. York, Nantes, and Venice suffered similarly in the twelfth century, as did Carlisle at the end of the thirteenth.

The seventeenth century saw much progress in awareness of fire hazards. The broadsheet (see Chapter 19) written by Gosling during the English Civil War of 1642–6 included instructions on procedure and equipment in communal fire control, gave advice on the exclusion of onlookers, and emphasized the danger both to fire-fighters and to those unable to escape:

Orders that if fire should happen, either by wilde-fire, or other wayes, to prevent the miseries thereof.
Then the Bells going backward, doth give notice of fire: and that all Officers and others, must keepe the streets or lanes ends, that the rude people may be kept from doing mischiefe, for sometimes they doe more harme than the fire: and suffer none but the workers to come neere, and all

the streets from the fire to the water, may have double rowes or rankes of men on each side the street, to handy emptie pales, ports, or buckets, to the water, and to returne full to the fire, by the other rowe or ranke of people, on the same side the street: so as the streets affords, you may have divers rankes: and by this order, water may be brought to quench it, or earth to choake it, and smoother it, with that speed and plenty, as need requires.

All those of higher or levell ground, should throw downe water, to run to the place where the fire is, and there to stop it: and others to sweep up the waters of kennells towards the fire. If waterpipes run through the streets, you may open it against the house that is a-fire, and set another pipe in that upright, and two or three foot lower than the height of the head of the same water, sett in some gutter, trough, or pipe unto the upright pipe, to convay the water to the fire, for under the foresaid height, it will run it selfe from high ponds, or from Sir High Middletons water, or Conduit-heads, or from the Water-houses, without any other help, into the fire, as you will have it: you may keepe great Scoopes or Squrts of wood in houses; or if you will, you may have in the Parish a great Squrt on wheeles, that may doe very good service.

Where mild fire is, milke, urine, sand, earth, or dirt, will quench it: but anything else set a-fire by that, will be quencht as afore: if there be many houses standing together, and are endangered by a mightie fire, before it can be quencht, or choaked with earth, then you may pull down the next house opposite to the winde, and then earth and rubbish being cast upon the fire, and round about it, will choake the violence of the fire: besides the water you may get to do the like. Also it is necessary that every Parish should have Hookes, Ladders, Squirts, Buckets and Scoopes in a readinesse upon any occasion.

The broadsheet concludes with the observation that prevention of fire leads to a great saving of money which could be better used by the community in other ways.

New World colonists rapidly introduced regulations to reduce fire hazards. In 1630 Boston householders were required to have a ladder and a long-handled mop to fight roof fires. New Amsterdam, in the second half of the century, concentrated on prevention by banning wooden chimneys and appointing fire wardens. Those responsible for starting a fire were fined and a 'rattle-watch' patrol was set up to warn the inhabitants if a fire occurred. By the end of the century, inspectors were checking chimneys to see that they were not harbouring combustible soot. About the same time, Philadelphia banned the cleaning of chimneys by burning, the storage of more than 6 pounds of gunpowder within 25 feet of a dwelling, and also, repressive though seems to the modern reader, smoking on the streets.

England had to wait until 1666 when the Great Fire provided stimulus for greatly improved safety regulations. Some lessons had indeed been learned from the rapid spread of fire through warehouses stocked with oil, tallow, spirit, hemp, and fodder, up streets too narrow for pumping engines and crowded with dangerously flammable houses; and fought by few and ill-equipped volunteers, as most inhabitants were trying to salvage their belongings and flee. (The fact that only six deaths occurred in the fire itself is attributed to the fact that flight took precedence over fire-fighting.)

The new safety regulations included stricter control on dangerous trades and the storage of dangerous goods. Hot ashes were to be quenched before they were disposed of, and were not to be left near a staircase. Dangerous houses were to be demolished (by gunpowder) and indemnity paid for them; their replacements had to be built of suitable material and to a limited height. Fire-fighting equipment (including 'continuous-stream' engines) was to be provided at public expense and the water-pipes were to be fitted with plugs, so that they might be tapped. A bellman was to patrol at night and skilled men were to be available to extinguish fires. Leather pipes and iron-wired suction hose (imported from Holland) were soon introduced so that the fire-fighters could stand a safe distance from the flames.

The rebuilding of a city after destruction by fire naturally affords great opportunity for modernization and improvement, although total replanning of a city is seldom possible. London was rebuilt with wider, straighter streets, and raised quays. The new markets were more suitably sited and the many small parishes made into fewer bigger ones, with fine Wren churches. The City of Hamburg similarly acquired a fine sewage system after the large fire of 1842 (which also produced the world's first news photograph: C.F. Stelzer's 'Charred Waterfront').

The 1666 fire of London is credited with stimulating the development of organized fire insurance, and indeed of property insurance in general, since the rudimentary marine insurance available at that time took much longer to evolve. Financial help after fire loss was previously restricted to money obtained from begging (which needed permission from the King or the Church) or from assistance offered by one's guild. The first fire office opened in 1680 and insured London houses at a premium which depended both on the size of the house and the fire hazard involved. A brick house could be insured for 2.5 per cent of its annual rent, and a frame one for 5 per cent.

Over the next one hundred years fire offices were established throughout Britain, insuring all types of contents in addition to buildings.

The early fire insurance companies soon built up a good reputation for honouring their contracts, largely because they co-operated in assessing actuarial risks and in charging a realistic premium. In Britain, formalized agreements between companies started as early as 1826 and became more centralized as the Fire Offices' Committee in 1868, but were not covered by national legislation until 1909. The only legal interference before that date was the requirement of the insured to pay stamp duty, which was so heavy that it sometimes exceeded the premium.

This book is no place in which to explore the labyrinth of legal minutiae in a fire insurance contract, but it is worth noting that the first policies were confined to material loss occasioned by fire. Compensation is never provided for loss of objects of purely sentimental value, but nowadays insurance cover can often be obtained against 'consequential loss' of profits, if a business is damaged by fire. Standard fire insurance policies may have exclusion clauses for fires caused by such factors as earthquakes, war, and 'riot and civil commotion' (i.e. political or industrial action), and special conditions relating to explosions and to water damage. Private dwellings and their contents are now more usually insured under a comprehensive policy, in which fire is only one of a possible number of hazards against which the property is covered for a single premium. Here, too, consequential expenses, such as temporary alternative accommodation may be provided by insurance cover. Agricultural fire insurance poses different problems. Sweden was one of the first countries to tackle the insurance of forests against fire, but in those areas, such as North America, where there is a high risk of vast forest fires, insurance is out of the question.

The aim of the early fire-insurance companies was to relieve the loss which one individual incurred by fire by sharing the financial hardship amongst large numbers of potential other victims, the majority of whom would never become actual ones. It was obviously in the interest of the companies to reduce the claims made on them, and we have seen that they designed their premium rates in order to encourage fire safety. They were also concerned to minimize the damage caused by such fires as did occur. Since the municipal fire-fighting services were often ineffective, the insurance companies formed their own and also did much to further the development of the fire-engine, which they used from about 1722. Each corps had its own livery, with a large arm badge, and wore protective helmets of horsehide and metal, padded with wool. There was great competition to be the first corps to arrive on the scene, largely for the purposes of advertisement. It became the practice for buildings to carry the badge of the company they insured with, and naturally a company would direct its best efforts towards protecting its own buildings.

In the early nineteenth century, larger fire brigades were formed in London by combining those of several insurance companies, and by 1865 all London fire services had been taken over by a central London Fire Engine establishment, to which the insurance companies still had to contribute. Elsewhere in Britain, many towns had municipal brigades; and many private establishments, such as big houses and firms, maintained their own fire-fighting service. For example, Oxford University had its own fire-engine and crew from 1809–80, and the Oxford University Press is recorded as buying a fire-engine in 1830. In 1879, the students of Girton College, Cambridge, then restricted to women, had their own fire brigade, soon to be followed by the all-women brigade of forty to fifty students of Holloway College, London, who drilled in blue serge uniform and sailor hats. It was not until 1938 that Britain required all local authorities to provide fire services to a specified standard. These local fire brigades were short-lived, as they were centralized into a national fire service throughout the Second World War, although they were decentralized and improved soon afterwards.

In the USA, the first organized fire brigade was founded in 1736 in conjunction with Benjamin Franklin's insurance company. Each member supplied six buckets and two strong linen bags at his own expense. Other brigades followed rapidly and, as in Britain, competed for clients. To the consternation of the householder, the fire-fighters sometimes fought off a rival corps before attacking the fire. The subsequent history of fire brigades in the USA and Canada closely follows that in Britain, although in small towns volunteer fire brigades persisted much longer.

The need for accessible water for fire-fighting resulted in the present situation where most urban buildings are within hose-distance of a hydrant. By the end of the nineteenth century, there were 30 000 in London alone. The mere presence of a hydrant is not, of course, a prophylactic against fire damage. In the New York City fire of 1835, they were frozen, as was the water in the hoses. In Baltimore in 1904, fire companies from Washington DC, Wilmington, and Philadelphia came to assist the local fire services. But as their hose couplings would not fit the Baltimore hydrants, they had to pump water from the waterfront, or transport it from there to the scene of the fire. The water in the hydrant must be of sufficient pressure to reach to the top storey of every building it serves. This was not the case for the ten-storey office block of the Equitable Life Insurance Company in New York, which was destroyed in 1912. Much more recently, in 1985, there was an aircraft fire at Manchester in which fifty-five people died. The subsequent enquiry showed that all the hydrants at the airport had been turned off simultaneously for repairs.

Many fires which cause casualties or serious damage are subject to investigation of why they started and how they burned. One aim is to establish whether the ignition was intentional. The presence of, for example, matches or paraffin would suggest arson, but much can also be learned from the way the fire progressed. An extreme example is a haystack fire, which, if spontaneous, starts in the centre and burns a channel to the outside; when the fire-fighters open the stack, the increased access of oxygen to the partly pyrolysed hay may cause the whole stack to blaze. An arsonist would of course be likely to ignite the outside of the stack, and so create a quite different pattern of burning. A burned house provides much evidence, not only of where and how the fire started, but the way in which it proceeded. Chromium, for example, becomes discoloured by fire, due to the formation of a thin film of oxide. The thickness of this surface layer, and hence its colour, varies with the temperature, and so any chromium-plated object provides a record of the highest temperature reached. Depth of charring of wood depends on the time it has been exposed to a particular temperature. A 2.5 centimetre char at 815 °C indicates an exposure of about 40 minutes. If the windows are very stained, but unbroken, the fire has built up slowly; further slow heating to a very high temperature would melt the glass, first at the corners. A faster build-up to a high temperature would leave clean windows with many cracks, whereas an even faster build-up would produce a few very large cracks. Further research is likely to show that useful information can also be obtained by analysing the tar produced in accidental fires.

Present-day fire services do not restrict their activities to fires. Just as fire insurance companies extended their business to all forms of property insurance, the fire brigades which these companies developed now operate rescue services wherever they are needed, in fires, accidents, or natural disasters.

We have seen that the fire insurance companies have, since their foundation, sought to minimize the damage caused by fire, as well as to insure against the financial losses it produces. It is therefore no surprise that the first formal work on fire research was initiated by an insurance company, who in 1894 set up Underwriters' Laboratory Inc. to investigate the fire hazards associated with various types of electrical lighting and other equipment. British fire research, also sponsored by the insurance companies, started slightly later and was mainly directed at testing the efficiency of fire-fighting equipment and the combustion properties of doors and shutters.

The Second World War provided much impetus for research on fire. The USA investigated its prevention and control in military and naval contexts, and later in forests. After the war, research sponsored by the National Academy of Science and the National Research Council extended the studies to peacetime situations. Fire research has been proceeding throughout the industrialized world since the 1950s, with different countries often investigating complementary aspects of the problem. Canada, for example, developed both theoretical models of fire spread and observational studies of mock-up buildings, which could fortunately be extended to some real buildings which were scheduled for demolition. Work in Japan, which has suffered much from fires caused by earthquakes, has long been concerned with the outbreak of mass fires and the effect of wind on their spread. The earliest study was that following the Kanto earthquake of 1923, which destroyed nearly 50 square kilometres of central Tokyo at a cost of £200 million. It revealed that the mass fire had its origin in at least eighty independent ones, presumably arising, as in the San Francisco earthquake fire of 1906, from fractured gas pipes and burning fuel from spilled lamps and heaters. Workers in the UK have studied the conditions needed for ignition and subsequent growth of combustion, with a view, of course, to its suppression. The theoretical interpretation of such results requires knowledge of the detailed mechanisms and rates of the many individual pyrolysis and oxidation reactions.

As we have seen the chemistry of combustion is extremely complex and attempts to unravel it depend on fundamental research being

25 Candles for private devotion. Moscow, 1991

26 'The Martyrdom of St Lawrence'. Mosaic in the church of Galla Placida, Ravenna, mid 5th century

carried out in laboratories throughout the world. If these results are to be used to make our environment less prone to fire hazards, the fire-fighter, architect, builder, furnisher, garment-maker, factory owner, user of electrical appliances, and buyer of many everyday goods, all need to know whether the materials and objects they are using are safe. And if they are, how safe in fact is 'safe'?

Attempts to develop standard test procedures were initiated in Sweden, where the first work was concerned with flame spread in building materials. It is of course very difficult to get international agreement on any topic, but safety testing might seem particularly intractable, even though its aim is surely good. Will it be agreed, for example, that slow flame spread is an important criterion for the safety of building materials? If so, how should it be defined, by what method should it be measured, and under what conditions? How can some important conditions of a real fire, such as reradiation from nearby surfaces, be simulated in the test? How should the hazard of speedy flame spread be balanced against other desirable safety properties such as sluggish ignition or low toxicity of combustion fumes? Ease of ignition is itself a concept which can be expressed in a number of ways, and depends on how long a material must be exposed to a particular energy supply in oxygen of a particular concentration. Any one of these three quantities can be measured at fixed values of the other two in order to rate materials by 'flammability'. Another criterion is the concentration of oxygen needed, under fixed conditions, to *sustain* combustion, once ignition has occurred. Flame spread can be assessed by measuring the angle which the advancing flame makes with the surface. The ease with which a material burns is also affected by the total heat which is actually released.

A complementary aim for safety testing is the study of the smoke and fumes produced. In what quantity are airborne products given off and what do they contain? How much oxygen remains? The most important question about the smoke and fumes is, of course, their effect on people. As humans are unsuitable subjects for toxicity experiments, mice and rats have been used to find out what levels of various substances produce irritancy, patho-physiology, morbidity, incapacity, and eventually death. 'Incapacity' may be assessed by the animal's inability to swim, to run a maze, or to avoid an electric shock.

Although laboratory tests under controlled conditions give much useful information, the results cannot be used for direct prediction of the course of any real fire, in which there may be dramatic local gradients in temperature, pressure, and gas concentrations. These can result in turbulent transfer both of heat and of pyrolysis products, and can bring unexpected chemical pathways into operation. A difference of only a few degrees between the temperature of the test and that of a real fire can make a nonsense of some safety predictions. One furnishing material may be almost unchanged below a particular temperature, but when it is 1 °C hotter it may blaze furiously; a second material may burn, but slowly, at a much lower temperature, and continue to burn slowly until the temperature is far in excess of that necessary to consume the first fabric. Obviously at lower temperatures the first material is the safer, but at high temperatures, the reverse is true. Such behaviour illustrates the difficulty of setting up standard safety tests, and may account for the low correlation of safety ratings from one country to another. For example, 'very similar' tests were applied to twenty-four wall coverings by several European countries; that rated 'least flammable' by Germany was rated 'most flammable' by Denmark. Laboratory toxicity studies also give an incomplete picture of what happens in a real fire. Experimental fires often generate lethal atmospheric temperature and lethal oxygen depletion before any toxic product reaches a lethal level; but post-mortem examinations of victims of real fires strongly indicate that the majority die of carbon monoxide poisoning.

More realistic predictions can be made if tests are carried out on as large a scale as possible, in scaled-down mock-ups of rooms, or if possible in full-sized rooms, or even combinations of rooms with corridors. The properties of the material are then expressed in terms of its 'fire-performance', and although such information is pragmatic rather than fundamental, it is what we need for safety planning. Large-scale tests are, however, extremely expensive. (But the cost of *not* doing such tests, even in purely financial terms, may be higher still.)

A different approach is large-scale theoretical modelling, pioneered with the supercomputer at the National Bureau of Standards, Washington. The work has since been greatly developed in the UK at AEA Harwell and the Fire Research Station. Input includes the detailed geometry of the room, the pyrolysis and combustion properties of the fuel, the thermal properties of all materials present, and so on. The room is treated as composed of about 70 000 subvolumes, and containing up to 12 000 representative soot particles. The program is able to generate a model of changes in temperature, turbulent flow, and soot concentrations with time, by considering changes which occur in each of the subvolumes, and using the results to assess the influence of these changes on all the other subvolumes. The predicted course of a fire is very similar to its observed development and for some simple room geometries which have also been tested in full-scale experimental fires, the predicted and observed intervals between ignition and flash-over agree within 10 per cent. The method of fire modelling would seem to hold great promise for prediction of hazards, with reference both to room dimensions and to new materials, and is now being extended to differently-shaped enclosures, such as tunnels, aircraft cabins, and sports stadia. Predictions show pleasing agreement with medium-scale (1:6) experimental simulations. They are, however, very expensive in computer time, and are still hampered by vast gaps in our knowledge both of the flaming regions of the fire and of the type and concentration of toxic products. We need to learn much about how real materials burn and how real flames spread over real solid fuels (see Plate 21).

Our increased knowledge of fire science does not of itself decrease fire hazards. Results of fire research must first be synthesized into practical recommendations, which must then be transmuted into accepted practice. In much of the industrialized world, considerable success has been achieved in improving fire safety at work. New buildings are subject to such stringent regulations as regards design, construction, and materials that they may almost be regarded as 'fireproof'. Older buildings used for employment or multiple occupancy must often be modified in order to conform to legal requirements about smoke-free exits, fire-resistant doors, alarms, and sprinklers. Buildings of great historic interest pose a special problem, as any alteration to the structure would be deemed inappropriate by architectural purists. Some buildings of this type are no mere monuments, but may house a large working population, together perhaps with objects of great value. Ancient libraries and museums are cases in point. While for most buildings, prevention is the most important defence against fire, for historical monuments it is the sole defence, and vigilance must therefore be maximal. Many countries now require adequate provision and maintenance of fire extinguishers and regular checks of electrical equipment. The manufacture and sale of electrical appliances is often covered by regulations designed to

KNOW WHAT TO DO IN CASE OF FIRE!

- DON'T PANIC
- KEEP CALM!

3 BASIC INGREDIENTS of a fire
...take one away and FIRE STOPS!

AIR + (Cover -- fire SMOTHERS)
HEAT + (Control heat -- fire COOLS)
FUEL (Shut off gas -- fire DIES OUT)
= FIRE!

How to FIGHT SMALL FIRES:

Aim extinguisher or hose at BASE of FIRE.

YOUR SAFETY COMES FIRST! Stay near exit--low and out of heat.

EXIT

FLOOR FIRES -- sweep from edge in.

WALL FIRES -- sweep from bottom up.

ELECTRICAL FIRES -- disconnect power source, if possible. Use an extinguisher appropriate for what is burning.

But if fire gets LARGE-- **GET OUT!** (And close all doors behind you.)

① SOUND ALARM

Learn the location of the nearest Fire Alarm Call Point. Follow instructions for raising the alarm.

F
I   break glass here
R
E

② EVACUATE PEOPLE

Follow instructions for your building. Know evacuation procedures, primary and alternate escape routes.

EXIT

KNOW YOUR FIRE DRILL.

For different kinds of FIRES...

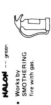

WATER for:

ORDINARY COMBUSTIBLES
Fires burning in wood, cloth, paper, rubbish, rags, shavings, packing materials. Do not use on electrical equipment.

FOAM, DRY POWDER for:

FLAMMABLE LIQUIDS and GASES
Fires fuelled by petrol, oil, grease, paint, paint thinners, propane, ethers.

CO², **HALON** or **DRY POWDER** for:

ELECTRICAL EQUIPMENT
Fires occurring in motors, controls, wiring; or involving live electrical current. Where possible, disconnect electrical supply and treat as appropriate for burning material.

OTHER WAYS TO FIGHT A FIRE

| **DRENCH** a fire with water from hose reel or fire bucket. | **SMOTHER** a fire with a blanket or sand. | **BEAT** out a fire with a shovel. |

3

...there are different kinds of FIRE EXTINGUISHERS.

Find out WHERE THEY ARE and HOW THEY WORK. Read instructions often so you'll be prepared to use every type. . . . NOW, _before_ a fire starts.

They may be coloured predominantly red, with a small colour code showing the type of extinguisher. Or, they may be coloured as indicated here.

FOAM — cream

- Works by SMOTHERING fire with blanket of foam.

HALON — green

- Works by SMOTHERING fire with gas.

DRY POWDER — blue
- TYPES: stored pressure: cartridge operated.
- Works by SMOTHERING fire with blanket of powder.

CO₂ (Carbon Dioxide) — black

- Works by SMOTHERING fire with gas.

WATER — red

- TYPES: stored pressure: cartridge.
- Works by COOLING fire.
- Do not use on electrical equipment.

- **KNOW** how fires are caused.
- **REPORT** or repair unsafe conditions.
- **PRACTISE** good housekeeping.
- **LEARN** emergency procedures.

Oxford University Safety Newsheet 1990.

protect the users not only against electric shock, but also against the hot-spot generated by a faulty circuit.

In addition to regulations designed to promote general fire safety at work, there is a multitude of regulations and codes of practice which govern dangerous trades and hazardous substances. All dangerous materials must be clearly labelled using accepted symbols which identify the particular hazards involved. Flammable liquids used, say, in paint manufacture must be transported, dispensed, used, and disposed of according to safety regulations which also refer to the heating and ventilation of the plant and the maintenance of equipment. Many fire codes cover not only the manufacture and use of flammable materials such as liquid fuels, dry cleaning solvents, matches, fireworks, and timber, but also heating, ventilation, and maintenance of the plant and more general practices such as the removal of grass and rubbish and the accessibility of exits. Regrettably, accidents do still occur at work, as in the explosion which destroyed the chemical plant at Flixborough, UK, in 1974, killing twenty-eight people and injuring eighty-nine others. A temporary pipe ruptured, releasing the highly flammable vapour of cyclohexane into the air, at a rate of more than 1 tonne per second. In the enclosed space of the plant, the deflagration became a detonation (see p. 129). The resulting fireball and shock waves damaged buildings up to 3 kilometres away.

Most of us, however, are exposed to fewer fire hazards during our working hours than during the rest of the day. About 64 per cent of US fire deaths occur at home and another 16 per cent in hotels and places of entertainment. As early as the mid-nineteenth century, fire escapes on tall buildings in New York were mandatory (although often ineffective, see Chapter 20). Building regulations for homes are often much less stringent than those for other buildings and much more difficult to enforce; and there is no requirement for house-owners to equip their homes with fire detectors, sprinklers or even extinguishers. Recent hotel fires in the USA on the other hand, cannot be attributed to absence of safety regulations. The eighty-four people who died in the MGM Grand Hotel fire in Las Vegas, Nevada, in 1980 were probably victims of the construction defects of the building, which did not meet the safety requirements which were in force when it was built seven years earlier.

Theatres have been particularly at risk from fire on account of the early use of naked flame for lighting, and the hazard, which still exists, of stage sets with a very high ratio of surface area to mass. Some of the methods used by stage hands were markedly hazardous, for example the oxygen and hydrogen needed for the production of limelight (see p. 61) were supplied in bags on which the operator sat to control the pressure. Iron cylinders became compulsory in the UK after a severe fire in Drury Lane Theatre, London. The death of 602 people in the fire at the Iroquois Theater, Chicago, in 1903 led to more stringent safety regulations in theatres throughout the world. However theatres, dance-halls, and night clubs and discos are a continuing hazard since they assemble large numbers of people in a small area in buildings which may have low fire-resistance and inadequate exits. The plastic ceilings often used in places of entertainment are particularly dangerous since they both melt on to any people trapped below and burn, emitting thick toxic smoke.

Regulations about the fire safety of house contents (like those about building) are fewer and less stringent than those in force for public buildings or places of work. The difficulties of reaching agreement about safety standards and the increased cost of supposedly safer materials are disincentives to enforcing their use. However, the increased use of smoke detectors in private houses has been claimed to have caused a significant reduction in the number of deaths in home fires.

Most of society's efforts to combat accidental fire are directed towards groups of people, be they manufacturers, builders or workers. More could surely be done to modify the behaviour of individuals; over half the fire deaths in the UK are attributed to personal carelessness, of which three-quarters are blamed on misuse of equipment, often despite clear safety instructions. Economic, as well as human benefits might be gained by publicizing the dangers of, for example, playing with matches, interfering with extinguishers, smoking in bed, hoarding flammable rubbish and blocking exits.

Little research has been done into the way people behave when they are involved in a fire. Many derive great excitement, often accompanied by sexual arousal, at watching a fire from a distance. When they are too near and need to escape, they may behave unwisely, either through the 'lack of judgement' observed in the early stages of intoxication by fumes, or because they do not know what they should be doing. Some may be overcome because they linger to consider what to do next or to collect a few valued possessions. Others panic, rush to an exit, and may get crushed in the stampede.

Although psychologists have been unable to provide a satisfactory definition of panic, the layman would claim to recognize it easily as undisciplined and often counterproductive activity, generated by fear. Such activity may itself cause death, as is thought to be the case in the Iroquois Theater fire (p. 221) and also the Lakewood grammar school fire in Collinwood, Ohio, which claimed 175 child victims in 1908. It is easiest to evacuate a burning building calmly if as many people as possible know what they are meant to be doing. When a building has largely the same occupants every day, panic can be minimized by holding regular fire practices. The Japanese authorities celebrated the 1990 anniversary of the Kanto earthquake by holding evacuation drills of smoke-filled shops and stations in the Tokyo district; thirteen million people were involved. In a residential institution, such as a boarding school, drills should be held at night. If a real fire were to occur, most people would then know what to do, and where to go, and would appreciate how quickly a building can be evacuated without mishap, provided that the proper procedure is followed. When occupants cannot escape unaided, each member of the staff must know exactly whom they must help, and a rehearsal procedure is even more necessary. In the past, tragic fires have occurred in hospitals and residential homes for the old and the handicapped, often because their old buildings did not comply with fire-safety regulations.

Hotels, theatres, and aeroplanes pose different problems as the gatherings are only temporary. All the emergency exits must be clearly marked and the sensible visitor will consciously note them on arrival, and work out at least two escape routes. Gamble claimed in 1925 that the best way to prevent panic if fire started in a theatre was for someone to come to the front of the stage and crack a few jokes with the audience, after which the orchestra should play the national anthem. The heroic themes of many national anthems, combined with the familiarity of the tune, might indeed generate a state of purposeful, calm confidence. Staff should of course be trained thoroughly; but not too rigidly. There is a story that, during a restaurant fire, all the waiting staff efficiently escorted their own customers to safety. When they had finished, they themselves stayed outside, making no attempt to help colleagues who still had guests at many more tables.

The aim of minimizing casualties by informing people what they should be doing is as important for the professionals as for those who are trying to escape. The co-ordination of fire-fighting services is obviously a role of key responsibility, as indeed is the role of co-ordinating the different emergency services; but in the Manchester airport fire of 1985 (see p. 213), the fire and ambulance services went to one rendezvous while the police went to another. Although modern technology should make light work of communication, such blunders are not infrequent.

Even though a fire may cause no casualties and the financial loss involved is spread infinitesimally thin by insurance, it must be stressed that *all* unwanted fire causes financial loss by destruction of resources and the liberation of energy which escapes unharnessed. It has been estimated that the Great Fire of London destroyed property to the value of £10 730 500, at 1666 prices. The Chicago fire of 1871 consumed one hundred and ninety million contemporary dollars. Material losses from the incendiary air raids of the Second World War must have been exceedingly heavy; in an earlier wartime conflagration, it was estimated that twenty million pounds worth of property was burned during the fighting between the Greek and Turkish armies in Smyrna in 1922. Turkey has, over the years, suffered considerable fire losses, its capital (then Constantinople) having been subjected to seven large fires in the second half of the eighteenth century, and to large or fairly large fires almost annually during the half-century from 1870–1920.

Statistics of casualties and financial loss do not, of course, even approach a description of the suffering which fire can cause. They give no indication of distress, except perhaps that of the bereaved and injured. It would indeed be difficult to take into account the feelings of those fire-fighters who did not manage to save all the occupants, of the owner who sees a lifetime of creative effort reduced to a charred skeleton, of the custodian of rare books defaced or consumed by fire, of the construction engineer who had designed his work to be safe. These examples are but a few. Even in a small house-fire, the feel and the stain of the omnipresent tar can oppress and depress those concerned in cleaning up salvageable items, and the smell can linger, acrid, for months or even years inside cupboards or between the pages of infrequently used books. The loss of small familiar objects may assume disproportionate importance, even if they were of neither sentimental nor financial value.

We have seen, however, that some good may come out of unwanted fires, however tragic they may be. The great fires which laid waste whole cities also cleared them for fresh planning with more gracious streets and better drainage; and they stimulated preventative and protective measures. In our own times, big fires are usually the subject of an enquiry, which often leads to adoption of more sensible practices. The fire at the London underground station of King's Cross (see p. 196), found to have been started by an unextinguished match or cigarette, led to a total ban on smoking throughout the whole underground railway network. But the match might not have led to tragedy had the grease been cleared from the escalator more frequently, had wooden boards not been stacked in the ticket hall, and had the warning been heeded at the outset. All too often, enquiries of this type show that tragedies occur through a series of avoidable malpractices, some of which are already known to the authorities.

Sometimes new lessons are learned from fire disasters; more often old lessons must be relearned. The collapse of an exhibition hall through softening of metal girders was dramatically demonstrated in New York in 1858 (see p. 193), but almost identical fates befell the London Crystal Palace in 1936 and the Chicago McCormick Place exhibition hall in 1967. A disaster can, however, increase professional and public awareness and more care is then taken, at least for a short while. More resources are used for research on various aspects of fire, and more money is used to implement recommendations. The research is no longer limited to the physical science and technology of combustion. Psychologists are learning more about the relationship between fire and people, the different ways in which people behave when confronted with fire, and the reasons why some people have a strong urge to start it. Psychiatrists and social workers are exploring ways of helping those who have been bereaved or distressed by large-scale tragedies, and are using their new craft of 'disaster therapy' to develop the potential phoenix within us.

22

Nature and fire: towards symbiosis

A rampant forest fire (see Plate 22) may look very similar to a fire raging through a large hotel; but there are a number of important differences between the two. We have seen that, given an adequate supply of air, confined fires burn more rapidly than open ones; since less heat is lost to distant surroundings, a higher proportion is re-radiated to the fuel, and the combustion is accelerated. All rural fires, unlike urban ones, involve the burning of extremely similar fuel, which is solid, of recent vegetable origin, and whether from forest or grassland, composed largely of cellulose. However, in a burning building, even a residential one, there may be gaseous and liquid fuels and a plethora of solid synthetic polymers and animal fibres in addition to the cellulose provided by wood, cardboard, paper, cotton, and linen. Even so, fire modelling has been much less success-ful for forest fires than for confined urban ones, partly because wildfire is subject to a much wider variation in environmental con-ditions. Moreover, the flammability of the fuels of rural fires varies enormously, depending on resin content, moisture content, and size and shape. Coniferous wood is more flammable than similar deciduous wood. Living plants differ in dampness from their dead counterparts which may be either drier, or more sodden. The moisture content of a particular material varies with the season, and even with the time of day. For a given moisture content, the flammability of the fuel decreases with increasing size: dry leaves ignite more readily than dry logs. Once ignited, however, a log contributes a more concentrated output of heat and burns best if surrounded with other burning logs, while dried grass or leaves burn better if not too compact. Living wood of diameter more than a few centimetres is unlikely to burn, but, on the contrary, acts as a heat sink.

The rate at which fire spreads through a forest depends also on the continuity of the flammable material, as does the intensity of the heat generated. Initially, a rural fire travels mainly on the surface of the ground, which may be generously loaded with such combustibles as fallen twigs and leaves, and dry grasses and ferns. Curled dead oak leaves and tufted pine needles are rapid carriers of surface fire (but single pine needles form a compact mat which burns more slowly). Underground material, consisting of roots and compacted leaves, is difficult to ignite but, once alight, is so difficult to extinguish that it may continue to smoulder for weeks. Surface fires can be contained in particular areas of forest by adequately wide fire-breaks kept free of combustible ground cover.

Wildfire does not travel only along the forest floor, however. The flames from the surface fire rise and ignite suitable brush and shrubs, and from this middle region, leaves from the forest canopy may ignite if they are no more distant than one and a half times the flame height. On a still day, the fire may travel up a single tree in this way, but should a wind blow up, this 'torching' effect can rapidly turn into a crown fire which spreads through the canopy, consuming living foliage. A gap in the canopy of 100 metres or more is usually enough to stop the spread of a crown fire and bring it down to the surface layer. A forest fire, if unchecked, can destroy whole towns in its path. In 1811, sixty-four villages and hamlets were destroyed in the Austrian Tyrol. In 1871 in Peshtigo, Wisconsin, 1152 people died, while the Minnesota fire of 1918 claimed 569 lives in twenty-six towns.

In many ways, fire in a forest and within a closed room represent the two limiting cases of fire behaviour. Within a room the oxygen supply is limited, the heat is trapped, and the development of the fire is largely uninfluenced by external factors such as the weather. There is a moderate to high mass of fuel per unit area and so the fire burns in one place for an appreciable time. A forest fire, on the other hand, has a limitless supply of oxygen but much of the heat it generates is lost to the atmosphere, both by convection and radiation. Moreover, the fuel per unit area, even in an old decayed forest, is much less than that in even the least heavily fuel-loaded building. Unless a whole pile of lumber is burning, only those regions very close to the flame will be pyrolysed by the heat of the combustion products. For this reason, wildfire moves rapidly and the rate at which it travels over the surface of the ground is very sensitive to any factor which can spread the flame.

A surface fire travels up a bank more quickly than along or down it, because the flame warms a larger area of the slope above it than below it, or to either side of it (see Plate 2b). Wind enlarges the flame area in the same way and increases the supply of oxygen, so greatly accelerates the spread of the fire (unless the fire is so small that wind blows out the flame). Fires always create their own draughts and in large forest fires, the upward convection currents are very strong. Cold air is sucked in to replace the hot air so forcefully as to rotate, causing at first a 'fire-whirl' and then, as the force further increases, a cyclone. 'Fire-storms', as they are called, accompany not only forest fires (such as those at Peshtigo in 1871 and at Sundance, Idaho, in 1967), but also large incendiary air raids (as on Dresden and Tokyo in 1945) and atomic explosions (as happened in the attack on Hiroshima, also in 1945).

One of the many difficulties in modelling a forest fire is the complex interaction between the wind, which may of course vary moment by moment, and the convection currents caused by the fire itself. Given an initially unstable turbulent airflow, prediction is well-nigh impossible. Forest fires are, of course, retarded by rain, which cools the fuel, provides a transient protective coating between the fuel and the air, and generates steam which dilutes the oxygen. However, the retardant effect of light rain on the burning of wood is less than might be expected because the rain is converted immediately to steam, which absorbs much less heat from the fuel than does liquid water and does not provide even a momentary coating. Wildfire is also somewhat sensitive to sun, which in hot climates can cause appreciable preheating of the fuel and so make it more flammable.

For many centuries, fire-guards have been used to protect hearth-rugs from being set on fire by burning fragments which might be ejected from the fire by hot combustion gases; and chimney fires were often caused by flaming paper being wafted upwards against the hot soot. In forest fires, too, burning matter can be transported upwards by convection currents and fall, still burning, to start a fire elsewhere.

There have been accounts of dramatic examples of the spread of forest fires by this phenomenon of 'spotting', as when a flaming bush, two metres long, passed the cockpit window of a pilot flying 1000 metre above a fire in Northern California. Long distance spotting occurs frequently in Australia where the curled up bark strips of Eucalyptus candle-bark form cylinders which would have made a good substitute for Prometheus' fennel stalk. They are stripped off the burning tree by convection currents, carried upwards for 3–4 kilometres, and may land up to 30 kilometres away, still burning on the inner surface. The moisture content must be high enough to prevent burn-out whilst in flight, but low enough for easy ignition; about 4 per cent is optimal. Shorter range spotting of up to a few kilometres is much more common and fire can be spread in this way by a number of types of bark, cone bracts, and clusters of leaves or needles. The spotting which occurs in grass fires is of even shorter range but may none the less be adequate to cause the fire to cross a road or river.

Although some unprescribed forest fires are started by human carelessness, accidents or arson (see Chapter 7), the great majority are attributed to lightning. Some are caused by volcanic action, but none, so far as is known, by the frictional action of branches, favoured by some classical writers (see Chapter 4). In many areas wildfire seems to occur at regular intervals, which represent the period taken for the burnt area to regenerate and to accumulate enough combustible fuel to sustain a fire under the climactic conditions to which it is subject. The length of these fire cycles varies enormously. The prairies of Missouri often burn annually, the pine forests of Washington every decade, picea forests in Alaska and Canada every century or alternate century, and the alpine tundra of the Rockies or the arctic tundra of North America only two or three times a millennium. Tropical rain-forests never burn.

The flammability of a particular type of plant can be influenced by other living things. Trees can be killed by insects or fungi, and so burn more easily. Their tops can be stripped by squirrels, leaving bare twigs which are readily struck by lightning. Squirrels build flammable dreys out of pine-cone scales, and chippings from woodpecker nests can allow fire to travel more rapidly across the forest floor. But animal action can also retard fire; flocks and herds often use familiar routes, trampling the ground cover and eating young shrubs, so creating natural fire-breaks.

A rural fire, especially a large forest fire, can have a dramatic effect on both the living and the non-living parts of the environment. Loss of the forest canopy exposes the soil to more sun and wind, and so increases the rate of evaporation of rain. A small rainstorm therefore increases the moisture content of the soil to a lesser extent after a fire; and heavy rainstorms cause more surface erosion, since there are fewer roots and dead leaves to absorb the moisture. A severe fire may produce a water-repellent surface layer, which may persist for years. These effects may alter the drainage pattern of a whole region. The quality of the water declines, as it contains more silt from the increased erosion, more cations, and more phosphates. Stream ecology is also affected by the increased sunlight which follows the destruction of waterside plants. The chemistry of the soil is changed, both by the burning of the surface layer and by the ash which falls from above; a burn produces an increase in the nitrogen and phosphorus present and a decrease in acidity. The soil surface is sterilized from fungi and bacteria, but its rapid recolonization often produces populations greater than before the burn. Rural fires usually produce a great deal of smoke, which is unpleasant for nearby inhabitants and a hazard to motorists. Prescribed burns, whether of tracts of forest or merely of one field of stubble, should of course be carried out when the wind is such as to minimize the hazard and nuisance caused.

A forest fire obviously causes a cataclysmic environmental change, which marks the start of a new cycle of ecological progression, which in fire-prone regions is often the beginning also of a new fire-cycle. Some species of plant are able to survive fire because their buds are protected by thick tufts of leaves or are formed underground on roots or rhizomes. Others are quick to colonize the nutrient-rich burned ground, now freed of former competitors. Fire may act as a stimulant to a stage in the reproductive cycle, by stimulating, for example, flowering (usually in monocotyledons), opening of cones, splitting of seed pods and expulsion of the seeds, or germination of seeds which are already lying on or in the soil. Many of those species which are well adapted to surviving fire contain volatile oils which have a high heat of combustion and favour ignition and propagation of fire, thereby gaining a great evolutionary advantage over competitors which are less well adapted to survive it. As these first fire-adaptive plants die, their remains form humus, the soil starts to return to its former state, and the wider variety of species which can grow on it compete with the fire adaptive species for water, light, space, and nutrients; the ecological wheel of change is in full motion.

Although a severe fire can kill a great many animals, there is no holocaust. Many survive by escape (by land or air), and others by burrowing or hiding in crevices. Some predators find a ready supply of food at the edge of a fire. Lions and leopards hunt at the margins of savannah fires, much as we shoot rabbits running from burning stubble, and some birds fly towards fire to catch escaping insects, lizards, and rodents. The spirit of Prometheus is not restricted to *Homo sapiens*; some of the apes are attracted to abandoned camp-fires, apparently out of pure curiosity. The instinct which activates smoke-flies to approach a fire is thought, however, to have some connection with mating. Fire beetles have infra-red detectors which sense glowing wood at a great distance and enable the females to lay their eggs on hot charcoal, where biological competition is surely minimal.

The series of modifications which fire produces in the environment naturally makes survival at any one moment easier for some animal species and more difficult for others, and so causes progressive changes in the relative populations. For many types of bird, the outcome of a fire depends on exactly when it occurs relative to the nesting season. An important feature for animal survival is the ability to adapt to the different foodstuffs available after a fire, and in some species health is improved by the fire which may destroy the parasites which normally afflict them. As one example of the effect of fire on population, we shall consider its role in increasing the mineral content of stream water. Algae thrive on the high concentration of nutrients, and the increased detritus produced decreases the concentration of oxygen dissolved in the water. This results in a decrease in the population of the trout which cannot function well at low oxygen concentrations, but an increase in the population of its competitor, the catfish, which is more tolerant of slight oxygen deprivation. The increased efficiency of fire prevention has been held responsible for near extinction of the Californian condor because the non-fire terrain undergrowth is now too thick to support a thriving population of the small mammals on which it formerly preyed. Reduced to a diet composed solely of large carrion, the condor now suffers from a deficiency of calcium, which was previously provided by the small bones of rodents and which is required for the production of strong eggshells and chicks with sturdy bones.

27 Cremation of Rajiv Ghandi

28 Demon stoking the flames of hell (French, 1863)

Since fire has such a decisive effect on ecology, it presents man with a powerful tool for modifying his environment. From earliest times, fire has been used for land clearance (see Chapter 7) and, unlike modern mechanical methods, it leaves the soil undisturbed and uncompacted. However, burning is incomplete and wood more than 5 centimetres thick is unlikely to burn unless it is first felled and left several months to dry; and the loss of income over such a period may well be uneconomic. More often fire is prescribed in an attempt to alter the distribution of species, rather than to destroy as much plant life as possible. Light burning can be used to kill off undesirable annual weeds from amongst tougher wanted perennials, and to prevent young woody shrubs from taking over areas of grassland. The grass regenerates quickly after the burn, but the woody species take much longer to re-establish themselves.

Wildlife is often encouraged by prescribed fires of low intensity which destroy parts of the habitat and create 'edges' between different ecological areas. Many species thrive on the diversity provided. The burning of heather on parts of Scottish grouse moors has been carried out for centuries to maintain a high population of game birds (see Plate 9). Naturally, such attempts to manipulate the balance of nature will only fulfil their aims if there is a deep understanding of the ecological interaction between all the species involved. An equally sensitive task is the use of fire to 'freeze' an environment in order to preserve it for posterity in the state in which we enjoy it today. One area of 'preservation' in which prescribed fire is particularly useful is that of managing coniferous forests. Controlled burning of the forest floor destroys seedlings of hardwoods which would later compete with the conifers, and also the layer of fallen branches, cones and needles which, if left, could fuel a large-scale wildfire. A low intensity burn does not affect either the trunks or the needles of the mature trees, and it leaves the soil not only unharmed but enriched. Prescribed burning is often initiated by workers on foot, carrying drip-torches which are designed to prevent accidental spillage and deliver controlled amounts of burning fuel. In Australia, however, burning fuel or incendiary capsules are dropped from low-flying aircraft. All prescribed burns must of course be carried out under an optimal combination of conditions (season, time of day, wind, and weather) and attended by a full team of fire-workers able to ensure that the fire is kept under proper control.

Management of wildfire presents some problems which do not face urban fire-fighters: control of rural fire may be neither possible nor even desirable. Some conservation areas are set aside so that they may develop by unhindered ecological progression, and any attempt to interfere with fire in such a region would be contrary to this primary aim. For example, in 1988, natural fires in parts of Yellowstone National Park, USA, were allowed to burn unchecked. When fires occur in areas which are used for leisure activities the first concern, as in urban fires, must be the protection of human life and health. But wildfire often occurs in the absence of anyone except the fire-fighters and any potential resources for its control must compete with other claims. However, in view of the long-term consequences of wildfire on the environment, it would be an oversimplification to weigh the cost of the fire services solely against the economic productivity of the land.

The cheapest way of reducing the loss and damage caused by wildfire is prevention, both of ignition and of spread. The control of a small rural fire is a comparatively simple and economic operation; suppression of a large area, high intensity forest fire is not. Since there is little we can do to modify either the hot-spots caused by lightning or the supply of atmospheric oxygen, attempts to prevent forest fires must be directed towards reducing both the hot-spots caused by human activities and the supply of readily ignitable fuel.

Much effort has been spent on education to reduce the number of forest fires caused by human carelessness. In most fire-prone areas publicity campaigns exhort forest users to extreme care when smoking, cooking or operating machinery. Some countries use cartoon animals as mascots, the most famous being Smokey the Bear, launched in 1945 in the USA where, later, forestry youth clubs were introduced to encourage care of the forest. Accidental forest fires have been further reduced by improvements in the design of stoves, chainsaws, vehicles, and even railway engines to minimize flying sparks or fuel spillage; but there is as yet no marketable self-extinguishing cigarette.

The rapid spread of wildfire can be avoided by reducing the availability of flammable fuel. One approach is to make potential fuels less flammable by increasing their moisture content. Extra precipitation is initiated in spring and autumn by the seeding of individual cumulus clouds, but since ground-based rain-generators are ineffective, seeding must be carried out by rockets or aircraft, which seldom justify their high cost. Another strategy is to reduce the total amount of low level fuel in the forest. Bottom branches are lopped off, and the forest floor may be cleared, often by prescribed burning.

If various parts of the forest are separated by boundary strips which are very low in fuel, it is difficult for fire to spread from one region to another. Fire-breaks, in which such strips are almost free of any vegetation, are useful for protecting buildings from fire, but are very expensive to maintain, since they must be cleared once, or even twice, a year. It is much more practicable to use fuel breaks that support low growing plants which are not excessively flammable. Attempts to increase the moisture content of these ground-cover plants by irrigation have proved very expensive, even with water. Irrigation by sewage has the further disadvantage that it may lead to an undesirably high concentration of heavy metals in the soil.

Low flammability of ground cover can in principle be achieved by use of plants with a very high moisture content. Large areas of fuel break in California were planted with succulents such as mesembryantheumum around 1930, but these plants were ill-adapted to forest life. A better approach is to use native species, but to shift the population balance in favour of the less flammable ones. Perennial grasses can for example be increased at the expense of annual ones, which are better adapted to fire and burn more readily.

Despite all efforts at prevention, accidental fires do occur on wild land, as elsewhere. The principles of control are similar: rapid detection followed by combat to reduce one or more of the three necessities of fuel, heat, and oxygen. Some of the practices are, however, very different. In the USA, fire detection patrols used to circulate the forest by foot, on horseback, or by canoe. Later, lookout towers were built on high points and at first housed human observers who scanned the scene for smoke. Nowadays, smoke is more often detected by television cameras which are sometimes complemented by heat-sensitive infra-red detectors. Instruments which respond to microwave radiation are also being developed for fire detection. Since the 1920s, however, mobile patrols are coming back into favour; operating from the air rather than the ground, they can cover vast tracts of land. The efficiency of aerial patrol is enhanced by a computer program which, given the necessary information about the weather, terrain, tourist movements, and past fire history, can predict which areas are likely to be the most vulnerable to fire at a particular moment. The patrol can then pay particular attention to such places and, if a fire starts, it is likely to be detected and controlled before much harm is done; moreover, resources need not be wasted in over-zealous observation of regions where the risk of fire is low.

Attempts to control a wild-land fire which has been detected may often be hampered by the flame-spreading action of the wind and the lack of access for tankers of extinguishant. Small fires are commonly fought on foot, often by the age-old technique of beating the flames in order to disperse the hot combustion gases. Branches of green leaves, brooms, or specially designed beaters are all effective for diluting the pyrolysis products with air and cooling them to below the ignition temperature. Smothering a fire with earth also cools it, and in addition prevents access of oxygen. Water is of course an extremely effective extinguishant, acting both as a coolant and as a diluent of the oxygen; it can be provided in a rucksack equipped with a pump.

Small forest fires do not, however, stay small for long. Unextinguished wildfire spreads rapidly, provided that fuel is available. If a lighted match is dropped on to a flat forest floor, evenly covered with flammable debris, a small circle of fire will soon form and, on a windless day, the edge of the circle will expand while the central area, where the first ignition occurred, will burn out. The fire is now in the form of a ring of ever increasing external and internal diameters. Its progress could in principle be stopped by removing all fuel in its path, e.g. by cutting clear of vegetation a large ring so far outside the flame front that the outer circle can be completed before the fire reaches it. Fire ploughs, bulldozers, and explosives* can be used, and have the advantage that the fire-crews are working well away from the flames themselves. Alternatively, trenches may be dug, either mechanically or by hand, only just ahead of the advancing flames. The earth which is thrown inwards serves to cool the fuel and smother the flames, and the region from which it was taken forms a fuel-free barrier.

Real fires seldom occur on level, evenly fuel-loaded terrain, in the absence of any wind; and so they are likely to move more rapidly in some directions than others. Resources are seldom adequate for fighting a fire on all fronts, and fine judgement is needed as to where a fire should be attacked. The decision depends on the terrain, the

---

*The creation of a fire-break has also been carried out during the course of a city fire, as in London (1666) and Manhattan (1835), when houses in the path of the blazes were demolished by gunpowder.

wind, the speed and direction of spread, the men and equipment available, and the position of any buildings or other areas which may merit special protection. Small fires are usually attacked at their head, from in front of their main direction of progress. For larger fires, however, this may not be possible and it may then be better to concentrate resources on the flanks in an attempt to control sideways spread. In addition to the mechanical clearance of fuel from the path of a fire, flammable material may also be removed by back-burning, so that fuel is consumed by prescribed burning before the wildfire reaches it. Occasionally, wind machines are used to direct the back-burning, or to retard or change the direction of the wildfire itself.

Control of wildfire in dense forest is often hampered by lack of access by land, either for bulldozers or for tankers of water or other extinguishant. Air tankers, however, offer a rapid, if expensive, way of transporting water to where it is needed. Some can scoop up water while skimming the surface of the sea or a large lake, while land-based aeroplanes must fill up from a source near a landing strip. Vintage bombers were often used, but are being replaced by helicopters (see Plate 23) carrying buckets since they can deliver liquids with more precision and are more suitable for night use. Moreover, as no special adaptations or additions (such as water tanks) are needed, the helicopters can also be used for other duties. Chemical extinguishants, such as charring agents (see Chapter 20) sometimes complement water in the control of wildfire from both ground and air, but much less widely than for urban fires. Water itself is particularly useful in the mop-up operations which must be rigorously undertaken to ensure that no re-ignition occurs. Recently burned, partially dried-out forest is particularly vulnerable to rekindling. Any bits of smouldering debris, such as roots, which cannot be moved away from potential fuels are broken up by handtools and thoroughly doused. Burned-out areas are none the less patrolled for several days after a fire, to ensure that no hot-spot remains.

Special care must be taken of inhabited buildings which are threatened by wildfire. If the outer structure is of low flammability, the flammable contents are best protected by ensuring that no flame can enter the building through any opening. Doors and windows should obviously be tightly closed, ground-level vents covered with earth, and roof vents cooled by hose play. Good protection to chimney vents and windows is offered by a covering of blankets, constantly doused by hose-water until the wildfire has burned its way past.

Fighting a forest fire is a less hazardous occupation than fighting an urban one in that the number of lives lost per man hour is more than one third lower, although injuries, incurred by working in rough terrain at night, are appreciably higher. Wildfire, however, continues to take its toll. Whilst this chapter was being written, an airtanker succeeded in extinguishing a fire in a narrow valley near Marseille. Lightened by having jettisoned its cargo of water, and probably tilted by a sudden convection current, its wing-tip skimmed a tree top. The plane lost control and plummeted, killing the crew of two and starting a fire at least as intense as the one it had extinguished. Some might say that tamed fire had vanquished the primitive, which in its turn had reconquered the tamed, completing the circle, and maybe squaring the account; but that would take no account of the loss of the elderly aircraft and of two human lives. Man has not yet learned total control over fire and this must surely be part of the fascination of fire for mankind, not only for its more practical members but also for its seers and dream-mongers, whose ideas form the theme of the final part of this book.

V

Fire for contemplation

O thou who camest from above
The fire celestial to impart,
Kindle a flame of sacred love
On the mean altar of my heart.

There let it for thy glory burn
With inextinguishable blaze,
And trembling to its source return
In humble prayer and fervent praise.

Jesus, confirm my heart's desire
To work and speak and think for thee;
Still let me guard the holy fire
And still stir up the gift in me.

Still let me prove thy perfect will,
My acts of faith and love repeat;
Till death thy endless mercies seal,
And make the sacrifice complete
Charles Wesley

23

Fire and the gods

A fire raging through a dry forest or a bombed city is an awesome sight. Our distant forbears may have felt an even greater awe in the presence of fire, since they understood less of how it works, its benefits, and its destruction. It is not surprising that peoples who worshipped trees, rocks, heavenly bodies, and water should also worship the life-enhancing, and life-taking, phenomenon of fire, spewed mysteriously and dramatically from sky or mountain top. Primitive peoples, ignorant both of combustion chemistry and of the nuclear fusion processes which generate stellar energy, would readily assume that fire, which like our nearest star, the sun, provides warmth and light, should also favour the growth of crops. The act of producing fire by rapid movement of a hardwood stick in a depression in a static softwood block, so similar to the sexual activity which mysteriously created new life, seemed to imply a connection between fire and the fertility of humans and animals.

Whilst many early cultures venerated fire itself, others revered those materials which were employed to make it, such as flint, or the oak tree which provided the hardwood stick for the fire drill. The kangaroo, a less immediate candidate for worship as a fire generator, may have acquired this status by virtue of its leaping vitality, or by the suitability of its sun-dried dung for tinder. Naturally occurring fires and perpetually burning oil-wells were obvious sites for fire-worship.

Worship of purely natural phenomena developed into religions which venerated personalized fire-gods. The myths which arose about animals and demi-gods who obtained fire from the gods for the use of mankind represent the first step in our attempts to understand fire (see Chapter 24). As religions evolved, fire continued to play its part in sacred symbolism and liturgical practice, as Charles Wesley's eighteenth-century hymn (see p. 237) shows. Some fire rituals are still performed in the monotheistic religions while others have lost their spiritual significance but survive as secular customs.

Many of the physical characteristics of fire discussed in earlier chapters make it highly suitable both for deification and for ritual (see Plate 24). In addition to its seemingly mysterious origin and unpredictable behaviour, it brings the benefits of controllable heat, of light, and also of sound. But its intense heat can also destroy; bronze statues of the South Indian god Shiva often show him performing a dance of cosmic destruction within a circle of flames. Since fire causes intense pain it is a symbol of divine punishment in several religions, including Christianity and Islam. It consumes, almost totally, offerings made to it, but the small residue of ash increases the fertility of crops. The flames move as if alive and point heavenwards, as if to God. The hot gases above them also rise, carrying with them smoke and other light particles. By use of suitable fuels, a wide variety of smokes can be generated, some resembling clouds, others fragrant or foul-smelling. A fire can be preserved almost indefinitely, or it can be extinguished and rekindled at will. Strange dim and cold manifestations of fire, like the will-o'-the-wisp hovering over marshes and churchyards, appear unexpectedly and proceed randomly, like souls that have lost their way.

Many cultures evolved deities who were associated with particular aspects of fire. The Egyptian goddess Sekhet, for example, represented destructive heat, while the Sumeno-Akkadian Nusku was the god of fire-light. The Ainu people of prehistoric Japan worshipped the fire-goddess who lived in the volcano; the name of the famous Mount Fuji is derived from their word for fire. Later, the Shinto god Kagutsuchi had the power to protect against, or destroy by, conflagration which is a constant hazard in a region prone to seismic and volcanic action. The Roman equivalent, Vulcan, played a much smaller role since Vesuvius had been dormant for several centuries before its notorious eruption in AD 79. The Romans built their fire-temples to Vulcan on the outskirts of their cities, doubtless to maximize the chance of success of their prayers for deliverance from conflagration; and to this day many a rural community has its bakery

Natural gas burning at Baku, eighteenth century (the phenomenon had been described by Marco Polo in 1272)

and communal cooking oven on the periphery of the village. The Icelandic Surtr was probably also a god of volcanic fire, and the Indian goddess Devi dwelt in the natural fires of oil fields and in jets of flammable vapours.

Tamed, domestic fire also had its guardians. The ancient Japanese worshipped the cooking-oven, apparently without personification. The Greek goddess Hestia and her more famous Roman counterpart Vesta, who presided over the fires in home and temple, are thought to have been deities of the hearth stones and the altar, rather than of the fire itself. The idea of the hearth as a symbol of family well-being extended to include the welfare of the wider community, and at its heyday the altar of Hestia at Delphi represented the civic hearth for all Greek people. The Lithuanian god Dinstipan had narrower responsibilities: his sole activity was that of directing the smoke up the chimney.

Some gods combined several aspects of fire. The Babylonian Girru personified both the technological power of the smith and the holier fires used for sacrifice and for the destruction of evil. The Greek Hephaistos, god of volcanoes, used his subterranean fires for the manufacture of weapons. The most comprehensive fire-god was, however, Agni, whom the ancient Hindus revered as high priest of sacrificial offerings. He was depicted with two faces, one malignant and one beneficent, and with three limbs representing his three manifestations: as the sun, promoting the growth and fertility of crops; as lightning, bringing vengeance; and as earthly fire, providing humanity both with warmth and with rising smoke which bore its prayers to the other Vedic gods.

Religious rituals involving fire formed the focal point of early Zoroastrianism in Persia and later in the Parsi communities in India. The holy prophet Zoroaster was engaged in spiritual contemplation on a mountain top and escaped unscathed when the entire mountain was destroyed by fire. For his followers fire symbolized both sacred purification and the transport of prayers to their god.

Early man's difficulties in kindling fire (see Chapter 3) are reflected in the importance of perpetual fire in many religions ranging from North American camp-fires to the Mediterranean hearths of Vesta and Hestia and the Asian altars of Zoroaster. Some rituals demand the preservation of fire for a defined period. The fire by which Agni blessed a Hindu marriage should be preserved to light the funeral pyre. Greek orthodox Christians preserve an icon lamp from one Easter to the next and the Jews light one candle from another throughout the eight day festival of Hanukka. The need of nomadic peoples to transport embers has also passed into rituals accompanying movement to new land or property. The fire may have been taken from a previous house (as in recent Russian custom), from the bride's house as in various marriage ceremonies, or from a public civic hearth, as in Greek colonization customs. The Vikings claimed land or property by carrying fire round it, or by shooting lighted arrows at it. Amongst some North American peoples, the borrowing of fire from neighbours symbolized cautious negotiation.

The great importance which is often attached to keeping a ritual fire 'undefiled' may have its origin in the primitive need to supply it with appropriate fuel. Zoroastrian fire, for example, became impure if contaminated by a corpse, while for some North American tribes, fire became defiled if spat into. Since those who tended sacred fires had, by definition, a priestly role, high moral virtue was expected of them, whichever god they served.

The emphasis necessarily laid by primitive peoples on kindling techniques has been preserved in the particular requirements for the method of ignition. To the Zoroastrians, the holiest fire was that which had been produced by lightning, but many cultures prefer 'need-fire' kindled by the sexually symbolic fire-drill. The present-day Olympic flame is, however, obtained by concentrating the sun's rays with a parabolic mirror (see Plate 4).

One of the most significant aspects of fire for sacred ritual is the liberation of destructive heat. Offerings of food to the gods of hearth and altar were widespread; convection took the steam and smoke upwards, bearing the offering to the god, often together with prayers. Many marriage rituals involved such offerings. The Greek word for sacrifice is related to the terms for smoke and burning, a reminder that in every Greek household Hestia received a daily share of the main meal. One may speculate as to why the secular use of candles in our own electrically lit homes is restricted largely to the dining table; perhaps Hestia lingers still.

Offerings to the fire were not restricted to food. Live sacrifice, both of humans and animals, was also common, as recalled by the biblical account of the divine intervention to prevent Abraham from offering his son Isaac to the fire-altar. Some societies replaced live victims with images, for example the small Greek clay figurines, or in Boethia, a huge log effigy dressed as a bride. Live animals were, however, sometimes used. Mrs Gaskell's novel *North and South*, written in 1855, refers to the belief that the screams of roasting cats were efficacious against the forces of evil, and it may have been for this reason that live cats were thrown into bonfires in some parts of rural Europe as recently as the early twentieth century.

There may well have been an element of religious sacrifice in the all too recent Hindu practice of suttee where a widow was required to accompany her husband to the afterlife by allowing herself to be burned on his funeral pyre. Some wives even committed suttee in anticipation when their husbands went off to battle. Self-destruction occasionally occurs in our own day, often in protest against ideological injustices, as in the suicides of the Buddhist monk Quang Duc in 1963 and the Czechoslovak student Jan Palack in 1969. In Greek mythology, the hero Heracles was burned on his funeral pyre still alive, so that he might become a god without having been subjected to human death.

The destructive power of fire has frequently been exploited as an instrument of execution, for example for adulterous Hindu husbands. (An adulterous Hindu wife, however, was subjected to the more ignominious death of being torn apart by dogs.) Death by fire was considered particularly suitable for spiritual offences, such as heresy and sorcery, from which society needed purification. Legend claims that St Lawrence was martyred by being roasted on a gridiron (see Plate 26) although it is more likely that, as a Roman, he was executed by the sword; but death by roasting was probably the actual fate of St Vincent of Saragossa. Joan of Arc was burned at the stake as a heretic at Rouen in 1431, and over several centuries, large

Granite cross in Broad Street, Oxford, marking the site of the stake where the martyrs Latimer and Ridley were burned

numbers of unfortunate women must have been burned as witches, both in Britain and continental Europe, by people who genuinely believed that they were thereby eliminating evil. Several churchmen were martyred by fire in Oxford during the fifteenth and sixteenth centuries. In 1555, Bishop Latimer, sent to the stake for his support of the Reformation, exhorted his fellow victim: 'Be of good comfort, Master Ridley, and play the man: we shall this day light such a candle by God's grace in England as I trust shall never be put out'.

Ritualistic execution of criminals by burning has now happily been largely replaced by the burning of their effigies, much as animal and human sacrifice was superseded by offerings of clay figures. The ancient Slavs celebrated Spring by burning an effigy personifying winter, and in our own times Christians in Latin America and in Greece and Cyprus burn Judas Iscariot every Easter. In Britain, Guy Fawkes meets a similar fate on November 5th on the anniversary of the discovery of his plan to blow up the Houses of Parliament in London in 1605. The burning of books, papers, and national flags provides us with an easy and dramatic means of public demonstration of religious, political or moral outrage. Late twentieth century examples are provided by the books of Salman Rushdie which offended some members of the Muslim faith, by a women's prayerbook which offended those Christians opposed to women priests, and by the flags of overthrown regimes such as the dictatorship of Romania.

The use of fire to destroy human corpses was an obvious way for our nomadic forbears to dispose of their dead, and the practice of cremation has long been widespread (see Plate 27). It was believed that total destruction of the body prevents its coming to further harm, such as mutilation by enemies, use in witchcraft, or natural decay, and frees the spirit, which is warmed and carried upwards by the fire; a spirit thus well cared-for would surely not wish to return to earth to haunt the living. The Vikings' funeral pyre of a burning longship must have been a particularly impressive transition from earth to Valhalla. We ourselves can feel something of the same awe when television enables us to share the solemnity of the cremation rites of the Indian Prime Ministers, Indira, and later her son, Rajiv Gandhi, both victims of assassination. It is understandable that some peoples, particularly those in volcanic regions, believed that fire would one day destroy not only their own bodies but the entire world.

Fires at graves both tend the spirits of the departed and protect the survivors against the evil power of death. In our own times, candles and lanterns are often used for remembrance. Perpetual fire adorns the grave of many a nation's unknown warrior. But death rituals are not the only rites of passage to be celebrated by fire. A Hindu ceremony involves the initiation of a student, together with his tutor.

Purification through fire magic plays an important part in folk medicine. Flaming wands may be waved over the patient to exorcize the evil spirit of illness, and the Chinese even placed burning cones of incense on sick children as a cure. On the other hand, the illness itself is sometimes considered to be a form of fire, and indeed the Greek words for fire and fever are cognate: we still take antipyretics to bring down the body temperature in illness, as we take anti-

Drinking glass as tomb lamp, Greece 1991

Candles at the shrine of St Thomas Aquinas, France, 1991

inflammatory drugs to ease diseased joints. In some cultures, the patient kindled fire with the fire drill, so that the fire passed out of his body into the fire stick. Fire had its place also in legal ritual: oaths sworn over a candle were thought to be particularly binding, being presumably free of impure intentions.

The unpredictability of many aspects of combustion has made fire a fertile area for belief in manifestations of the divine. Some of the fire-legends, such as the bush which appeared to burn but remained unburned, may have pragmatic explanations. (The plant *Dictamnus fraxinella*, cultivated in some English gardens, emits a flammable vapour on hot summer evenings. As an after-dinner trick, the vapour can be ignited by a flick of a cigarette-lighter, but the plant is as unscathed by the enveloping blaze as a Christmas pudding which has been flamed in brandy.) The unexpected ignition of the Vestal virgin's girdle on a cold altar was deemed to demonstrate her purity, as the destruction by fire of Elijah's altar showed the divine presence; but combustion which occurs spontaneously and spreads ravenously is all too common, especially in hot dry regions. We cannot, of course, tease the fire-science from the mythology: is the Ethiopian account of the River Jordan flaming during Christ's baptism a spiritual metaphor, a poetic description of sunlight on rippled water, or the factual report of combustion of a slick of crude oil? We do however know that 'St Elmo's fire', which appears in stormy weather round church spires and tall masts is not true fire, but a discharge of lightning, although believed by Mediterranean sailors to be flames manifesting the guardianship of their patron saint, Erasmus (corrupted to 'Elmo'). It has also been reported around the heads of

29 Hogmanay celebrations in Scotland

30 Midsummer feast of St John, Greece, 1986

people, perhaps giving rise to myths about haloes, or tongues of fire (see p. 248).

Failure of fierce fire to consume was often attributed to divine intervention; there are many stories of Greek church fires which miraculously stop just short of a holy icon. Fires were sometimes used for the express purpose of demonstrating, or testing, the god's support. The Old Testament tells of Shadrach, Mesach, and Abednego who were saved by their god from the 'burning fiery furnace' and, in a similar legend, a cloak which had belonged to St Patrick had saved its wearer from fire and therefore demonstrated the saint's holiness. Buddha showed his superiority to the Taoists by allowing their holy books to burn while changing his own scriptures into waterlilies which floated on the flames. Various ordeals such as walking through fire and touching red-hot objects were widely used to elicit guilt or innocence in the sight of a god. Those who suffered injury were deemed to be guilty; and many of the guilty (and possibly also of the innocent) preferred to confess rather than to undergo the ordeal. The legendary Roman, Gaius Mucius, did not, however, plunge his right hand into the fire to establish innocence, but to show his contempt for the death to which he had been condemned: but his courage was so admired that he was pardoned.

Since the combustion of solid fuel is so complex a process (see Chapter 2), an almost infinite number of unpredictable states can be reached during burning. Such apparent randomness is a fruitful area for pyromancy. Divinations have been made from sparks, from the flickering and flaring of a flame, from the way the smoke rises, from faces seen in the fire, and from the way in which an object curled when placed on hot coals. On Karpathos, Greece, a child's patron saint was chosen from the fastest burning of a number of named candles.

Extinction of fire commonly plays a part in rituals which mark the passing of definite periods of time, as in many European countries where the Yule log was extinguished at the end of the Christmas festival. Maybe the custom in which a child blows out the candles on his birthday cake also symbolizes the completion of fixed period of time. Our forbears would surely have been amazed and delighted had they known the self-relighting candles available to us today. Since the temperature around the wick of a freshly blown-out candle is high enough to reignite the remaining vapour, the candle relights spontaneously almost immediately. It would be hard to find a more appropriate manifestation of renewal. But some ritual extinctions are final, as in the rite of excommunication from the Catholic church. During the fourth century AD in Persia, the Christian fanatic, Narsai, extinguished the sacred fires of his Zoroastrian neighbours to stamp out their worship of false gods (and was martyred for refusing to relight them). The extinction of fire sometimes seems miraculous. Many a fire-fighter would have envied St Fabian the divine aid which enabled him to extinguish a burning house in Rome with a single bucket of water.

Various American peoples viewed the extinction of fire from a perspective quite different from that adopted in Indo-European cultures. Observing that heavy rain could extinguish fire, they supposed that ritual extinction of fire would induce rain, a belief enhanced by the similar appearance of heavy clouds and smoke from a doused fire.

By definition, fire emits light as well as heat. A burning torch is a frequent secular symbol of learning, enlightenment, and education. Some modern rituals involving lamps and candles, such as the lighting of candles by catholic and orthodox Christians (see Plate 25) and the candle-lit procession at Greek Easter, doubtless contain both elements; but sometimes the symbolism seems restricted to the light of the flame, as in the pillar of fire which led Moses through the wilderness at night. The flames which descended (apparently painlessly) on the heads of Christ's followers at Pentecost denoted inspiration, while the candle used at Christian baptism signifies shining spiritual example.

Many current fire-rituals take place around the winter solstice and are probably much older than the events they purport to symbolize. The candles on a Christmas tree, or those crowning Swedish girls on St Lucia's day (December 13th) may have their roots in rituals performed to encourage the return of light after winter. Perhaps Guy

Lamp-shaped badge of Christian evangelical group, 1970s

Fawkes (see p. 58) would be less famous today if his Gunpowder Plot had been discovered in summer, rather than in dark northern November.

Ritual may also make use of the sound which some combustion produces. Fireworks, though used in recent centuries to promote civic and national status, were probably introduced into family and community rituals in their native China to frighten away evil spirits, who disliked the noise of firecrackers, as did the monster who ate the sun and moon during eclipses. Later, muskets added to the din. Fireworks, firearms, and less formal explosive devices were widely used in Christian celebrations. Robert Browning writes of a religious festival in nineteenth century Italy:

> All round the glad church lie old bottles
>   With gunpowder stopped,
> Which will be, when the Image re-enters
>   Religiously popped.

Similar religious celebrations still occur in rural Cyprus and in Malta where the overt rationale of the noise was to alert a busy god to the village's humble festival. In communist Bulgaria fireworks and trace fire contributed to the impressive national remembrance ceremony.

Some fire rituals emphasize the material products of combustion rather than the energy liberated. Not only does fire generate hot gases which rise heavenwards by convection, but it can produce a wide variety of smokes. Some ritualistic uses of smoke to deter evil beings may have grown out of its secular efficacy as a fumigant and repellent of insects and vermin. One Australian tribe burned grass during its funeral rites for fumigation and Tyrolean fairies understandably avoided the smoke produced by burning an old shoe. In Orkney, inhalation of smoke from a hide burnt at the festival of Samhain was believed to bring good luck. At Greek Easter the smoky flames of candles are used to write the protective sign of the cross in soot above doorways.

The fragrant smoke of gums and herbs has been widely used as incense. The components may be thrown on hot coals or powdered and often cast into spirals or joss-sticks (see Chapter 15). Incense counteracts the smell of burnt offerings, pleases gods, scares off demons, represents divine presence, creates a devotional frame of mind, and may even generate hallucinations or trance. Incense was burned in Syria for the solemnization of vows, and is much used by

Christians to this day. In the Chinese liturgy, it is stolen by the forces of evil and later reclaimed. The ancient Egyptians used incense smoke to purify their mouths, and also their hands after washing. The use of 'moxa' incense cones for sacred branding of monks and pilgrims was carried out in Tibet up to 1945.

On the other hand, fire is also associated with the forces of wickedness. The exhalations of a witches' cauldron are often a prerequisite for the casting of an evil spell, while the fires of hell are traditionally stoked by Satan and his minions (see Plate 28).

Many North American peoples make ritual use of tobacco smoke: to invoke rain (see above), to propitiate gods and the souls of slain animals, and to produce dreams. Smoking the calumet symbolized mutual trust when negotiating an armistice or treaty, or exchanging hospitality; the breaking of a covenant made in this way could be fatally serious. Hashish and marijuana are, like tobacco, widely smoked for relaxation; they also induce trance and are used to generate prophetic power.

Ashes from sacred fire also find use in ritual, their reputations doubtless enhanced by the beneficial effect of the potassium-rich wood-ash on the growth and fertility of crops. Mildly alkaline, softly abrasive, and absorbent, they were used for ablutions, cleansing, and drying. Rubbing with ash supposedly improved the circulation and strengthened infants' knees; and hot ashes were used as a poultice. Magic benefits were also claimed. The faces of some African warriors were painted with ashes before battle, possibly in order to scare the adversary as much as to hearten or protect the anointed. However, ash often symbolizes the less positive states of submission, humiliation, mortality, and mourning. At the beginning of the Christian season of Lent, palm crosses are distributed and those of the previous year are burned; the worshippers are anointed with the ash as a reminder that they, too, will become dust. Ashes of the dead are often regarded as sacred and may become talismanic relics.

Mythology, unconstrained by the laws of thermodynamics, is free to resurrect ashes into a living being at a stroke of divine, or popular, will. When the Titans killed, boiled, roasted, and ate Dionysos (Zagreus), a thunderbolt was sent down to consume them by his father, Zeus. From the rising soot appeared men who rebelled against the gods. The remains of the feast were collected, and lo-and-behold Dionysos rises from the dead. The famous mythical bird, the phoenix, is named after the palm tree which, with its spherical top of flame-shaped leaves, was sacred to the sun-god Apollo. Despite much scholarly argument about its lifespan, it was generally agreed that only one phoenix existed. At the end of its appointed span it was consumed by fire, but rose again from its ashes. The asbestos clothes used by Arabian fire-warriors (see p. 82) were popularly believed to be woven from its gorgeous feathers. The myth that a salamander can withstand fire is thought to have arisen by an etymological confusion with the Arabic word for phoenix (although it is likely that salamanders have indeed survived forest fires by hiding underground, cf. Chapter 22).

While the phoenix is a widespread symbol of renewal and resurrection, the other main member of the fire-bestiary, the dragon, often represents evil. Although the flames they exhale may represent 'burning' snake venom, or a more abstract evil, they have also been attributed to halitosis. The large predatory and carrion-eating lizards, now confined to the island of Komodo, may well have had forbears who earned their immortality in folk memory by virtue not only of their ferocity but also of their foul breath. If its smell was as acrid as that now popularly attributed to the 'Komodo dragon', fire might indeed be an apt metaphor.

Twentieth century secular fire-rituals have much in common with former religious practices. The opening ceremony of the Olympic Games is a modern revival. The torch-bearing run was originally a contest, after which the victors lit the fire on the Promethean altar; as today, it burned throughout the games.

Some New Year customs in Scotland and Northern England, which appear to be survivals, involve carrying fire around the village (see Plate 29). One may have its roots in the stone age, as half a tar barrel (a 'clavie') must be fixed to a stave by a nail made with a stone hammer. The embers from the burning clavie are distributed for good luck, and used to light the domestic fires. Other rituals involve whirling burning baskets around the head, or parading with lighted barrels on top of the head. This last custom continued throughout the Second World War despite the stringent black-out regulations; a single barrel was lit and carried round inside a metal trunk supported on the head of one stalwart villager. In Latvia, a lighted tar barrel on a pole is used to forecast fertility; the further its light spreads, the more productive will be the fields.

The burning of the yule log has obvious connections with fertility rites, as in Bulgaria where the log is anointed with oil, incense, and wax, and burned on Christmas Eve. The flames connect the log to heaven, allowing the god of fertility to descend. The log may be hit to produce a multitude of sparks which bring or foretell fertility. An unburnt (and so hardened) piece of log may be kept and incorporated into a new plough, or used to poke a visiting priest, again to increase fertility. In industrialized countries, where many households have only token hearths or none at all, the yule log is still a folk memory, on Christmas cards and as cakes, suitably shaped and decorated; and the first visitor to the house at the start of a new year may bring a symbolic offering of a piece of coal.

Rituals involving bonfires may have elements of mimetic magic, of sacrifice, and of purification. At the Celtic Beltane and Latvian mid-summer festivals, burning cartwheels are rolled downhill to help the sun to run its course. Samhain (see p. 249) recalls animal sacrifice; while the drawing of lots from the fire during the Beltane ceremony is thought to survive from the choosing of a human victim. Some ceremonies, as in France, Cyprus, and Ireland, involve rushing through or leaping over fire, the close contact with the flames giving spiritual purification and protection from misfortune (see Plate 30). Slavic and Greek Midsummer fire festivals may be associated with St John the Baptist through confusion between the Russian word for the ritual (meaning 'heat' or 'ardour') with that for baptism. No moral basis can be claimed for the bonfire-leaping which takes place in the author's city after races on the river, when the victors jump over burning boats in a spirit of inebriated jubilation. Exploits with fire have great spectator appeal from a safe distance and motor cyclists or dogs leaping through hoops of burning paper make popular circus acts; contact with the hot gases is so brief that the sensation must be similar to that of passing a finger rapidly through a candle flame. An even more impressive skill is that of blowing a stream of flammable liquid (such as paraffin) from the mouth and igniting it. A long apprenticeship, starting with pure water, is said to be needed before the act can be accomplished without disaster.

The ritual of walking or dancing on red-hot coals was known in India in 1200 BC, and was widely used for expelling evil spirits. In ancient Rome, fire-walking prowess brought exemption from military service. In modern times, religious firewalking has been practised in Spain, Natal, and throughout Asia; it still survives in Bulgaria and Northern Greece. In most rituals the participants are believed to be under divine protection and so must be in a state of moral virtue. Some firewalkers carry holy objects and may be in a state of religious trance. The fire is lit from a sacred source and the ashes used for cures and divination.

Scientific speculation about the possibility of walking unharmed on red-hot embers was previously centred on the protection of the soles of the feet by callouses, sweat, or some applied coating. The Romans were known to have anointed their feet before firewalking and a recipe containing wine, egg-white, and various plant juices appears in Mark the Greek's *Book of fires* before AD 800. Now,

Walking on red-hot coals, North Greece, late twentieth century

however, it is thought that the most important factor is the low thermal conductivity of red-hot carbon, which prevents heat from travelling rapidly from the embers to the foot during the short period of contact, provided of course that the fire-walker proceeds with the unhesitating confidence which preparation and faith provide. Steady progress across the hot coals must be much helped by the impressively even layer of embers which results from centuries of experience of firemaking.

Fire walking is not now restricted to religious festivals, but has recently been performed in Greece in football-stadia for a combination of money, bravado, and mockery, with women's underclothes or waiters' trays replacing the icons and sacred cloths, and to the accompaniment of bawdy songs. In Britain and the USA on the other hand, one or two isolated groups have started the practice, with the aim of helping the participants to develop their personalities through fostering courage and confidence on the coals which are claimed in one US fire-walking trench to reach temperatures approaching 3000 °C. Some participants seek, and indeed obtain, strength to overcome wider problems such as illness and phobias. It seems that, even in our industrialized and supposedly rational society, the gods of fire are unextinguished (see Plate 31).

24

Fire and the thinkers

Part of the fascination of fire is its variety: of appearance, of use, of behaviour, and of the response which it elicits from us. It is easy to appreciate the appeal to the spiritual side of man's nature of this beautiful, fickle, life-enhancing, life-taking phenomenon. But mankind also has the need to understand, to explain, and to predict. In this chapter we shall explore some of the attempts to fit fire into a coherent view of the natural world.

The first 'explanations' of fire were concerned not only with such general issues as its appearance on earth and its use by mankind, but also with specific observations such as its production by sparks from stones, its consumption of wood, its blackening effect, and its extinction by water. Wood and flints were often thought to have fire lodged in them, and myths of the renewal of fire commonly involved black birds or other animals which, since they were the colour of charcoal, must have been previously burned, and so carry the fire within them. Many myths ascribed the origin of fire to theft. The ancient Greeks' Prometheus stole it from the gods and carried it down to earth in a dried fennel stalk, an ideal structure which provides air and fuel in the right proportions for smouldering and a thick outer cover to prevent excessive loss of heat. Prometheus, like fire-stealers in many other mythologies, was sorely punished for his effrontery, which gave to mankind god-like powers (and with them, greatly increased opportunities for moral choice). Prometheus must have assumed that mankind would preserve his gift, since the myth says nothing about rekindling. In the northwest Pacific, however, the god Yehi, in the form of a raven, stole a burning brand, and the stones and wood on which it fell retained the fire. The New Zealand hero, Mani, kindled flame from a nail of his divine grandmother, but he extinguished it, and had to return to beg another. The same happened again, and again, until all her nails had been used. She then became angry and pursued Mani with fire. He was saved by the rain, and some of the sparks lodged in the flints and the wood. When the Japanese fire-god was killed by his father, his blood fell on sticks and stones; and it is not hard to see why such a myth arose in a region familiar with streaming lava and falling volcanic embers. In non-volcanic regions it would be natural to believe, like the ancient Slavs, that fire is born in heaven and carried to the earth by lightning.

As cultures became more cerebral, mythologies based on anthropomorphic explanations ceased to satisfy. Understanding based on rational thought was required. In ancient Greek communities ranging from Sicily to Asia Minor there appeared philosophers who used their powerful intellects to construct coherent views both of the natural world and of our own place in it. Some created their cosmologies on foundations of thought alone; others, like Aristotle, used their eyes as well, and more fruitfully based their systems on observable fact. But, coming as they did from societies in which most of the manual work was done by women and slaves, experimentation was contrary to their tradition.

Some of the earliest thinkers considered that every type of matter was a different manifestation of the same substance. Around 600 BC Thales, doubtless noting that water could become either steam or ice, opted for this as his universal element. Two centuries later, Heraclitus too concerned himself with material changes and took the view that the sole constancy of matter is in fact change, apparent stability being achieved only by the occurrence of equal and opposite changes. In his scheme, all forms of matter (including the human soul) were different manifestations of fire, itself a constantly changing instrument of change. 'All things' he claimed 'are an exchange for fire, and fire for all things, even as wares for gold and gold for wares'. The purest form of cosmic fire, situated in the firmament above the air we breathe, changes the sea into vapours and rain, which it then expels from the sky to replenish the sea. The oceans dissolve the land, and the land is redeposited from them. His writings, which are both cryptic and obscure, seem to have baffled his contemporaries and still concern philosophers today. Lucretius, writing four centuries later, dismissed Heraclitus as 'light-witted' and his ideas as 'utterly crazy'. He was expounding the ideas of Epicurus, who was a younger contemporary of Heraclitus, and believed that matter was composed of different types of atom, circulating in empty space. Burning involved the emission of 'fiery' atoms.

The most influential cosmology of that period was, however, undoubtedly that of Aristotle, who built on the earlier views of Empedocles that all matter is made up of four elements, earth, air, fire, and water, combined in varying proportions, which are determined by a balance of 'love' and 'strife'. The Four Element hypothesis, as extended and expounded by Aristotle, governed scientific thought for nearly two thousand years. He considered that all matter behaved according to its relative proportions of two pairs of opposed qualities: wetness and dryness, hotness and coldness. Each of the four elements combined two of these qualities as follows:

Air represents hotness and wetness
Earth represents coldness and dryness
Fire represents hotness and dryness
Water represents coldness and wetness

These days we might represent the behaviour of any substance as a point on a two-dimensional grid representing temperature and humidity. The four elements would then occupy the corners of the grid. In this system, the elements are not immutable, but can be changed one into another by keeping one quality the same, while altering the second variable. So if fire (hot and dry) is cooled, it becomes earth, while if it is wetted without cooling, it becomes air. An Aristotelian element is not identical to its natural manifestation, but is rather a purer form, or essence, of it. Thus, for Aristotle, elemental fire was the 'essential quality' of real fire. Such ideas were

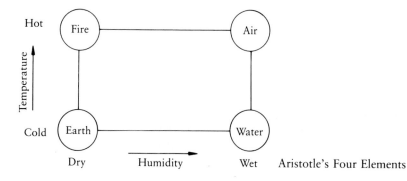

Aristotle's Four Elements

not restricted to Western thought; the Buddhist cosmology is also based on the same four elements, save that air is replaced by wind. Nor need the number of elements be restricted to four. Aristotle extended his system by introducing a fifth element, the aether, to account for the behaviour of the heavenly bodies.

The Stoic philosophers, whilst basically accepting the Four Elements hypothesis, believed that the world is a living entity, animated by fire, which is both a material substance and the breath of a rational, vitalizing god. This fire governs the inter-transformation of the elements and from time to time destroys the cosmos, leaving only a seed. From this, a new but identical system will develop, itself to be destroyed by conflagration, and then reborn. Such a picture echoes the views of Heraclitus, and recalls natural forests with their periodic fires and subsequent regeneration (see Chapter 22). The Stoics' idea of rebirth from ashes is part of the familiar mythology of the phoenix, and their belief that every human being contains a spark of divinity, to be vitalized into flame by the breath of a god, has been carried forward into Christianity, where it manifests itself at Pentecost and in the texts of countless hymns.

The ideas of the Stoics illustrate the complex interdependence of scientific and theological thought, which has continued, with fluctuations, throughout the centuries. Teutonic philosophers, in particular, often incorporated contemporary alchemical imagery into their more metaphysical cosmologies. Boehme (1575–1624), for example, took fire as the fourth of his seven 'forms of nature', claiming that it burns and hurts but does not purify. Its dull light represents the dawn of awareness, which at this stage is full of greed, wrath, and pride. This is the point at which evolution can branch towards light, love, and Jesus, or towards the fires of self-destruction and Lucifer. Such musings do not, of course, throw any light on the physical nature of combustion, but emphasize man's continuing fascination with fire as a symbol of moral choice. Our own speech also contains fire-metaphors in the context of everyday morality, and with roots which stretch further than images of Hellfire or the Holy Spirit. We can toss off such phrases as 'he hasn't got much spark' or 'she's in her element' without a conscious thought for the ancient Greeks. The author has been assured by educated non-scientists that the Four Element hypothesis (see Plate 32) is the obvious, indeed the 'natural' way of looking at nature. Bachelard uses fire as a prime example of his persuasive hypothesis that scientific progress is hampered at a subconscious level by the emotions, symbolism, mythology, and fallacies of the past. Although much of his material dates from the seventeenth and eighteenth centuries, he writes, in 1938, 'When one asks ... even eminent scientists "What is fire?" one receives vague or tautological answers which repeat the most ancient and fanciful philosophical theories'. Over half a century later, the same seems to be true.

The first tremors to shake the apparently immovable Four Element hypothesis came from the alchemists. In the early centuries of the Christian era, Greek intellectuals in Egypt rubbed shoulders with the indigenous metal-workers and from this cross fertilization grew alchemy, which spread through the Arab world. Some of the practitioners were mystics, some magicians, some charlatans, and some seekers after truth. Many were certainly assiduous experimenters. We do not know where, or when, or by whom, the first hints of doubt about the Four Elements were expressed, but we do know that, from about the eighth century AD, information was being amassed throughout the Middle East about the effect of heat on a variety of substances. The Four Elements hypothesis, which supposed that one substance might be transformed into another by changing the amount of its fiery component, must have encouraged those alchemists who sought to transmute base metals into gold. But the more observant experimenters noticed that many minerals emitted a smell of burning sulphur if heated in air, and that some yielded their metal if cast on to hot coals. (Sulphide ores are, of course, changed to the more stable oxides if roasted in air, and the oxides may be reduced to their metals by sufficiently hot carbon.) Sulphur itself was found to burn particularly vigorously. Some metals, on the other hand, are unchanged by fire, and were therefore thought to be 'noble'. Mercury had the virtue of being vaporized by the fire; since the vapour could be collected and condensed, the mercury could be purified by distillation. Other 'less noble', or 'base', metals did not survive fire unchanged but were changed into a powdery oxide of 'calx'.

These observations led some alchemists to think that all matter consisted of two principles, one of which conferred combustibility on the substance, while the other conferred metallic nobility. As sulphur burned so easily and completely, it was thought to consist almost entirely of the first principle. Mercury, which was unchanged by fire even after distillation, was an almost perfect manifestation of the second, while base metals and minerals contained both principles in varying proportions. Since removal of the Sulphureous Principle changed a base metal into a noble one, this Two Principle hypothesis led further generations of alchemists into their quest for the transformation by fire of lowly metals into gold.

There was much medieval discussion as to the relative merits of the Two Principles and the Four Elements. The Two eventually vanquished the Four, only to be joined by a third 'saline' or 'earthy' principle, useful for distinguishing salts and mineral ores from base metals. Leonardo da Vinci (1412–1519) showed that air contained at least two components because it was not completely consumed by combustion or respiration. But his work was too far ahead of its time to receive any attention, and the idea of combustion as the loss of the Sulphureous Principle held unchallenged sway until the mid-seventeenth century when it was subjected to both theoretical criticism and experimental scrutiny. In several works by Robert Boyle, including his famous *The Sceptical Chymist* (1661), the Four Elements and the Three Principles were attacked with equal vigour on the grounds that chemistry should be founded on observation rather than dogma. If the chemists wished to maintain that fire was an element, the onus must be on them to demonstrate its indivisibility experimentally.

Around that time, experiments on combustion were indeed being carried out by various investigators, including Robert Hooke. One of his preliminary reports, prosaically entitled 'Of Charcoal and Burnt Vegetables' (in *Micrographia*, 1665), is thought to have shown that, when charcoal is burned in a glass vessel, it consumes air, and that the combustion ceases both when the air is spent and when it is pumped out. If air is pumped in, the charcoal can be reignited with a burning-glass. Later, he found that saltpetre ('nitre') could support combustion in the absence of air. From the following extract from Sprat's history of the Royal Society of London in 1667, we might think that combustion was well on the way to its current theoretical footing:

That there is no such thing, as an *Elementary Fire* of the *Peripatetics*; nor *Fiery Atoms* of the *Epicureans*: but that *Fire* is only the Act of the Dissolution of heated *Sulphureous Bodies*, by the *Air* as a *Menstruum*, much after the manner as *Aqua Fortis*: or other sharp *Menstruums* do work on dissoluble Bodies, as *Iron*, *Tin*, *Copper*: that heat, and light are two inseparable Effects of this dissolution, as heat, and ebullition are of those dissolutions of *Tin* and *Copper*: that *Flame* is a dissolution of *Smoak*, which consists of combustible particles, carry'd upward by the heat of rarify'd *Air*: and that Ashes are a Part of the *Body* not dissoluble by the *Air*.

There was, however, confusion even amongst the best scientific minds of the period. John Mayow, working, like Hooke, in Oxford in the early 1660s, believed that combustion (and also respiration) depended on some 'nitroaerial' spirit or particles common to nitre and air. He was also aware that several investigators had reported that metals such as lead increase in weight during combustion. Although these views seem to anticipate the concept of oxidation, he also held that his nitroaerial particles were present in iron, and that if agitated they produced heat. The sun was seen as a vast chaotic mass of such particles, here closely akin to the 'fiery atoms' of the Epicureans. The time had not yet come to leap the large conceptual gap between the emission of some essence and the uptake of oxygen. Indeed, although air had been shown to be a material substance, its component gases had not yet been identified.

The process of burning was also under scrutiny in Germany. Becher, in 1669, expounded and expanded earlier views that combustion of a substance involved loss of a fiery component and formation of a calx. Stahl, in 1702, sought, with apparent success, to rationalize most known chemistry in terms of this hypothesis, which in addition to combustion covered dissolution of metals in acids and extraction of metals from their ores by means of hot charcoal, which consisted almost entirely of the fiery principle. This 'essence of fire' he called phlogiston, from the Greek verb 'to inflame'. The phlogiston hypothesis was widely accepted. The need for air to be available during combustion was attributed to its ability to absorb the phlogiston liberated. The associated increase in weight was explained by endowing phlogiston with negative mass, so that loss of it from a burning metal would increase the mass of the resultant calx. The hypothesis flourished until the 1770s, despite the pioneering work of Boyle, Hooke, and Mayow over a century earlier.

The second round of spade-work for the overthrow of the phlogiston theory had started in Edinburgh in the mid-eighteenth century when Joseph Black had, by careful handling of gases and precise measurements of changes in weight, demonstrated that air contained a substance which could be absorbed by alkali. Rutherford, a colleague of his, found that air also contains a high proportion of matter which can neither be breathed nor absorbed by alkali, indicating the presence of at least three components.

Priestley was concerned to explain why air continued to support combustion and respiration despite the fact that it was continuously being used up by these processes. He found that the component concerned could be regenerated by green plants; a sprig of mint, kept in a closed vessel in which a candle had burned out, had in ten days so changed the air that the candle could be reignited. By a chance heating of both mercury oxide and red lead, Priestley also generated a gas which supported combustion and respiration spectacularly better than air itself. The Swedish chemist, Scheele, had in fact prepared the same gas about two years earlier by heating a number of oxygen-containing substances but, due to the 'inexcusable negligence' of his publisher, his results were not made public until 1777. Priestley, like Scheele, was a confirmed phlogistonist and so had the greatest of difficulty in explaining his observations; but since the new gas supported combustion so well, it must be a splendid absorber of phlogiston, presumably because it contained none at the outset. He therefore called his gas dephlogistonated air, and tried to reconcile its existence with the phlogiston hypothesis; the lack of clarity in his attempted explanation may well reflect the confusion in his own mind. Happily, he dined with M and Mme Lavoisier in 1774, and despite his 'speaking French very imperfectly and being little acquainted with the terms of chemistry' he managed to tell them of his discovery.

Antoine Lavoisier had already observed that there was no overall change in mass when a substance was burned in a closed vessel; and since the calx weighed more than the metal, some (weighable) substance must have been taken from the air. Lavoisier showed (after some delay, for he had been appointed to a new job betweenwhiles) that the calx formed by gentle heating of mercury in a fixed volume of air could be decomposed at higher temperatures, and that the gas which was then given off exactly reconstituted the spent air to its original quantity and quality. But phlogiston was not yet vanquished; and indeed it seemed to have been isolated in the form of the gas which we now call hydrogen. When an electric spark was passed across a mixture of this gas and air, water was formed, and four-fifths of the air remained. Lavoisier immediately predicted that water should be able to give off hydrogen under the right conditions, and succeeded in making it do so by passing steam over red-hot iron. The

31 Firewalking in England, 1992

32 'Ignis and Aer.' The elements fire and air from a 12th century manuscript

burning of hydrogen, as of metals, can then be understood in terms of the combination of these substances with Priestley's new gas, which Lavoisier named 'oxygen'. The phlogiston hypothesis was effectively dead, although Priestley clung to it until his own death in 1804. The phlogiston model was indeed remarkably resilient. Elegant work on the combustion of oxygen-containing materials in a vacuum was carried out in Russia by Petrow who died in 1834 without abandoning the concept.

We should not, however, judge the phlogistonists too harshly. Everyday observation assures us that most burning is indeed accompanied by emission of something, and very few substances (and *no* familiar organic fuels) burn to produce solid ash which weighs more than the original material. The two main combustible 'essences' in the history of chemistry, the alchemists' sulphur and the phlogistonists' charcoal, appear to be totally consumed, as they burn to give purely gaseous oxides. And, of course, something is indeed always given out; but that something does not have negative mass, nor does it have positive mass. It is energy. As we have seen, one of the driving forces for combustion is the fact that its products contain less chemical energy stored in their bonds than does the mixture of the combustible material with oxygen. Energy is therefore liberated and manifests itself as heat, as light, and often also as sound. It is outside the scope of this book even to attempt to outline the vicissitudes suffered by the various hypotheses which took root, and wilted, and sometimes re-established themselves, as physicists strove to understand the nature of energy. It is enough to say that we now envisage heat as motion of and within molecules, light as electromagnetic waves with characteristics also of weightless particles, and sound as a sudden perturbation of pressure.

So today, have we, who 'stand on the shoulders of giants', a thorough understanding of the nature of fire? We have certainly come a long way since Lavoisier put us on the right road. However, the policy for chemical education, at least in the UK, enabled the phlogistonists to fight back posthumously for about 150 years, with the result that generations of young teenagers, many of whom might have been fascinated to learn more of the workings of nature, had their enthusiasm quenched by the need to regurgitate ideas which seemed outmoded, irrelevant, confusing or plain daft. Despite this regrettable rearguard action, our understanding of combustion has flourished. We have now amassed considerable stores of information

about the mechanisms and rates of processes which occur in pre-
mixed flames, and can predict how the behaviour of such flames will
vary as we change the conditions. Our knowledge of various forms of
heat transfer and of the pyrolysis of many solid and liquid fuels has
also progressed so well that we are now able to perform computer
modelling of how an unwanted fire will spread within a room of
particular shape and furnishings, and even throughout a building.
Much progress (see Chapters 19–22) has been made in methods of
prevention and combat of unwanted fire. Are we then so near to
complete understanding that future research is likely to be a mere
tying up of a few loose ends without new areas to explore?

Any idea that we have now largely mastered the theory and need
only to extend its application somewhat is surely misguided.
Although we can now generate satisfactory computer models of the
spread of fire in some enclosed spaces of simple shape (see Plate 21),
we do not yet know enough to predict behaviour near a flame, either
spreading over a solid surface, or accelerating towards detonation in
a constrained gaseous mixture (see Chapter 12). We are also still a
very long way from success in modelling wildfire (see Chapter 22).

Another form of natural 'fire' which has so far resisted analysis is
the 'will-o'-the-wisp', appearing in previous eras as small colonies of
lights, each about the size and shape of a hen's egg, which hovered
or moved low over marshy ground. Also known as 'ignus fatuus',
supernatural explanations gave way to the idea that the light was due
to burning methane, generated by decaying plants. Mixtures of
methane and air are indeed flammable, but do not ignite spontaneously at atmospheric temperatures; if they did, flames would
frequently be seen around the tails of cows, who emit appreciable
amounts of methane. The spontaneous ignition has been ascribed to
the presence of phosphine, PH_3, which does not in fact ignite spontaneously in air, or to its common impurity, P_2H_4, which does.
Traces of these compounds might well be formed by underground
oxygen-free fermentation of wetland vegetation. But if the will-o'-
the-wisp were indeed due to burning methane, however ignited, the
flame would be hot, yellowish, and short-lived, whereas most reports
describe it as cold, bluish-white, and lasting for a few minutes. In
1853, a physics professor from Kiev claimed that the brass ferrule of
his stick was in no way warmed after having been held in the
luminous region for 15 minutes. Such an observation would suggest
that the phenomenon is a cool flame (see Chapter 12) caused by

some, as yet unidentified, unstable fermentation product which rises from the marsh and reacts with the oxygen in the air.

A phenomenon which was also attributed to supernatural causes is that where a human or animal body appears to ignite spontaneously from within. As yet, we know little about the ways in which a human body burns, and although a layman might think it unlikely that a material that is about two-thirds water would ignite of its own accord, experienced fire officers are of divided opinion. Some think that Spontaneous Human Combustion, which was the supposed fate of Mr Krook in Charles Dickens' novel *Bleak House*, is so unlikely that another cause of ignition should be sought. Others believe 'SHC' to be a real possibility, initiated perhaps by a solar flare which causes a massive surge in the Earth's magnetism. This could destabilize substances which are normally stable, or cause a brief electric discharge, turning the stomach momentarily into a microwave oven. An increase in temperature would inactivate the body's thermostating system, allowing energy-producing reactions to accelerate and so increase the temperature still further. In principle, evaporation of water from the tissues, vaporization of body fat, and pyrolysis of the vapour could occur, to be followed by ignition. Clothing or a blanket could act as an external wick. Spontaneous combustion has also been reported for dogs and for pigs living in hot regions such as Queensland. Both species have poor systems of temperature control and cool themselves mainly by panting. We, however, unlike the pigs, are able to sweat. It is clear that the last word on Spontaneous Bodily Combustion, as on many other aspects of fire, has yet to be said.

But the last word of this book should perhaps go to Scheele: writing over two centuries ago of the difficulties encountered during his research into fire, he emphasized 'the centuries that have elapsed without our succeeding in acquiring more knowledge as to its true properties'.

Main sources

============

GENERAL

1. *Encyclopaedia brittanica.* Many entries in 14th (1950 and 1968) and 15th (1982) editions. (Chicago.)
2. Science Museum, London. Permanent exhibitions.
3. Lyons, J. W., *Fire*, Scientific American Library, 1985. A general account, richly illustrated, covering Section I, Chapters 4, 6, 8–11, and Section IV.
4. Barnard, J. A. and Bradley, J. N., *Flame and combustion*, 2nd edn, Chapman & Hall, London, 1985. A 'primer' for the non-specialist scientist, covering Section I and Chapters 4, 10–12, and 17, with many useful references.
5. Faraday, M., *The chemical history of a candle*, Thomas Y. Crowell, New York, 1957. Written as instructive entertainment for nineteenth century twelve-year-olds, it still has much to offer their successors and seniors.

COMBUSTION THEORY

(Mainly technical works for the specialist, fully referenced; see also Refs 3 and 4 above.)

6. Glassman, I., *Combustion*, 2nd edn, Academic Press, Orlando, Florida, 1987.
7. Gaydon, A. G. and Wolfhard, H. G., *Flames*, 4th edn, Chapman & Hall, London, 1979.
8. Drysdale, D., *An introduction to fire dynamics*, Wiley, Chichester, 1985.

9. Lewis, B. and von Elbe, G., *Combustion, flames and explosions of gases*, 3rd edn, Academic Press, Orlando, Florida, 1987.
10. Williams, F. A., *Combustion theory*, 2nd edn, Benjamin/ Cummings, Menlo Park, California, 1985.
11. Kuan-yun Kuo, K., *Principles of combustion*, Wiley, New York, 1986. Mainly theory of modelling.

HISTORY OF TECHNOLOGY
(See also Ref. 3 and those in next section.)

12. Singer, C., Holmyard, E. J., Hall, A. R., and Williams, T. I., *A history of technology*, Clarendon Press, Oxford, 1954–8.
13. Derry, T. K. and Williams, T. I., *A short history of technology*, Oxford University Press, 1960.
14. Forbes, R. J., *Studies in ancient technology*, Brill, Leiden. Vol. V (2nd edn, 1966) glass; Vol. VI (2nd edn, 1966) heating, cooking, and lighting; Vol. VII (1964) mining; Vol. VIII (2nd edn, 1972) and Vol. IX (1964) metallurgy and metal working.
15. Forbes, R. J., *Man the maker*, Constable, London, 1958.
16. Hodges, H., *Technology in the ancient world*, Penguin, London, 1970.
17. Needham, J., *Science and civilisation in China*, Cambridge University Press. Vol. I (1954) proposed contents of whole work; Vol. 4(I) (1962) Section 26, physics; Vol. 5(II–V) (1974–83), Section 33, chemistry and alchemy. Repays serious browsing.
18. Hough, W., 'Fire as an Agent of Human Culture' in *Bull. U.S. Nat. Mus.*, No. 139, 1926.

TECHNOLOGICAL TOPICS
(See also references in previous section.)

19. Eveleigh, D. J., *Firegrates and kitchen ranges*, Shire Publications, Princes Risborough, UK, 1983.
20. Gledhill, D., *Gas lighting*, Shire Publications, Princes Risborough, UK, 1981.
21. O'Dea, W. T., *Making fire*, Science Museum, London. Her Majesty's Stationery Office, 1964.

22. O'Dea, W. T., *Lighting*, Nos. 1, 2, and 2, Science Museum, London. Her Majesty's Stationery Office, 1967–70.
23. Hero of Alexandria, *Pneumatics*, ed. B. Woodcraft (1851), introd. by M. B. Hall, Macdonald, London, 1971.
24. Brock, A. St. H., *A history of fireworks*, Harrap, London, 1949.
25. Partington, J. R., *A history of Greek fire and gunpowder*, Heffer, Cambridge, 1960.
26. Ellern, H., *Military and civilian pyrotechnics*, Chemical Publishing Inc., New York, 1968.
27. Urbański, T., *Chemistry and technology of explosives*, trans. I. Jęczalikowa, and S. Laverton, Pergamon Press, Oxford, 1983.
28. Dolan, J. E., 'Explosives' in *Chem. in Brit.*, August 1985, p. 732.
29. Bedini, S. A., *Trans. Amer. Philosoph. Soc.*, 1963 (new series) 53, pt. 5; Bedini, S.A. *New Scientist*, 1964, **21**, 537. Oriental fire-clocks.
30. *Vogel's qualitative inorganic analysis*, 6th edn, rev. G. Svehla, Longman, Harlow, UK, 1978.
31. Goffer, Z., *Archaeological chemistry*, *Chemical Analysis Series*, Vol. 55, John Wiley, New York, 1980. Attic pottery; thermoluminescence.
32. Moore, J. W. and Moore, E. A., *Environmental chemistry*, Academic Press, New York, 1976.
33. Ferguson, J. E., *Inorganic chemistry and the Earth*, Pergamon Press, Oxford 1982.
34. Wayne, R. P., *Chemistry in atmospheres*, Oxford University Press, 1991.

URBAN FIRE
(See also Refs 3 and 8 above.)

35. *Chemistry in Britain*, March 1987.
36. Gamble, S. G., *Outbreaks of fire*, Griffin & Co., London, 1925, repr. 1941.
37. Blackstone, G. V., *A history of the British fire service*, Routledge & Kegan Paul, London, 1957.
38. Barlay, S., *Fire*, Hamish Hamilton, London, 1972.
39. Cullis, C. F. and Hirschler, M. M., *The combustion of organic polymers*, Oxford University Press, 1981.

40. Bare, W., *Fundamentals of fire protection*, Wiley, Chichester, 1979.
41. Canter, D. (ed.), *Fires and human behaviour*, Wiley, Chichester, 1980.
42. Sansom, W., in *Fire and water, an NFS anthology*, ed. H. S. Ingham, Lindsay Drummond, London, 1942.
43. Firebrace, A., *Fire service memories*, Melrose, London, *c.* 1948.
44. Topp, D. O., *Medicine, Sci., Law*, 1973, **13**, 79. Arson and symbolism.
45. *New Scientist*, 7 July 1988. King's Cross Fire, p. 29; fire modelling, p. 44.

RURAL FIRE

46. Chandler, C., Cheney, P., Thomas, P., Trabaud, L., and Williams, D., *Fire in forestry*, Wiley-Interscience, New York, 1983.
47. Pyne, S. J., *Fire in America*, Princeton University Press, 1982. A historian's treatment.

PHILOSOPHY AND RELIGION
(See also Ref. 44 above.)

48. Hastings J., *Dictionary of the Bible*, T. & T. Clark, Edinburgh, 1899.
49. Hastings J., (ed.), *Encyclopaedia of religion and ethics*, T. & T. Clark, Edinburgh, 1908–26.
50. Lévi-Strauss, C., *The raw and the cooked*, trans. J. and D. Weightman, Jonathan Cape, London, 1970.
51. Frazer, J. R., *The golden bough*, 3rd edn, Part VII, Vols 1 and 2, Macmillan, London, 1930.
52. Frazer, J. R., *Myths of the origin of fire*, Macmillan, London, 1930.
53. Burkert, W., *Greek religion*, trans. J. Raffan, Basil Blackwell, Oxford, 1985.
54. Gunn, G., *Blackwood's Magazine*, 1962, Vol. 291, p. 193. Fire-walking.

55. Danford, L. M., *Anastenaria: a study of Greek ritual therapy*, Ph.D. thesis, Princeton University, June 1978; *Firewalking and religious healing*, Princeton University Press, 1989.
56. Wightman, W. P. D., *The growth of scientific ideas*, Oliver & Boyd, Edinburgh, 1950.
57. Holmyard, E. J., *Makers of chemistry*, Oxford University Press, 1931.
58. Bachelard, G., *The psychoanalysis of fire* (1938), trans. A. C. M. Ross, Routledge & Kegan Paul, London, 1964.
59. Lucretius, *The nature of the Universe*, trans. R. E. Latham, Pengiun, London, 1951.
60. Mills, A. A., *Chemistry in Britain*, 1980, Vol. 16, p. 69. Will-o'-the-wisp.

Acknowledgements

Permission to reproduce artwork has been obtained from the following sources:

Black and white illustrations

Page		
11	Soot	From *Atoms, electrons and chemical change*, by P. W. Atkins. Copyright © 1991. Reprinted by permission of W. H. Freeman and Company
13	Under-ventilated flame	Drysdale, D. *An introduction to fire dynamics* (1985). Reprinted by permission of John Wiley and Sons, Ltd
19	Davy safety-lamp	Singer, C., Holmyard, E. J., Hall, A. R., and Williams, T. I. *A history of technology* (Clarendon Press, Oxford, 1954–8)
22	Sticks laid for charcoal burning	The author
27A	Fire-saw	Singer, C., Holmyard, E. J., Hall, A. R., and Williams, T. I., *A history of technology* (Clarendon Press, Oxford, 1954–8)
27B	Fire-plough	
27C	Fire-drill	
27D	Bow-drill	
37	Egyptian goldsmiths using blowpipes	
44	Vitruvius' idea of the taming fire	
48B	Grate with register to adjust chimney opening	Eveleigh, D. *Firegates and kitchen ranges* (Shire Publications, Princes Risborough, 1983)
48C	Grate from c.1830	

50	Warming pan	Ashmolean Museum, Oxford
51	Pot-bellied stove, USA	Redrawn by permission of Culver Pictures, Inc.
54	Roman hypocaust, Silchester	Singer, C., Holmyard, E. J., Hall, A. R., and Williams, T. I. *A history of technology* (Clarendon Press, Oxford, 1954–8)
55A	A typical domestic gas burner	Barnard, J. A. and Bradley, J. N., *Flame and combustion*, 2nd edn.
55B	A fluidized-bed combustor	(Chapman and Hall, London, 1985)
60A	Candle and tapers, Egypt	Singer, C., Holmyard, E. J., Hall,
60B	Minoan candlestick	A. R., and Williams, T. I. *A*
60C	Mesopotamian shell lamp	*history of technology* (Clarendon
61A	Mesopotamian gold lamp	Press, Oxford, 1954–8)
61B	Mesopotamian calcite lamp	
61C	Phoenician pottery lamp	
62	Graeco-Roman lamps	
63	Flat-flamed gas burners	Gledhill, D. *Gas lighting*. (Shire
64	Advertisement for gas lamp, 1987	Publications, Princes Risborough, 1981)
79	Monastic oven	The author
80	Smoke-jack for turning spit	Singer, C., Holmyard, E. J., Hall, A. R., and Williams, T. I. *A history of technology* (Clarendon Press, Oxford, 1954–8)
81A	Kitchen range	The institute of agricultural history and museum of English rural life, Reading
81B	Gas cooker	Derry, T. K. and Williams, T. I. *A short history of technology* (Oxford University Press, 1960)
	Fishing lights	The author
87	Ignition of fire-damp in a mine	Singer, C., Holmyard, E. J., Hall, A. R., and Williams, T. I. *A history of technology* (Clarendon Press, Oxford, 1954–8)
90	Splitting rocks by fire-setting	
92	Greek fire used in naval battle	
97A	Reconstruction of ceramic kilns	Hodges, H., *Technology in the ancient world* (Penguin, London 1970). Reprinted by permission of John Johnson Ltd, London

98A	Attic black-on-red vase, showing forge	The Trustees of the British Museum
98B	Attic red-on-black vase, showing vase-painter at work	Ashmolean Museum, Oxford
100	Glass-making in Italy	Derry, T. K. and Williams, T. I. *A short history of technology* (Oxford University Press, 1960)
102A	The lost-wax process	Hodges, H. *Technology in the ancient world* (Penguin, London, 1970). Reprinted by permission of John Johnson Ltd, London
102B	The 'Gloucester' candlestick cast by the lost wax method	By courtesy of the Board of Trustees of the Victoria and Albert Museum
103	Distillation apparatus	The Bodleian Library, University of Oxford, Shelfmark MS. Bodley 645, fol. 11
104A	Tending the furnace of a	Singer, C., Holmyard, E. J., Hall,
104B	brandy still Sulphuric acid manufacture, 18th century.	A. R., and Williams, T. I. *A history of technology* (Clarendon Press, Oxford, 1954–8)
106A	Leonardo da Vinci's smoke jack	Rossotti, H. S. *Air* (Oxford University Press, 1973)
107A	Hero's door-opening machine	Singer, C., Holmyard, E. J., Hall, A. R., and Williams, T. I. *A history of technology* (Clarendon Press, Oxford, 1954–8)
108	Paddlesteamers racing on the Mississippi	The Bettmann Archive and Hulton picture library
109	Savery's Miner's Friend	Singer, C., Holmyard, E. J., Hall,
111A	Mobile steam engine driving threshing machine	A. R., and Williams, T. I. *A history of technology* (Clarendon Press, Oxford, 1954–8)
111B	Paddlesteamer	Kemp, P. (ed.) *Oxford companion to ships and the sea* (Oxford University Press, 1976)
112	World's first passenger railway (a) track	Derry, T. K. and Williams, T. I. *A short history of technology* (Oxford University Press, 1960)
	(b) Trevithick's engine	

113A	Steam tricycle 1887	Singer, C., Holmyard, E. J., Hall,
113B	Steam-propeller airship, 1852	A. R., and Williams, T. I. *A history of technology* (Clarendon
115	The *Turbina*	Press, Oxford, 1954–8)
120A	Benz motor-car, 1888	Derry, T. K. and Williams, T. I. *A short history of technology* (Oxford University Press, 1960)
120B	Petrol horse	Singer, C., Holmyard, E. J., Hall, A. R., and Williams, T. I. *A history of technology* (Clarendon Press, Oxford, 1954–8)
120C	The Wright brothers' flying machine	Derry, T. K. and Williams, T. I. *A short history of technology* (Oxford University Press, 1960)
120D	Bleriot landing at Dover	Derry, T. K. and Williams, T. I. *A short history of technology* (Oxford University Press, 1960)
127A	Jet engine	Barnard, J. A. and Bradley, J. N.
127B	Combustion chamber of jet engine	*Flame and combusion*, 2nd edition (Chapman and Hall, London, 1985)
135	Explosion of the airship Hindenburg	Popperfoto, Northampton
140	Charcoal burning	Singer, C., Holmyard, E. J., Hall, A. R., and Williams, T. I. *A history of technology* (Clarendon Press, Oxford, 1954–8)
141	Cannon	Derry, T. K. and Williams, T. I. *A short history of technology* (Oxford University Press, 1960)
149	Use of rockets for ejector seat	Redrawn from *The Times* 7 September 1991, © Times Newspapers Ltd, 1991
162	Smoking of salt red herring	Singer, C., Holmyard, E. J., Hall,
176	The assay of copper	A. R., and Williams, T. I. *A history of technology* (Clarendon Press, Oxford, 1954–8)
184	Factory chimneys	Derry, T. K. and Williams, T. I. *A short history of technology* (Oxford University Press, 1960)
186	Peppered moth	Kettlewell, B. *The evolution of melanism* (Clarendon Press, 1973)
192A	Pollution near rocket launch pad	NASA, USA

192B	Pollution of upper atmosphere by solid fuel propellant	NASA, USA
193	Pipesmoker of the year	From *The Times* January 16 1992. © Times Newspapers Limited, 1992
220	Great Fire of London consumes St Paul's Church	William Longman, *A history of the three cathedrals of St Paul in London* (Longmans, 1873)
226	Hand-pumped engine at the time of the Great Fire of London	The Master and Fellows of Magdalene College, Cambridge
249	Oxford University Safety Newsheet	Oxford University Safety Office, 1990
279	Natural gas burning	Singer, C., Holmyard, E. J., Hall, A. R., and Williams, T. I. *A history of technology* (Clarendon Press, Oxford, 1954–8)
285B	The shrine of St Thomas Aquinas, France	The author
297	Fire-walking in Greece	Yannis Kyriakides

The Plates

1	Fire at the houses of parliament	The Hulton Picture Company
2	Candle flame and match	Keith Waters
3	Gas – air flames of bunsen burner	Keith Waters
4	Olympic flame	Emmanuel Diakakis and Son, Athens
5	Campfire	Images Colour Library Ltd, Leeds
6	Burning of inorganic fuels	From *General chemistry*, by P. W. Atkins. Copyright © 1989 by W. H. Freeman and Company. Reprinted by permission.
7	Street brazier in China	Zeng Yun-Feng
8	Street lighting by gas	The Hulton Picture Company
9	Burning-off in Scotland	A. J. McLachlan
10	Burning-off on oilrig	Images Colour Library Ltd, Leeds
11	Burning oilwells	Schurr/Cedri/Impact Photos, London
12	Attic cup	Ashmolean Museum, Oxford
13	Launch of *Atlantis*	NASA, USA
14	Hot-air balloon	Mantis Studio
15	Fireworks	Images Colour Library Ltd, Leeds

16	Coloured bunsen flames	Keith Waters
17	Buildings on fire	Colorific, London
18	Smoke and vapour trails	Ministry of Defence
19	Fire action card	Signs and Labels Ltd, Stockport
20	Capping an oilwell	© Stephane Compoint, Sygma, London
21	Fire modelling	CHAM, London
22	Forest fire	Images Colour Library Ltd, Leeds
23	Aerial fire-fighting	
24	Tapestry in St Albans Cathedral	Photo: Jeremy Marks, (Woodmansterne Ltd): © St Albans Cathedral
25	Candles, Moscow	Associated Press
26	The martyrdom of St Lawrence	Dr N. Gendle
27	Cremation of Rajiv Gandhi	© Swapan Parekh/Black Star/ Colorific
28	Demon stoking the fires of hell	Images Colour Library Ltd, Leeds
29	Hogmanay celebrations in Scotland	Wood, The Stillmoving picture company
30	Midsummer in Greece	G. A. Akaterinides
31	Fire-walking, England	Carlos Guarita, Reportage photos
32	Ignis and aer	Images Colour Library Ltd, Leeds. After a 12th century illustration to Aratus in the National Library, Vienna.

Although every effort has been made to trace and contact copyright holders, in a few instances this has not been possible. If notified the publishers will be pleased to rectify any omissions in future editions.

Index

Index